Robert Altman's
McCabe & Mrs. Miller

Robert Altman's
McCabe & Mrs. Miller

REFRAMING THE AMERICAN WEST

ROBERT T. SELF

 UNIVERSITY PRESS OF KANSAS

Published by the

University Press of Kansas

(Lawrence, Kansas 66045),

which was organized by the

Kansas Board of Regents and

is operated and funded by

Emporia State University,

Fort Hays State University,

Kansas State University,

Pittsburg State University, the

University of Kansas, and

Wichita State University

© 2007 by the University Press of Kansas

All rights reserved

Leonard Cohen, "Sisters of Mercy," "The Stranger Song," and "Suzanne" © 1967 Sony/ATV Songs LLC. All rights administered by Sony/ATV Music Publishing, 8 Music Square West, Nashville, TN 37203. All rights reserved. Used by permission.

Bob Dylan, "A Hard Rain's A-Gonna Fall" and "The Times They Are A-Changin'" Copyright © 1965 by Warner Bros. Inc. Copyright renewed 1991 by Special Rider Music. All rights reserved. International copyright secured. Reprinted by permission.

All photographs are from Photofest.

Library of Congress Cataloging-in-Publication Data
Self, Robert T., 1941–
Robert Altman's McCabe & Mrs. Miller : reframing the American West / Robert T. Self.
p. cm.
Includes bibliographical references and index.
ISBN-13: 978-0-7006-1551-3 (cloth : alk. paper)
1. McCabe & Mrs. Miller (Motion picture) I. Title. II. Title: Robert Altman's McCabe and Mrs. Miller.
PN1997.M4236S45   2007
791.43'72—dc22   2007015899

British Library Cataloguing-in-Publication Data is available.

Printed in the United States of America

10 9 8 7 6 5 4 3 2 1

The paper used in this publication meets the minimum requirements of the American National Standard for Permanence of Paper for Printed Library Materials z39.48-1992.

Goodbye, Bob

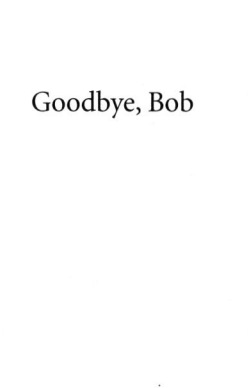

Contents

Preface, *ix*

Introduction: Negotiations and Deals, *1*

1 The Real and Mythic West, *14*

2 Revisionist Western, *46*

3 Countercultural Contexts, *101*

4 Altman's Art, *135*

Epilogue: Violence, Decline, and Death, *175*

Notes, *181*

Bibliography, *191*

Index, *201*

A photograph section follows page 90.

Preface

In the thirty-six years since its release many academic critics, journalistic reviewers, and Altman fans have recognized the importance of *McCabe & Mrs. Miller*. This book reflects and expands much of this knowledge in order to urge the film's importance for a larger audience. The inception for this work dates from the enthusiastic appreciation for the film by Mike Briggs of the University Press of Kansas, who first proposed the idea for such a study. His interest matched my long admiration for the film, which originated in research begun in 1977, and his support has been central to this project. I owe special thanks to another Atman admirer and my longtime colleague at Northern Illinois University, Lynne Waldeland, who gave detailed critical reactions to the manuscript. I am indebted as well to my colleague Jeff Chown for ongoing reactions to the ideas of the book. Bob Kolker, Lee Mitchell, and John Lenihan made extensive and invaluable suggestions both in the development and in the revision of the manuscript, and my nephew Robert O. Self gave me the very beneficial critique of an American historian. Andy Sidle ably assisted me with a survey of reviews and a detailed record of shots and editing in the film and with final proofreading. At the press, Jennifer Dropkin discerningly copyedited the manuscript, and Susan McRory and Susan Schott guided it smoothly through production. Carolyn Law once again professionally indexed my words. My sincere thanks to all these colleagues for their crucial assistance. And to my family, Lois and Sarah, whose love always inspires and supports my work.

I have conventionally used the literary present throughout this book to discuss Altman's work, and as I wrote, that present carried the aura both of the living film and the living auteur. I finished revising the manuscript on the day that Robert Altman died in November 2006, so these sentences retain for me now only the ghostly presence of the man who lives on in powerful works of art like *McCabe & Mrs. Miller*.

Robert Altman's
McCabe & Mrs. Miller

Introduction: Negotiations and Deals

The moaning sounds of a winter wind fill the soundtrack along with the haunting voice of Leonard Cohen intoning, "It's true that all the men you knew were dealers." The camera pans slowly across a moody gray landscape of mountain evergreens lit intermittently by the autumn gold and red of changing leaves. A lone rider materializes from this forest under a cold rain and turns into the direction and the rhythm of the pan. Swathed in a red bearskin coat, the rider slumps in the saddle as his horse and packhorse slowly pick their way along a faint trail against the steady moaning of the wind and the song. The camera tracks their progress as they approach a stately church steeple rising from the fir-lined mountain slopes, and the lyrics describe "that kind of man . . . who is reaching for the sky just to surrender."

So begins Robert Altman's traditional, and innovative, western film, *McCabe & Mrs. Miller*. As in countless other westerns, another lone horseman rides out of the wilderness and approaches civilization. It's a familiar story: the central character arrives at a wilderness mining camp, sees its potential for business, and begins working to change the backwoods camp into a mining town. John McCabe is a gambler with a gunfighter's reputation, and he quickly builds an entertainment business of casino, bar, and brothel. His efforts attract an unlikely partner, Constance Miller, an experienced madam, who operates the whorehouse, and their jointly successful enterprise soon defines the developing community of Presbyterian Church, Washington, in 1901. As both mine and town prosper, the Harrison

Shaughnessy Mining Company moves to consolidate its profits by making Presbyterian Church a company town. Unable to negotiate an acceptable price for McCabe's business, the company sends in three gunmen, a team of enforcers who will terminate his resistance to corporate interests. Without any law to protect his property, McCabe is forced to defend himself by taking up arms and confronting the forces of lawlessness that would rob him of his labor, his rights, and his life.

The constant variations on this oft-repeated story constitute part of the ritual reenactment of "how the West was won." Even its central figures reenact the lives of prominent western figures. Mark Twain wrote his way into national success with humorous stories about life in the mining town of Virginia City, Nevada. His popular account of the eccentricities, absurdities, and excesses of western life in *Roughing It* observes: "The cheapest and easiest way to become an influential man and be looked up to by the community at large, was to stand behind a bar, wear a cluster-diamond pin, and sell whisky.... To be a saloon-keeper and kill a man was to be illustrious."[1] At the same time in neighboring Montana, Irish immigrant Josephine Hensley was rising above her mean circumstances as an itinerant whore to become "Chicago Jo," one of the most successful madams in the old West. At the height of her career in the 1880s she owned the majority of "demimonde" buildings and property in the mining town of Helena and demonstrated that prostitution no less than bonanza ore provided a means of striking it rich on the western wilderness.

These figures enjoy continuing life in the art of Robert Altman's film. John "Pudgy" McCabe is the gambler and saloonkeeper with the reputation of a gunfighter, "the man who shot Bill Roundtree." Constance Miller is the cockney immigrant who parlays prostitution into the dominant business of Presbyterian Church. Their business enterprise of gambling, boozing, and whoring also constitutes the central business of Altman's film. Paul Arthur argues that "the subtitle of Altman's opus should be 'The Art of the Deal'" because of its heavy emphasis on business transactions.[2] Indeed, when McCabe asserts, "Deals I don't mind. It's partners I don't like," he voices a central irony of a film about deals and negotiations. These avatars of western history must negotiate their partnership and their relationship; they must negotiate with the community and the mining company. At the same time, Altman's film must also negotiate alternative artistic space within the western genre. The film cuts cultural deals whose terms continue to resonate over thirty-five years after its release in 1971. Myriad negotiations cross the film everywhere and reach beyond its narrative frames: into the historic time of its fictional representations, the culture contemporary with its theatrical exhibitions, the strategic conditions of Hollywood movie production, the generic context of popular narrative fiction, and now particularly into the present as an effect of its engaging artistic achievements. The film's story in a major way is about negotiation, and it depicts negotiating everywhere. In the making of this film Altman deals as well with the counterculture that surrounds its production. He must rethink the formal and ideological commitments of the western as a central national American narrative. He must further navigate the shoals of a movie industry under siege by independent filmmakers and changing modes of capitalization. He must examine western history as a revised ground for the field of emergent cultural values. He must negotiate indeed a space for himself as a middle-aged director just entering feature-film making with a craft, vision, and art that will prove critical to a renascent Hollywood in the 1970s and central to the establishment of an American Art Cinema.

The stories of *McCabe & Mrs. Miller* develop as a series of deals. McCabe negotiates the terms of running a card table in Sheehan's saloon, then proposes the first game among strangers as five-card stud and negotiates the value of a bet at "a nickel a game to start off with." ("Let's make it a dime," the miners rejoin.) Then he negotiates to buy three whores in Bearpaw to bring back to the mining camp of Presbyterian Church. Implicit in the condensed time between these first and second sequences of the film is his negotiation of successful gambling into the purchase of land in this nascent frontier town. Subsequently Mrs. Miller enters the town with the proposal that he can't refuse of a partnership to operate his brothel: "Do we make a deal or don't we!?" Essential to their story are the various negotiations that shape their partnership: over his willingness "to spend money to make money," over the mining company's offer to purchase their business, and over the threat the company finally poses to their aspirations and ultimately their lives. A central conflict of the plot revolves around McCabe's failed negotiations with the company and his inability to make a deal with the killers who arrive to negotiate from a position of "extreme prejudice." Legal negotiations devolve into political platitudes that force McCabe in the last instance to negotiate for his life, alone with his guns in a snowy showdown amid the labyrinthine streets of his now prosperous town.

These separate transactions further shape larger negotiations in the film. At a time when the dominant concepts of American masculinity begin to erode, the film reexamines understandings of masculine superiority and feminine inferiority. In particular, the relationship between men and women becomes a negotiation over sex. The development of community derives from the captivity of women in the sex trade. The film's major relationship between the title characters examines gender roles as the terms of a partnership. Anxiety about the efficacy of individual behavior emerges within a context of corporate relations. The entrepreneurial energies of the small business man and woman work within the capital interests of big business. The film begins under the lyrical contemplation of Leonard Cohen's meditation:

> It's true that all the men you knew were dealers
> who said they were through with dealing
> Every time you gave them shelter.

The action and the values of the film depict survival as dealing, negotiating, gambling—actions that are constantly tenuous and fraught with the danger of dealers who work for "the house" and thus hold the highest hand and run the biggest game.

Any film that tells a popular story like the western must also negotiate between the formal and thematic demands of this extremely popular American genre. Each conventional narrative genre displays a particular vocabulary and syntax, and the ritual repetition of similar plots permits audiences to participate vicariously in traditional, innovative, or changing patterns of cultural belief and understanding. The classical display of western settings, cowboys and Indians, guns and horses, in the opposition of values variously associated with frontier and society made it one of the major staples of Hollywood production from the silent era until the end of the twentieth century. Its various resolutions of the wilderness/civilization conflict reflect a wide range of changing American attitudes toward heroism, male success, and community development. During the late 1960s and 1970s the film industry began to revise dramatically the form and content of classical gangster, combat, science fiction, and detective genres. Sergio Leone's "spaghetti westerns" like *Once upon a Time in the West* (1968), Sam Peckinpah's *Wild Bunch* (1969), and Arthur Penn's *Little Big Man* (1970), for instance, all challenge dominant traditions of western films and popularly accepted national values.

In 1971 *McCabe & Mrs. Miller* was widely perceived, with its bleak, tragic, diffuse narrative, as an antiwestern. Action is motivated by vanity and incompetence, the community turns its back on religion, and prostitution motivates cleanliness in the town of Presbyterian Church. Its bearded and frock-coated hero hardly resembles the figure of John Wayne or Gary Cooper and is a dim shadow even of the romantic gambler played by James Garner in the long-running television western *Maverick*. The saloon-keeping Miss Kitty from *Gunsmoke* has become an assertive madam. The only Indian is a half-breed. The villain is a mining company, and the guns are not only the iconic Colt revolver and Winchester rifle but long-barrel hunting rifles, shotguns, and a derringer. Main Street is lost amid the chaotic and disorienting jumble of newly constructed buildings. The film elevates the woman to a place of parity in the narrative, even as it demotes the male, who has historically stood at the center of the form. In particular its representation of Mrs. Miller renegotiates the most venerable of all the western stories, the captivity narrative, casting the trade of prostitution as her confinement and white men as her captors.

McCabe & Mrs. Miller's negotiation with the western genre motivates a revised sense of narrative, style, and history. Unlike any other popular genre, the western depicts a specific time and place in American history. Ironically, its sense of history also plays a vital role in the representation of a mythic past. In part its mission is nostalgic: "Return with us now to those thrilling days of yesteryear." The cinematic western in particular, however, also contains a commitment to a truthful verisimilitude, to showing western space, the western past "as it really was." Indeed, some western authorities assert that "the western is American history."[3] Robert Altman's surgery on the genre extends to its conception of the story of the West not as history but as historiography, a competing way of telling the national story. The film rereads the past and marks that rereading as an essential characteristic of the generic process itself.

Revising the western carries a more significant weight, however, than rewriting other popular narrative forms. Because it so actively employs a particular history for its setting and action and because the western has been so involved in the discourse of national identity, its stories almost ritually engage a process of reimagining the frontier and its central impact on the American character. This process is significantly more challenging in the 1960s and 1970s. *McCabe & Mrs. Miller* shared the widespread revisionist impulse in Hollywood movies at a major time of transition in the movie industry as it undertook wholesale experimentation with classical narrative forms. Contemporary political and social unrest further drove a reconsideration of American values, especially as they were reflected in popular fiction. Historians of the American West began at the time to rethink the dominant paradigms of America's western expansion. Moreover, as a director, Altman consistently reflected in the film an aesthetic disposition to revision.

This rereading of generic structure is typical of the Altman film. "I'm always chasing genres,"[4] he says, surrounded by the evidence of a career that features remodeled science fiction, romantic comedy, murder mysteries, musicals, film noir, detective fiction, and combat film. Characteristically, his films establish reflexivity as a function both of the persistent transformations at work on the parent genre and as a stance within the film. In his other western, *Buffalo Bill and the Indians, or Sitting Bull's History Lesson* (1976), Altman self-consciously critiques the rewriting of western history by the entertainment values of the show business. Buffalo Bill and Sitting Bull, white man and Indian, have competing views of history, especially the nationally important scenario of Custer's Last Stand, in a film where numerous voices struggle over identity, authorship, and ownership of the past. The film suggests not only that the story of the West involved a conquest of the Indians but that motivation for that conquest evolved from the writing of history by showmen. The film literally begins with the rehearsal of America's national narrative as the sacrifice of hardworking pioneers "who made this nation what it is today." As the voice-over narrator intones these sentiments, the screen depicts another retelling of the most persistent and predominant form of the western, the captivity narrative. Indians attack a settler's cabin and carry off the women, just as the director's voice interrupts to call for another run-through of the performance. The film thus self-consciously grounds the origins of the western's stories in the competitive insecurities of masculine subjectivity.

National narratives rehearse the major desires and traumas, anxieties and ideals of cultural identity. The western as the American national narrative has for two centuries recounted the drama of western Europeans' mission into the wilderness as a religious, political, commercial, and personal journey that has uniquely shaped the American character. Its most persistent story recounts the struggle to reclaim and convert the savage wilderness, to find freedom, to strike it rich—all under the impetus of a "manifest destiny" to take possession of this continent. A sense of the West and an exceptional national American identity gets narrativized in the famous thesis of historian Frederick Jackson Turner at the end of the nineteenth century that conflates the settling of the frontier with the development of democracy. Within this context, the captivity narrative may be its quintessential incarnation. A perilous struggle for survival in the wilderness, an uncertainty about the efficacy of religious faith and physical prowess, a fear of the savage other: these are enacted in the kidnapping of the settlers' more treasured possessions—hearth, home, faith—all represented in the image of the woman. These stories encapsulate all the anxieties about safety, survival, and strength, where the woman is simultaneously a figure for security and a fear of its loss.

By the end of the 1970s western historians had begun to mount an assault on the traditional view of the West initially articulated in the Turner thesis. This scholar's famous conception of the West argued that white male Anglos moving steadily from the East into the free and empty land of the western wilderness forged the terms of American democracy. Personal initiative, the absence of class, individualism, pragmatic initiative along the ever-receding frontier inexorably shaped an exceptional character of independent American farmers. According to changing contemporary historical perspectives, however, the Turner thesis promoted a narrow sense of the West that omitted many of the major players in its development and masked the imperialist nature of a westward invasion and conquest. It hardly accommodated the industrial West of railroads, mining, urbanization, and large numbers of immigrant Europeans, Asians, and Africans. Certainly Altman's film is a compendium of the icons of both the generic West of myth and the Turner thesis. It also portrays a West more complex, however, than the classical narrative perspective of films like *Shane* (1953), with its celebration of the democratic community forged in the competition of homesteaders, cattleman, merchants, and gunmen amid fruited plain and purple mountain majesty. It reflects the contemporary western historians' complex sense of the West as a multiplicity of places. Films like *The Hanging Tree* (1959), *North to Alaska* (1960), *Ride the High Country* (1962), and *McCabe & Mrs. Miller* constitute a minor alternative to the classical depictions of the West. Here is the wet Northwest amid the commercial rain forests of the Pacific coast rather than the iconic setting of the arid plateaus of Utah or the grassy plains of Texas, here lovely redwood groves as the location of zinc to support the eastern metal industry, here the mountains of mining as opposed to the plains of cowboys and herding cattle.

It was not small farmers or independent stakeholders who "made" the West, but large corporations, the federal state, and turn-of-the-century industrialization. *McCabe & Mrs. Miller*'s West involves an intersection of towns developing to serve the mining industry; of the law developing around private, local, and national legislative interests; and of the sex and alcohol trade developing as an escape for the laboring class. Historians for the last two decades have posited the West as a crossroads of multiethnic cultures, rather than a site where white Anglo-Saxon Protestants fought the Indian to secure the national manifest destiny. *McCabe & Mrs. Miller* is populated by Irish and English and German and Mexican and Chinese men and women struggling to make a living. Sheehan's Saloon and Hotel is a home to immigrants attracted to jobs in the mines. Presbyterian Church is a dark, rainy, muddy mess of ramshackle huts that "don't look none too prosperous," set off against big, new, richly gleaming redwood construction. The film represents the church and the brothel as competing locales of progress in a mining camp that grows haphazardly into a town, and it examines the impact of both in the developing community. Its representation of prostitution, however, is its most dramatic contribution to an emergent view of the West that begins to include working women alongside the mythic "gentle civilizers" and the whore with a heart of gold. If once there were Indians in Presbyterian Church, they have long since disappeared. The classical captivity narrative revolves now around the captivity of women—fat, skinny, young, old, Caucasian, Asian—by prostitution or by mail-order marriages, and white men are the captors.

Popular narratives always develop in relation to the events and values of the contemporary culture as well as to a sense of the past. Since its release in 1971, *McCabe & Mrs. Miller*'s contribution to the multiple forces of the counterculture in the late 1960s has faded. A significant part of Altman's early popularity, however, with the large, young, moviegoing generation from the films *MASH* (1970), *Brewster McCloud* (1970), *California Split* (1974), and *McCabe & Mrs. Miller* derived from their experimental, improvisational style and their irreverent, caustic hostility to traditional values. The media stories about the community of actors and production personnel that characterized an Altman shoot, the hippie clothing and hair of the director and his staff, the stoned viewing of dailies, all gave the impression that an Altman production was one large "be-in." Part of the artistic power of *McCabe & Mrs. Miller* is that it transcends the times that produced it, but part of its power also resides in its resonance with the issues of its day. The film is aggressively antibusiness in its thematic construction of conflict; the world of the big-business Republican lies behind the gunmen sent to kill McCabe because he refuses to get out of the way of corporate expansion. The representation of the lawyer to whom McCabe turns for help is a parody of the John Kennedy persona, and his ambitious and self-serving platitudes reflect the antigovernment sentiments of the antiwar movement of the day. The film's depiction of Mrs. Miller's opium habit reflects issues of the contemporary drug culture. The antiheroic depiction of McCabe echoes the images of aimless, powerless, resistant little guys in *The Graduate* (1967), *Midnight Cowboy* (1969), *They Shoot Horses, Don't They?* (1969), *Little Big Man* (1970), *Harold and Maude* (1971), *Bananas* (1971), and *American Graffiti* (1973). The representation of Constance Miller as the strong, unconventional woman who is nevertheless ultimately dependent on the male is an image that reiterates the cultural critique of feminism. The representation, moreover, of John McCabe as a diminished version of the classical western hero reflects the film's contribution to a developing crisis in traditionally masculine narratives of power and control. The film significantly negotiates in 1971 a cinematic space for the social values that mobilized the civil rights movement, the antiwar movement, the environmental movement, and the feminist movement. It remains from 1971 one of the major events in the annus mirabilis of the counterculture.

The youth culture of the 1960s was described as a film culture as well, and the American cinema profited greatly on an aesthetic level from the introduction into Hollywood of the techniques and themes of the International Art Cinema. Altman's popularity, as well as that of Mike Nichols, John Cassavetes, Arthur Penn, Sam Peckinpah, Stanley Kubrick, and Francis Ford Coppola, emerged along with a perception of the director as the star of films that were modernist, iconoclastic works of art as well as political protests. Altman regularly employs an open and lyrical mode of storytelling; a persistent perception of social identity as fragile, fractured, and fragmentary; and a critical reflexivity about the nature of narrative communication itself. Altman's films systematically challenge the mainstream discourse of the movie industry in their play with story form and cinematic style, in their idea of character, and in their self-conscious distance from the industry. In *Buffalo Bill* the western hero is a man caught between William Cody's personal sense of identity and the public persona Buffalo

Bill manufactured by the publicity forces of the entertainment industry. The story meanders through documentary-like representations of William F. Cody's Wild West Show, reenactments of cowboy-and-Indian conflicts, and mystical interactions with Sitting Bull. It constitutes an essay on the storytelling process and business forces of the show business.

McCabe & Mrs. Miller reflects these same energies. Its central characters are debilitated, marginal figures, nomads along the far western frontier who struggle to make their way against the pressures of past failure, forces beyond their ability to confront and larger than their ability to control. The film is self-consciously experimental in style—employing Altman's trademark overlapping dialogue; graceful, constant, and inexplicable pan and zoom shots; a large repertoire of actors who improvise their lines; a musical soundtrack that works expressively along the lines of narrative. Its story replicates the tension between the foolhardy little guy with a big ego who pits himself against the suits of big business that has constantly characterized Altman's personal relationship to the Hollywood production system. Altman says that McCabe is a chance-taking fool with whom he empathizes. If *Buffalo Bill* is Altman's modernist essay on the nature of the western story, social subjectivity, and big-business entertainment, *McCabe & Mrs. Miller* is a poem about these same matters. The film is Altman's ode "To Autumn," but where Keats's famous poem celebrates the "Season of mists and mellow fruitfulness, / Close bosom-friend of the maturing sun,"[5] Altman's lyric charts the negentropic human energy that fruitlessly sets itself against the season's march into winter.

Artistry in the movies has not been a very popular topic in contemporary film studies. Questions of whether the film was worth making and whether it was well made are old-fashioned academic questions. Where classical literary criticism could evaluate poetry by its radiance, clarity, and harmony with some confidence that these qualities partake of the divine, film criticism understands these criteria as the politics of beauty that derive less from any eternal truths than from the coercive force of dominant ideologies. Nevertheless the great tradition in art is evaluative. Popular art especially enjoys its list of great works. The end of the twentieth century occasioned numerous lists of the best films of the century. The American Film Institute's "100 Greatest American Films" included Altman's *MASH* (at number 56) in 1998. The *Village Voice*'s "100 Best Films of the 20th Century" included *Nashville* (1975) in 2000. The *Los Angeles Daily News* readers' poll of the "Greatest American Films" included *MASH* in 1997. The National Film Registry of the U.S. Library of Congress (1989–2005) includes *MASH* and *Nashville*. To discuss the greatness of *McCabe & Mrs. Miller*—which is not included in any of these polls but ought to be—is necessarily to recognize its evocation of a minority set of aesthetic parameters that have canonized only a few innovative, modernist films like *Taxi Driver* (1976), *The Graduate* (1967), and *Apocalypse Now* (1979). *McCabe & Mrs. Miller* epitomizes the Altman film, and Altman's films both reflect and shape the formal and thematic contexts not of the universally enjoyed Classical Narrative Cinema but also of the more poetic and less popular International Art Cinema. Each form presupposes different norms of value, and each valorizes a different canon of great works.

One of the most particular characteristics of the art cinema is that it liberates the spatial and temporal dimensions of the film from the logical dimension; it is less a narrative than a lyrical cinema. In his commentary on the 2002 DVD version of the film, Altman makes some telling, and typical, observations about the narrative of the film. Choosing this generic western story is necessary on the one hand "because I'm not very inventive. I don't make up stories very well." On the other hand this "not typical shoot-'em-up western" is an aesthetical choice. "I wanted this to look a little different," with "an idea that you're peeking in on something" and that "it's not explaining too much." He says here what he has said in one way or another throughout his career: as a director who makes gloves in an industry that sells shoes, "I don't really care very much about story in a film. I think more of it as a painting." Employing the western genre, with its expected plots and iconography, means that "I don't have to waste any time with that, and I can then mess around in the corners, in the details, and it allows the film to develop in a different way."[6]

The graphic and rhythmic details of this film reveal its great success. The deathward-ness of life is matched by the narrative inclination toward winter's snow. The year's, the life's, the culture's entropy are caught in that inexplicably heavy descent and evoke James Joyce's famous conclusion of *The Dubliners:* "His soul swooned slowly as he heard the snow falling faintly through the universe and faintly falling, like the descent of their last end, upon all the living and the dead."[7] But running counter to this dreary fall is the ubiquity in the drama and in Leon Ericksen's set design of the still small golden lights of altar candles, of lanterns, of birthday candles, of campfires, of bathhouse fires, even of the reddish flecks of snow electronically laid over the final scene of the film. The buildings of the set design glow with the warmth of the freshly cut redwood trees: light, cleanliness, warmth, community, comfort against the inexorable dark. This "Tragedy of the Gambler's Defeat" is done as a cinematic tapestry full of the little gestures, the silent glances, the facial agitations, the last golden leaves of autumn, the sunset's sudden shadow—throwaway moments in the larger canvas of life's and nature's events, caught in the sudden cutaway or more often in Vilmos Zsigmond's slow zoom shots that carry the spectating eye through the dramatic space. The editing and cinematography are marked by a gracefulness and lyricism that emerges as well in the three soundtrack songs by Leonard Cohen. It blends the realistic and the expressionistic. It meditates with melancholy, humor, irony, and sympathy on the tragedy of contemporary social subjectivity. It structures the explanatory logic of story against the emotional logic of poetry. It makes the western into modernist art.

This book wants to document all these matters. *McCabe & Mrs. Miller* as a text negotiates among the history and historiography of the time and place it represents in the Pacific Northwest of 1901, the generic form and tradition of the western, the political and cultural rebellions of the time of its production in 1971, the vision and craft of the auteur Robert Altman. As in the film, the lyrics of Leonard Cohen chart the movement of this discourse. The first chapter, "The Real and Mythic West," examines the western as historiography and sees the film as a kind of museum that reflects the way recent western history thinks about gender roles in the extraction and service industries of the mining frontier. The second chapter, "Revisionist Western," reads the film against the tradition of the mythic West, where the national imaginary, in particular the captivity narrative, depicts the ideological parameters of American masculinity, "what a man's got to do." The third chapter, "Countercultural Contexts," understands the film as an illustrative voice among the many raised by protest movements against dominant cultural values in the 1960s, especially the feminist movement. The fourth chapter, "Altman's Art," values the film as simultaneously the definition and quintessence of the emergent American art cinema.

All these issues then feed into the recognition of *McCabe & Mrs. Miller* as a masterwork of American cinema. The western has played a central role in defining and debating American exceptionalism and other dimensions of national identity. Altman's western features prominently in that role. It dramatically negotiates what cultural geographers call the "third space"—between the then of 1900 and the now of 1970 and, indeed, the now of today; between the western and its revision; between dominant culture and counterculture; between the craft of fiction and the art of cinema. The film displays Altman's idiosyncratic play with story, social subject, and entertainment system fused within the power of a consummate work of art. It is a film that explores central issues in the postmodern environment—the role of myth in the sustenance of American identity, the economic exploitations of corporate capitalism, the power of desire within the sublime of nature and the seduction of drugs, the potential of artistic discourse within the mass productions of Hollywood. It teaches its audiences how to look and listen to narrative rhythms of life and art. It revels in the poetic dimensions of cinematic narration—the subtleties, the ambiguities, the resonances, and the depths of life's visual and aural surfaces.

The Real and Mythic West

Early in *McCabe & Mrs. Miller* an 1899 Case steam tractor lumbers screaming into Presbyterian Church, an event of shock and awe in the film that resonates with American history and myth. The mining camp recoils before the invasion of this small cargo train that extends industrial transportation from the East to the furthermost reaches of the West. Steamboat, locomotive, tractor—the steam engine and the industrial revolution have carried white Europeans from the Atlantic to the Pacific. They continue the colonial enterprise of extraction that fueled the earliest settlements of the West in the two-year fur trade of French goods for beaver pelts at Michilimackinac. Only now the Indians are gone, the voyageurs are miners, and the wealth of the New World is zinc. The tractor's astonishing intrusion also signifies the machine in the garden. Henry David Thoreau dramatically describes the invasion of the train into his reverie at Walden Pond: "When I hear the iron horse make the hills echo with his snort-like thunder, shaking the earth with his feet, and breathing fire and smoke from his nostrils . . . it seems as if the earth had got a race now worthy to inhabit it." He recognizes the disruption of the wilderness by this commercial energy, and its costs: "If the enterprise were as heroic and commanding as it is protracted and unwearied! . . . All the Indian huckleberry hills are stripped, all the cranberry meadows are raked into the city. Up comes the cotton, down goes the woven cloth; up comes the silk, down goes the woolen; up come the books, but down goes the wit that writes them . . . . so is your pastoral life whirled past and away."[1] The steam tractor completes this fantastic invasion of lush, nurturing nature by the unnatural, mechanical, and monstrous machine.

This moment in Robert Altman's film performs a lot of work. It marks a particular historical time—Pacific coast, northwestern Washington, 1901, zinc mining. It characterizes the human presence in this mountainous forest as intrusive and violent. It recalls the romantic sense of loss as the sublime world of nature gives way to the crass world of commerce. It also reveals the film's approach to history. The pulp western of fiction or the B western of the movies may only employ the West as a site for the melodramatic play of its traditional plots. Genre critics, however, locate the power of the form in its ritualistic recreation and celebration of some historic western time, particularly in its classical form summarizing the manifest destiny of the European mission in the wilderness to build God's "city on the hill." The history of the genre also reveals the extent to which the past is always a creation of the present, a kind of imaginative etiology that explains the situation, events, and beliefs of today. Whether as melodrama, or art, or social ritual the western is always about history—its realization and its representation, its authenticity, illusion, and its significance. *McCabe & Mrs. Miller* strikingly reveals the western as historiography, as a way of thinking about history, a way of constructing history out of past artifact and event with contemporary hindsight, a way of selecting and displaying historical objects and events that denote historicity.

Historiography is metahistory. It seeks to define history and examines ways history can be known, discovered, revealed. It pluralizes its subject and articulates the variety of histories. It renders visible the ideological and methodological processes that generate any history. It argues data and authenticity, and it makes history self-conscious. Such historiographic enterprise is dramatically visible in museums, where history is simultaneously palpable and absent, real and invisible, the self-conscious interplay of physical objects and imaginary settings. The curator mounts an exhibit in a liminal space, the physical hall serving as the portal between this physical present and some vanished yesterday. The exhibit begins in artifacts from that past, or in the vision that collects and organizes those artifacts, or in an understanding that discards, resurrects, and rearranges artifacts. Museums put on display memorabilia of the past in both their power and paucity, and the spaces among those objects are filled in by the reminiscing, reasoning, and recollecting of the historian and the imagination of the visitor. The museum dramatizes historiography, the facts of some past, its physical and discursive reconstruction, and its present reconceptualization. "Imagination and presence come up against each other in a way that allows us to test the strength of each against the claims of the other."[2]

Movies thinly veil their status as museums, but the western purports to take us to exhibits of an actual West. Thus the theater screen becomes the site and the genre film the exhibit where the ritual movement of historiography occurs again, the space outside the daily present where the viewing becomes the self-conscious act of reaching out for the unreachable—studying these faces and behaviors, looking at these places, watching this process and those deeds, touching these hard and ghostly objects. The western as a popular genre is always a retelling of a popular story. As a genre firmly rooted in the specific time of the late nineteenth century in the specific space of trans-Mississippi North America, the western is also a retelling of a historic moment in the four hundred years of the settlement of the continent. And as the needs of the national present change, westerns both generically and historically are revisionist—recalling, repressing, or challenging earlier ways of representation in comparison with narrative here and now.

Like the museum, the western has always inclined toward the capturing of the real, with a "drive to make the past come alive."[3] William S. Hart, in his recorded introduction to the sound release in the 1930s of his silent classic *Tumbleweeds* (1925), sentimentally recalls the impulse of the early movie western, full of actors fresh from cattle ranges and frontier towns, to capture the facts and significance of the "true West." John Ford famously conveys the ability of film westerns to document an actual West in his continual shoots in Monument Valley, Utah. *Winchester '73* (1950) and *Colt .45* (1950) chronicle these real tools of the arms industry. *Heaven's Gate*'s (1980) disastrous budget overruns derive in part from production efforts to reconstruct exactly the railroad town of Cheyenne, complete with actual locomotives of the day. Roy Rogers's movies reveal that heroic western behavior dressed in high-heel boots with embroidered red, white, and blue eagles, and Gene Autry established that cowboys carried guitars and sang. Homesteading, ranching, and railroading; sheriffs, cowboys, and schoolmarms; uniforms, hats, and war paint; law, order, justice, and government—the western provides history lessons in all these matters, constantly revising them to get it right—where it was, what actually happened, who did it, and—as Ernest Hemingway's brand of realism put it, "how the weather was."

The Man Who Shot Liberty Valance (1962) famously remarks, of course, on the mythological impulse of the western when it asserts the oft-repeated line, "When the legend becomes fact, print the legend." The desire for the real also generates a process, according to Hart's rhapsodizing in the sound release of *Tumbleweeds*, that transposes the gray dust of reality into a golden haze. Both processes of making history and mythologizing go awry in the 1960s, however. Under the interrogation of national values occasioned by the antiwar movement, the recognition that western mythology and ideology always masquerade as history becomes a self-conscious aspect of movie westerns. Historiography, not history, becomes the new focus of both westerns and western historians. Much as Leonard Cohen's music is inextricably entwined in the discourse of its fiction, the historicity of *McCabe & Mrs. Miller* is engaged in the discursive enterprise of the new western history.

A NEW WESTERN HISTORY

The starting point of this history is the nationalistic conceptualization of the West. Richard Slotkin recounts this traditional ideological perspective at the end of the nineteenth century as the tension between Theodore Roosevelt's *Winning of the West* (1889–1896) and Frederick Jackson Turner's Frontier Thesis.[4] On the one hand, Roosevelt's racialist perspective of Anglo-Saxon superiority in the evolution of mankind saw the West as the proving ground for the American man. The West under this aegis violently pits white man against Indian to take possession of the land, to renew the vigor of his Anglo-Saxon heritage, and to discover his heroic place in the hierarchy of the human race. The major avatar of this divinity is Buffalo Bill, whose Wild West Show ritually performed this triumphal renewal in Buffalo's Bill's nightly defeat of the famous Sioux chief, Sitting Bull. On the other hand, Turner measures the frontier as the dividing line between wilderness and civilization where the exigencies of opportunity and survival in nature foster creativity and self-reliance, equality, and democracy. The historian Richard White argues that by the turn of twentieth century stories of the West and discourse about American identity actively engaged either Buffalo Bill or Turner: "They had divided the narrative space between them."[5] Turner and Buffalo Bill told separate stories; indeed, each contradicted the other in significant ways. Turner's history was one of free land, the essentially peaceful occupation of a largely empty continent, and the creation of a unique American identity. "Cody's Wild West told of violent conquest, of wrestling the continent from the Indian savages who occupied the land.... Turner took as his theme the conquest of nature; he considered savagery incidental. Buffalo Bill made the conquest of savages central; the conquest of nature was incidental."[6]

New western historians have been concerned variously to revise the ways such historical perspectives have dominated thinking about the American West. Turner's West was rural, classless, and agrarian. According to Elliott West, "Under the older frontier interpretation the story shimmered with a romantic, heroic glow. Suffering and tragedy were redeemed by the glorious results presumed to have followed—the nurturing of American individualism and democracy and the coming of a civilized order into a wilderness. The new themes, by contrast, emphasize a continuing cultural dislocation, environmental calamity, economic exploitation, and individuals who either fail outright or run themselves crazy chasing unattainable goals."[7] Recent versions of the West categorize the white Anglo-Saxon movement west as neither destiny nor divine but as conquest. They record the disparate race, class, and gender of the multicultural populations that intermingled in the West. They connect the energies of the region to larger national and global networks of government, economy, and technology. This West was industrial and urban and developed with railroads and precious and base mining; its growth depended on capital from large corporations and the federal government. Patricia Limerick claims that writers of the West had two options—either to tell stories about "white men riding in the wide open spaces and sometimes shooting at each other" or to "write stories that reflected the actual human complexity of the region—stories about towns and cities, mines and boarding houses, ethnic barrios and Indian reservations."[8] Here in part of course is that same revisionist desire of the western to tell the history correctly: "What you are about to see is a true story." Truth is a function of perspective, however, and the emergent history of the frontier recognizes that while this space meant the West to the United States, it was the North to the Hispanic culture of Mexico, the South to the French and English cultures of Canada, and Here to the Native American. Trans-Mississippi America manifests not an empty, "virgin land," but a crossroads of contesting cultures, differing ambitions, and competing power structures. Much of recent western history, then, resides in both self-consciousness about the methodology and process of writing about the West and recognition that the stories told must inevitably be diffuse, contradictory, ironic, and incomplete.

Two conflicting perspectives shape criticism of western narratives, the dominant arguing that westerns reflect history, the other that westerns essentially tell stories of ideology. But western films engage in historical interpretation no less than western history employs ideological narrative. Both the westerns of the American cinema in the 1970s and 1980s and the narratives of contemporary western historians develop what Robert Burgoyne calls "*counternarrative* of nation."[9] Janet Walker argues in particular for an understanding of the counterhistorical narrative: "We can see some westerns as fulfilling a historiographic function by evincing self-consciousness about the history writing process at the same time that they share in it. Through the lens of history, we come to realize that westerns incorporate, elide, embellish, mythologize, allegorize, erase, duplicate, and rethink past events that are themselves—as history—fragmented, fuzzy, and striated with fantasy constructions."[10] Altman's second western, *Buffalo Bill and the Indians* (1976), is "historiographic metafiction" that works aggressively to reveal the relationship among western history, western narratives, and the entertainment industry. *McCabe & Mrs. Miller,* in contrast, demonstrates the western as historiography in particular ways that echo new western history. It consciously expands the focus of western history to redefine the frontier as a "contested zone of cross-cultural meetings."[11] Its story of Pudgy McCabe reflects how "as a depository of enormous hopes for progress, the American West may well be the best place in which to observe the complex and contradictory outcome of that faith."[12] Its story of Mrs. Miller presages Limerick's insistence: "Acknowledge the human reality of Western prostitutes, and you have taken a major step toward removing Western history from the domain of myth and symbol and restoring it to actuality."[13] As historiography, *McCabe & Mrs. Miller* self-consciously employs the tropes of classical westerns and "points up gritty realities that were a feature of actual life on the frontier and it highlights, by contrast, the prettification engaged in by classical westerns."[14]

ANOTHER WESTERN MUSEUM

On the main street of Virginia City, Nevada, home of the famous Comstock Lode, richest of all the mining ventures in American history, sits the Way It Was Museum. Artifacts of the mining industry litter its front yard. Pictures of miners, maps of streets and mines, old bottles of whiskey, ore samples, period garments, rifles and pistols fill its display cabinets and adorn its walls. And down the street is the Red Light Museum, memorializing Julia C. Bullette, one of the West's most famous madams, with an assortment of nineteenth-century contraceptive devices, prostitute garb, and opium paraphernalia. Virginia City itself is today a museum. The site of actual events in a boomtown of 30,000 in 1863 on the old mining frontier is now the space of recollection—its churches, its saloons, its opera house, the rail line of the Virginia & Truckee Railroad to Gold City, its empty mines. Virginia City today exhibits parts of its past as history and entertainment.

McCabe & Mrs. Miller is another museum. Its narrative gallery is laid out with representative physical objects from the turn-of-the-century West: that steam tractor, the elegant music box and the mechanical carpet sweeper in the brothel, the huge cast-iron heater in McCabe's saloon, the fashionable attire of a gentleman and the grimy attire of a mine worker. There's the church that gives the camp its name, and over there is the House of Fortune, McCabe's saloon, around the corner from Mrs. Miller's brothel. Guns abound in this western museum. McCabe's pistol looks like a Swedish model 1887 Nagant revolver. He conceals a derringer. Kid shoots a .44-40 Colt Single Action Army revolver, popularly known as "the Peacemaker." Butler carries the 1874 Sharps Long Range .50-90 hunting rifle with a 34-inch barrel. The film's soundtrack exhibits the musical artifacts of nineteenth-century dance hall ("Ta-ra-ra Boom-de-ay!"), church ("Silent Night"), and popular culture ("Beautiful Dreamer"). Scattered amid all these objects collected from the past are the icons of western characters—gambler, prostitute, saloonkeeper, preacher, eastern businessman, cowboy, gunfighter. The temporal dimension of the narrative puts on display the transformation of Northwest redwood cedar into the social structures of business and domesticity. The film exhibits the exterior construction of a frontier town and the interior decoration of a brothel parlor.

Nevertheless, like visitors to the museum, viewers "are required to assent to the historical authenticity and reality of what they see, while they simultaneously recognise its artificial, fabricated nature."[15] The motive of this museum's curator lies in its display of these objects, these characters, and their stories through the impressionistic filters of prefogged film. The film works not to document how the West looked but to capture how moving pictures of that West look. The display emerges through the painter's palette of reds and golds, blues and greens; the editorial blur of civic construction; and the recursive strains of Stephen Foster's popular song,

"Beautiful Dreamer." Furthermore, the sadness of Leonard Cohen's popular contemporary music casts the whole narrative project as a retrospective tragedy.

The death of McCabe and Mrs. Miller's apparently subsequent opium delirium at the end of the film shapes the film from the outset. It thus illustrates what Janet Walker calls the "'traumatic western,' in which past events of a catastrophic nature are represented so as to challenge both the realist representation strategies of a genre that often trades on historical authenticity and the ideological precepts of the myth of Manifest Destiny . . ., in which the contradictions of American conquest—a kind of generalized trauma—become invested in particular narrative scenarios."[16] She argues that many western narratives depict the present story in terms of some violent past that intrudes into this present in a variety of expressionistic ways. She cites in particular the traumas of Indian captivity in films like *The Searchers* (1956) and *Dances with Wolves* (1990), of a murdered brother in *Once upon a Time in the West* (1968), and of murdered women and children in *Unforgiven* (1992) to illustrate how "certain ostensibly classical westerns depart from strictly realistic conventions to depict catastrophic events in a subjective style marked by nonlinearity, repetition, emotional affect, metonymic symbolism, and flashbacks."[17] The expressive subjectivity of Cohen's "Stranger Song" as the film begins foreshadows this lone rider's addition to the plaintive chronicle of "all the men you knew" and anticipates that in McCabe we will "see just another tired man / lay down his hand." Such a retrospective narrative draws less on the optimistic tales of western mythology than it envisions the hard-eyed research of a new western historiography: the doubled death of cowboy and gambler and the drugged recollections of a fallen prostitute. Walker argues that the need to separate the realistic from the impressionistic elements of such discourse is both historiographic and psychological: "Traumatic westerns feature the American mind and bodyscape in history; their internal pastness doubles the western's historical setting, interpolating the spectator into the terrain of history and memory."[18] Such western narratives employ impressionistic devices to convey realities of historic and individual trauma. *McCabe & Mrs. Miller*'s historical exhibits reconstruct a falling and fallen time set in a darkling wood at the beginning of a new century; it displays recent western history's sense of ordinary people, their desires and failures, caught in and destroyed by forces of nature and commerce they cannot control.

THE MINING FRONTIER

Presbyterian Church has all the features of the mining camp, where "dreadful living conditions were a tradition."[19] At the beginning of the film McCabe encounters its "stern climate, primitive facilities, shattered landscape."[20] Its main street is a messy, muddy canyon trail that meanders among tents and half-finished shacks. Mining debris and cut trees litter the sloping wayside. His horse picks its way over mining-car rails that curve off to mine shafts. The film script elaborates on the scene of McCabe's arrival: "The town is alive—or rather—struggling to survive. A tiny, rude community, it sprawls along a muddy street. . . . Calling Presbyterian Church a community is giving it all the best of it. There are a few ramshackle wooden structures, some on stilts and a few tents. It is a town that happened hurriedly, thrown up along a main street that is little more than a muddy bog."[21]

The two dominant structures are the unfinished church and Sheehan's saloon, "a rickety, ramshackle structure, haphazardly set at the edge of a small dirty lake."[22] Elliott West in *Mining Frontiers of the Far West* also describes the kind of camp introduced here: heavy drinking and gambling were "commonplace and quite unashamed. . . . Saloons appeared immediately, as if materializing from the ozone. Church services were usually not far behind."[23]

In Frederick Jackson Turner's earlier paradigm of the frontier that shaped American identity as practical, resilient, and democratic, he defined the rural and pastoral frontier as any region where the population was fewer than two people per square mile. He lamented the closing of the frontier and its crucially shaping influence on American character in 1898 after the government announced the end of open and "free land" in the continental United States. Patricia Limerick, however, conveys the different phenomenon of Presbyterian Church: "Mining, throughout the West, meant a rapidly urbanized kind of settlement, with concentrated populations, in quite a contrast to the more dispersed, rural pattern of settlement in farming and ranching." In such a place then, "one would have to declare the mining frontier closed virtually the moment it opened."[24] The dominant economy of the West proved to be an economy of extraction, and the mining frontier proved to be the "shaping pattern" for the western future. However, it represented "a conspicuous contrast to an otherwise well established pattern in the perception of the West: a place where ailing people went to recover their health."[25] That the film's grim mining town lies at the furthest backwater even of this common mining enterprise is reflected by the fact that in 1900 no more than 4.44 percent of the population was involved in mining the "far West."[26]

Presbyterian Church has a population of 125 (not counting women and Chinese) and thus, like all mining camps in Turner's sense, was closed frontier. Sheehan and McCabe denote the prominence of Irish immigrants frequently straight from the famine fields of Ireland; in these camps everywhere in the West they generally constituted a quarter to a third of the population of miners.[27] They also suggest ironically the lucky Irish in western mining: the Irish immigrant Marcus Daly became the bonanza king in Montana of Anaconda copper, and his fellow Irishman John Mackey (a name tellingly and ironically close to the film's John McCabe) was the principal beneficiary of the Comstock Lode in Nevada. In Montana in the 1870s, the Irish composed 20 percent of mining communities; in Nevada they composed 40 percent. Two other ethnic groups, additionally, represent the bottom of both the film's and the West's racial hierarchy. The film's one black couple, the barber Sumner Washington and his wife, accurately reflects the 1 percent African American population in Washington at the time of the film; it also reflects the 1,500 African American barbers in the West who with train porters, hotel maids, cooks, and servants filled major service roles by the turn of the century.[28] In another play on a name the barber's name is both a town south of Seattle and the name of the prominent Massachusetts senator who championed emancipation prior to the Civil War.

The Chinese ghetto in the camp reflects the other dominant immigrant population in western mining communities where the Chinese counted for 30 to 50 percent of the population. In Presbyterian Church "all you have to do is turn over a rock" to find one, says Sheehan. Paul writes that "the mining frontier was always more ethnically and racially diverse than even the immigrant-filled cities in the eastern United States,"[29] and Altman's museum reflects this diversity. The polyglot cast of characters in the film includes English, Irish, Scandinavian, Indian, Hispanic, and African American groups and reflects what Elliott West calls the "World's Convention" in the mining West.[30] The animosity against Asians within this international community was widespread throughout the West and the United States, and Congress passed the Chinese Exclusion Act in 1886 to prohibit Chinese immigration for a decade. The film's representation of the Chinese ghetto in the camp as visually disconnected from the rest of the camp indexes this widespread hostility to Chinese immigrants and of course comprehends how the numerous Chinatowns developed in American cities all over the country. Its closing scene in the opium den accurately depicts the Chinese, who not only provided much menial labor in the developing West, especially in the construction of railroads, mining, and prostitution, but also conducted much of the opium trade throughout the West.

Contrary to this marginal, and visually disconnected, part of the camp, the saloon is central. Sheehan's Saloon and Hotel characterizes one of the most important aspects of the immigrant West, not only for Irish but other immigrants as well. Saloons provided a place of community in environments of deprivation, a place for liquor and food, a site of camaraderie, of news, and even for banking and the mail. The publican was minister, postmaster, lawyer, translator, and writer, and the saloon was the closest thing to home for the immigrant miner. At Sheehan's the Irish Mrs. Dunn echoes the image of the immigrant western woman as cook and boardinghouse keeper recently documented by developing western history; she provides the meals and minds the general store. Sheehan of course supplies the booze and the tables for gambling, but his saloon also is the first place of worship in Presbyterian Church. Sheehan keeps in the wine cage off his main floor a small grotto that contains a statue of the Virgin Mary where in the opening sequence of the film he kneels, lights a candle, and prays for moral strength. Perhaps equally important is the role of the saloon politically; some historians argue its value on a par with Turner's view that the frontier encouraged the development of democracy: "The saloon was actually a 'democracy' of sorts—an *internal* democracy where all who could safely enter received equal treatment and respect. An ethic of mutuality and reciprocity that differed from the market exchange mentality of the dominant society prevailed within the barroom."[31] The film peoples this camp with a diverse array of individuals and takes this kind of community for granted.

EXTRACTION INDUSTRIES

By the turn of the twentieth century, the state of Washington dominated the "great age of Pacific Northwest lumber production."[32] Douglas fir and western red cedar—the forests of the Northwest proved a great resource for the entire nation. *McCabe & Mrs. Miller* references this industry in little exhibits across the film. McCabe approaches Bearpaw in the second sequence amid great stacks of felled trees waiting to be milled. The camera catches him riding into town through the smoke and production of a coastal sawmill. The steam tractor arrives in Presbyterian Church to power the branch operations of the Bearpaw Sawmill. The great deforestation of the upper Midwest in the early nineteenth century spread to the far West by the end of the century, and its transformation of timber into housing is repeated throughout the middle of the film. The once-surrounding trees of Presbyterian Church become the center of its newly constructed sites of commerce. Logging and the sawmill are hidden from the screen, but their product is continually visible; the great redwood forest bleeds into the carpentry of progress everywhere.

Mining is another constant backdrop to the narrative of *McCabe & Mrs. Miller,* but this far-western backwater extracts not precious metal but zinc. Important for eastern industries, zinc was largely used in the manufacture of the outermost layer of wire and cable. The telegraph, the technology of electricity, and the telephone, like the steam engine, are part of the transportation and communication revolutions that circumnavigated the globe in the nineteenth century and that would bring humanity closer together more than ever in the twentieth century, which is just beginning in the film. This gray base metal was an offshoot of lead mining, which itself was an offshoot of silver mining; its noxious smelting process is invisible in the film, but its ugly piles of tailings just visible in the background dot the landscape of this mining camp. Walt Whitman in "Passage to India" exulted over the Suez Canal, the transcontinental railroad, and the transatlantic cable as the major engineering events in humanity's western movement around the earth. Finally arriving at the Pacific Ocean, facing now back to the Orient, humankind looks backward to its origins and forward to its future and stands ready for a new and mystical phase of human development. But there is nothing mystical or romantic about this westcoast mining camp full of gray men whose drudgery in a gray light produces the gray ore for the wire. In the film, the mining company's enforcer Butler also notes the significance of technological progress when he praises dynamite as the "fantastic stuff" just coming onto the mining scene. He also measures the growing gap between the "distant concentrations of wealth"[33] in the East and the cheapness of life in the mines when he jokes about digging a hole, giving dynamite to a Chinese, and dropping him in the hole as a doubly convenient and economical way of expanding a mine.

At the outset of *McCabe & Mrs. Miller,* placer mining of surface minerals by prospectors has already given way to the more complex and difficult process of mining underground. The windfalls of early prospecting have given way to a wage economy; prospectors have become workers, and economic power has "shifted to companies and corporations with large labor forces."[34] Mining speculation, development, and corporate profits depend on cheap, impersonal, plentiful, and dispensable labor. And even greater profits can be achieved by consolidation, as the name of the mining company Harrison Shaughnessy indicates. But the people of Presbyterian Church who watch McCabe's entrance at the beginning of the film, according to the film script, "are difficult to tell one from the other for the pale gray zinc dust that covers them . . . . They are filthy to a man. Mud-caked boots, sweat-stained hard clothing. We can almost smell the rag-tag bearded group."[35] Steam engines and the telegraph are among the great inventions of the industrial revolution and the development of the American West. *McCabe & Mrs. Miller* depicts the costs of converting western resources to industrial wealth as the tragic lives of its two protagonists in the marginal world of miners and prostitutes on the mining frontier.

SOCIAL ECONOMIES

McCabe & Mrs. Miller is set at a point early in the career of the town, when the bulk of its residents are miners. The typical mining community would eventually support a population in which 50 percent would be miners and the other 50 percent would be service people—the merchants, lumbermen, blacksmiths, lawyers, teamsters, and others that would support a vital town.[36] Presbyterian Church, however, reflects a more primitive stage of development, between the establishment of the mines and the establishment of the town, all at a significant remove from civilization. Bearpaw, the nearest real town in the film, is located down on the ocean six hours, or "a good day's ride" away. Part of the film's museum display is the temporal representation of the mining town's growth whose pattern of settlement, Limerick claims, "turned out to be the most shaping pattern for the region."[37] The growth of Presbyterian Church runs parallel to the story time of the film, which Altman shot serially, "in dead sequence," as the set was actually being constructed; thus the temporal movement through the story is measured by the size of the set. From the moment of McCabe's arrival amid tents and huts to the end of the film, the town grows from a small camp to a thriving community with a tobacco shop, a drug store, a bakery, a hardware store, a dry goods shop, a harness maker, a hairdresser and barber, and an undertaker.

A significant aspect of *McCabe & Mrs. Miller* is the literal depiction of western development, in both its speed and its haphazardness. Continuing construction constitutes a major backdrop to the story; buildings crop up without regard to street layout or zoning, just as maturing towns frequently showed the signs of their willy-nilly growth in their crazy-quilt work of streets and buildings. Paula Petrik describes this phenomenon in the growth of mining town Helena, Montana: "The community was unplanned and set in a poor location. The bulk of Helena's early population never intended to stay, so street planning, platting, and constructing were abandoned to whim, the dictates of geography, and the preeminence of the miner's discovery claims, with no discernible plan of organization."[38] As a function of both set design and camera placement, the developing layout of Presbyterian Church is never easily determined; where Mrs. Miller's house stands in relation to the church and to McCabe's bar and Sheehan's saloon is purposively obscure. Altman's temporal display is a perfect case of phylogeny recapitulating ontogeny: the gestation of the set mirrors the development of the mining town.

Recent western historians have noted that by the last third of the nineteenth century the West was fully integrated with the industrial, legal, economic, and cultural dimensions of life in the East. "By the beginning of the twentieth century the linkages between the western economy and larger world and national economies were firmly in place. . . . All communities in the West existed within the framework of an increasingly modern and centralized society."[39] *McCabe & Mrs. Miller* exhibits artifacts of this integration everywhere. Hairstyles, beards, and mustaches reflect the current styles in turn-of-the-century East. A small part of the film's display of social interaction self-consciously represents the transition from bearded to shaved faces. McCabe and Mrs. Miller too wear clothes that reflect both their economic level in the town and the latest in fashion from the big western cities of San Francisco and Seattle as well as the East. Mrs. Miller derides McCabe's desire to be a "fancy dude" in his dress because of the "cheap jockey club cologne" he wears. As one historian asserts, "Proper deportment and fashionable attire imported from Paris were serious matters."[40] McCabe's joking about Sears, Roebuck and Montgomery Ward reference the great mail-order houses in Chicago that had with the help of

THE REAL AND MYTHIC WEST 27

transportation like the steam engine greatly facilitated the awareness and availability of eastern products in the West for almost a quarter of a century by 1901. Thus McCabe can dress like a Gilded Age gentleman of means in far-away Presbyterian Church, but his cheaper bearskin coat contrasts sharply with the more elegant apparel of the mining-company representatives. He is not so drunk in his negotiations with them as to miss the latest fashion in expensive sealskin coat and hat worn by the young urban businessman who works to buy him out.

Politically, too, the East-West relations had reached similar levels of integration. The gold rush influenced California's admission into the union by 1850, and pioneers following the Oregon Trail had pushed Oregon to statehood by 1859. In 1901 Washington had been a state for twelve years. When McCabe runs afoul of the Harrison Shaughnessy Mining Company, he turns for legal help in Bearpaw to a lawyer who has aspirations to be the next senator in Washington, D.C., from Washington State. The film's historiography here is pointedly self-conscious as it names the lawyer Clement Samuels and as it reminds the audience of turn-of-the-century politics. In the 1896 presidential elections, Washington had voted Democratic in the contest between William Jennings Bryan and William McKinley. Lawyer Samuels alludes to the populist potential of McCabe's case for aid in the little man's confrontation with the large mining company and busting trusts. His political bombast also of course imports into this display of contemporary politics the bipartisan Progressive movement and its impulse toward trust busting that would neutralize the unbridled power of companies like Harrison Shaughnessy. The Anaconda Copper Mining Company was similarly powerful: "By the mid-1890s the company not only owned huge reserves of ore, coal, and lumber, but also the world's largest reduction works and a modern refinery. It owned farmland and city lots; it owned real roads and hotels; it owned waterworks and electrical work."[41] Harrison Shaughnessy want similarly to own Presbyterian Church, by legal contract or by illegitimate force.

The film's treatment of McCabe's powerlessness before the mining company mirrors the political sense at the time that "individualism had lost meaning in a society of powerful corporations and bureaucracies in which individuals clearly did not determine their own fate."[42] Part of the very subtle irony in this moment of the film is that in 1901 the United States had just won the Spanish-American War with the help of Teddy Roosevelt and his Rough Riders. These dramatic heroes epitomized the Anglo-Saxon masculinity that Roosevelt touted as a consequence of the western "regeneration through violence." Roosevelt's national prominence earned him a spot as vice president on William McKinley's campaign for a second term as president, and in 1901 he would upon McKinley's assassination become the youngest president in the history of the United States. The picture of the doomed president hanging in Samuels's office represents an ironic nexus of ideas, from the generally friendly climate toward rapidly growing corporations during the McKinley administration, to the values of Roosevelt's western philosophy, and finally to McCabe's impending death as well. The weak gambler and saloon owner is no Rough Rider, nor is he heroic enough to survive the shootout with the eastern mining combine.

Political references, period costumes, and societal integration are not new historical dimensions of the western. But from the minute the archetypal lone rider arrives amid the tall Douglas firs and the sodden skies of the Pacific Northwest, *McCabe & Mrs. Miller* self-consciously removes us from the stereotypical high plains and deserts of the classical western. Norman Maclean loved to tell the story of his difficulty in finding a publisher for *A River Runs through It,* his collection of modern western short stories, because editors would exclaim, "These stories have trees in them!"[43] Certainly Anthony Mann in *The Far Country* locates his fiction in these environs, but it's still a cattle picture. And while the Cartwright family roams among the ponderosa pines in the Lake Tahoe mountains, *Bonanza* is another western empire series. When the gambler enters the unusual geographic space of this film, it registers its historiographical distance from the western genre itself. Altman's arrangements then of his ill-fated characters in this wet, cold Northwest in 1901, three years after Turner announced the closing of the frontier to the American Historical Association, call attention to the very historicity of his production design. A mining frontier, rapid growth, eastern fashions, social transition, and contemporary politics—the persistence of their distribution throughout *McCabe & Mrs. Miller* suggests that rather than a subtext for the fiction the story exists as a motive for their display.

The first of these important exhibits occurs in the second shot of the film that links the fur-clad gambler with the unfinished church. The film's trajectory might be called "development of the mining town," and the church first signifies the pattern of transition from mining camp to town. It foreshadows as well the conflict that plays out repeatedly on the mining frontier: the initial mineral rush brings the prospectors who build the first rudiments of society. The saloon follows almost immediately; gambling and prostitution quickly arrive thereafter. "First came the miners to work in the mine. / Then came the ladies to live on the line," went the song in Montana.[44] "Church services usually were not far behind."[45] *McCabe & Mrs. Miller* presents Presbyterian Church on this historic cusp—barely emerging from the primitive world of camps and slowly pointing the way to a mercantile and civil society. Men largely populated the camps, and the first significant female population was made up of prostitutes. Part of the power of *McCabe & Mrs. Miller* is its representation of ways the bordello filled the human needs of the miners not just for sex but also for community. Elliott West argues, "Men longed for female company, but the sex ratios were so out of balance that men were often compelled to find recreation in gambling, drinking, and whoring." He further notes that "workers in mining camps craved order, and they struggled to create a sense of community even though they were transients."[46]

In a wilderness regularly characterized by pioneer women as infinitely lonely, churches later become the locus of female companionship, as well as the center for efforts to improve social morality, largely led by the next wave of pioneers, the women who represented the Victorian ideal of "true womanhood." Historians note, "The struggle to make and sustain connections between isolated western households—the work of constructing a community—was perhaps the most difficult of all pioneer tasks."[47] But the church presages the next stage of civic development. For now in the narrative present of the film, it stands empty, being built solely by the labor of the preacher, Reverend Elliot. Elliot is hostile, misanthropic, reclusive, bent over apparently by the burden of the sinful humanity he reviles in the film's funeral scene; he represents that negative view of the minister in the West as "gospel sharks" and "gospel sharps."[48] Even when mining towns like Leadville, Colorado, gained some size as a town, the church was outnumbered by the more popular scenes of vice. The town in 1879 "boasted 120 saloons, 19 beer halls, and 188 gambling houses and club rooms and only four churches." Nevertheless, "Ministerial assaults on gambling, prostitution, and saloons usually marked the opening volley of the Protestant campaign to redeem the West."[49] Churches and schools routinely centered social and cultural affairs in western communities.

As the community matured, their allies in this effort were the representatives of female propriety: "Families and respectable women took on enormous importance in the context. The idealized family summed up the best virtues of the Victorian moral order, and the woman who stood at its center defined the cultural high ground." Nothing could seriously improve towns like Presbyterian Church as one miner wrote but "an influx of the chaste wives and tender mothers that bless our other seaboard."[50] Indeed, under the aegis of the Victorian "cult of domesticity," the woman's role was "in the inculcation of high and pure morals."[51] From the perspective of virtue and morality, mining towns revealed the worst of social trends apparent in the country at large, not just the western frontier. But such "true" women are few yet in this mining camp. The reformist energies of the late nineteenth century characterize a key aspect of the Gilded Age. As Richard White notes: "Reformers, who drew heavily from middle-class merchants and middle-class Protestant women, propounded stability instead of transiency, 'respectable' women instead of prostitutes, thrift instead of gambling, temperance instead of saloons, and the family instead of the world of single men."[52]

The Christian church became the predominant symbol of emergent civil stability in those mining towns like Helena, Montana, which survived the boom-and-bust cycle of mineral discovery and depletion. Historians point out that the West nevertheless was and remains the most unchurched region of the United States, and the empty church in *McCabe & Mrs. Miller* reflects that phenomenon. The historian Anne Butler asserts that "the images of comfort and forgiveness that spring from spiritual concepts made local church groups appear to be the likely places for prostitutes to turn for relief." Tellingly, only the prostitutes know the words to the hymn "Asleep in Jesus" at Bart's funeral. She points out further, however, "that the churches, influenced by nineteenth-century sexual values and a belief in the basic desirability of family life, failed to provide a practical haven for prostitutes."[53] Certainly it is ironic that the townspeople work so hard at the end of the film to put out the fire in the church they otherwise have ignored, but its deliverance and the subsequent celebration foreshadow an inevitably subsequent stage of western social development. There are no children in Presbyterian Church and very few families, but when Mrs. Dunn indignantly brushes by McCabe's whores upon their arrival from Bearpaw, when she spits out angrily, "More whores!" upon the arrival of Mrs. Miller's Seattle women, the film foretells the potential of another day when moral rectitude will direct the fortunes of the town. Of prostitution in Helena, for instance, Paula Petrik writes that its "economic and social opportunities diminished as the frontier period ended and families replaced single young men as the dominant population."[54]

The film then locates its historic objects and sets its exhibits of iconic characters at a critical juncture in the time and space of the mining frontier. Its historiographic energies appear in the linkage of gambling and prostitution with the drive for community and in its imagistic filters of romance and tragedy. Narratively the film centers on two relatively marginal figures in the pantheon of western dramatis personae, and historically the film indicates that stories about these characters, on the one hand, and the exploration of their historic time in the sun, on the other, have been little examined in the history books. *McCabe & Mrs. Miller* is a film whose self-conscious history foregrounds the period and represents gambling and prostitution during their momentary heyday. It enlarges on the moment of transition between primitive camp, with its "collection of people not overly committed to bathing,"[55] and social community on the mining frontier. It self-consciously puts on display a reading of that moment which suggests that the bordello, and not the church, cleaned up the town.

One of the most ubiquitous figures in the West is the gambler, especially in the early nineteenth century on the riverboats where gambling was a favorite entertainment. In the mining towns and the cattle towns, where young male workers had few means of entertainment or ways to spend their wages, saloons and gamblers regularly appeared to meet their needs. The inevitability of gambling in the mining community derives from the very quality of chance and risk surrounding the whole enterprise of mineral discovery and extraction. Mining itself "was essentially a lottery," according to one contemporary investment prospectus.[56] Prospecting was always a matter of luck, and "where every man expected to beat the odds in prospecting, leisure-time wagering became a passion."[57] Customers bet on every conceivable game from poker to roulette and every possible competition from dog fights to racing body lice. Mark Twain, who got his newspaper start in Virginia City, gained his first writing fame from a story about jumping-frog contests in Calaveras County in California. Mining in the West was hard, dirty, and dangerous work, and games of chance as entertainment went hand in hand with those conditions. Elliott West recounts:

> Gambling was a prime example of the creativity behind frontier community-making, at once perverse and conservative. On one hand it summed up every enemy of a collective sensibility—self indulgence,

greed, and the relentless drive to grab wealth and deny it to anybody else. But it also brought men together, often in continuing relationships. And gambling was an active metaphor of what brought these men there in the first place.[58]

Historians point out that the gunfighter was far less prominent in the West than the mythology of westerns has portrayed them, but the gambler was everywhere. His smooth and educated manner, his expensive and stylish dress, and his entertaining conviviality communicate distinction and success in an otherwise rough and primitive environment. When McCabe enters Sheehan's saloon, he steps into this social subjectivity. The men know from his dress that he is a gambler, and when he spreads the red blanket over a table, they scramble quickly to compete for a seat at the poker table and the new game McCabe brings to town. The character who early remarks in the film, "You know I don't gamble with no professionals," indicates the gambler's reputation for slick dealing that is revealed as well by McCabe. He shares his flask, lets them count the cards in the deck, jokes with them congenially, buys them a bottle of whisky, and initially allows the men at the table to win in order to ease any suspicions they may harbor toward him: "You boys don't know nothing about me and I don't know nothing about you, so what do you say we make this a nickel game to start off?" The excitement and energy are high, and the men are hooked: "How about a dime?"

SISTERS OF MISERY

McCabe's derby hat and his frock coat, his red tablecloth, his unbroken deck of cards, his manner of confidence—these are the exhibits in the film's historiographic project that localize the familiar frontier signs of the gambler. They are signs, however, that the curator very quickly moves beyond in favor of his most important subject, Mrs. Miller and prostitution. *McCabe & Mrs. Miller* appears before the major work of the new western historians, but its representation of Constance Miller and prostitution anticipates and participates in the work of these historians "to understand the variety of women's frontier experiences."[59] The film appears at a time in historical study when, according to Patricia Limerick, "few of the important economic enterprises resting on women's labor registered in the occupational frontier model. The Poultry Frontier, The Laundry Frontier, The

Sewing Frontier, The Boardinghouse Frontier, The Sexual Services Frontier all await their authors."[60] When the film appeared in 1971, the three basic stereotypes of frontier women described by Sandra Myres still dominated the representation of women in western history and western fiction. One is the tired, reluctant, careworn wife and mother; the second is the "Madonna of the Prairies, the Brave Pioneer Mother, the Gentle Tamer so familiar in western literature"; and the third is the bad woman, "the backwoods belle . . . the soiled dove or female bandit. . . . She was the antithesis of the civilizer helpmate; she was more masculine than feminine in her behavior, but she always had a heart of gold."[61] Altman's historiographical project recognizes this last stereotype and insists that there is more to the persona. The film thus joins in the historical research that has "found a new western woman; through her eyes we see a new view of the West."[62] Indeed, the central structure of *McCabe & Mrs. Miller* is the delineation of ways to rethink the roles of women in the West and to understand prostitutes and the bordello at this cusp of community development. Limerick notes that "the prostitute was as much a creature of Western stereotype as the martyred missionary, and in many ways a more appealing one. But while the colorful dancehall girl held sway in the movies, Western historians either looked discreetly away from this service or stayed within stereotypes of a colorful if naughty subject."[63] Altman's gaze is steady and sympathetic, and it actively participates in the historical energies that have examined the subject since 1971.

The traditional western since the end of the nineteenth century, according to any number of interpreters, posits the fraught ways of masculinity. It conveys the changing terms of what it means to be a man, revising them as the United States enters into its authority as a world power after World War I, as it faces depression in the 1930s, and as it confronts fascism in World War II and then Communism in the 1950s and 1960s. Jane Tompkins aggressively asserts that the western as it emerged in the late nineteenth century Gilded Age is a form of resistance to the feminization of American culture: "The western answers the domestic novel. It is the antithesis of the cult of domesticity that dominated American Victorian culture," and it seeks in particular "the destruction of female authority."[64] The robber barons and the captains of industry after the Civil War were building a great industrial nation with steam dynamos, vast natural resources, new technology, and the physical labor of large numbers of immigrants from Europe and Asia. Men and machines, capital and commerce march on.

Along Teddy Roosevelt's frontier the Anglo-Saxon male and his savage foe "were the archetypes of the universal and world-wide opposition of 'progressive' and 'regressive' races."[65]

Roosevelt and Turner variously write the history of the American western frontier as the space where the values of the hero "who knows Indians" and the agrarian democrat shape the racial, middle-class values. They must resist the plutocratic trusts above and the immigrant and savage hordes below in this march of American progress. Consequently the politics of political progressivism, the masculinist parables of western literature, and the hunter-farmer-fighter paradigms of western history conspire to marginalize women and displace them from any authority in public life.

At the same time, the role of women was becoming increasingly domesticated. The "Cult of True Womanhood" and the "Cult of Domesticity" are historians' terms "to summarize complex nineteenth-century ideologies regarding women's roles."[66] Women were ideally to be mistresses of the home and to uphold the virtues of submissiveness, self-sacrifice, selflessness, passivity, maternity, moral purity, and dependency. Much of the popular literary culture of the Gilded Age "concerns the interior struggles of the heroine to live up to the ideal of Christian virtue—usually involving uncomplaining submission to difficult and painful circumstances, learning to quell rebellious instincts, and dedicating her life to the service of God through serving others."[67] Building on the moral authority accorded them by this ideology, late nineteenth-century women extended their franchise of virtue into reform outside the home. They worked to improve society in an extensive number of arenas, including the "prohibition of alcoholic beverages; ending prostitution; sterilization of criminals; improvement of prison; physical education for girls and boys; sex education as a means of ending 'vice.'"[68]

Neither conceptualizations of the middle-class woman had much interest in telling the complex story of the frontier woman. The tired stereotypes of madonna and whore effectively served their divergent ideologies until the revisionist energies were unleashed in the 1970s by a revised western history and reflected in the exhibits of Altman's film. Indeed, the historian Anne Butler writes explicitly: "The Warren Beatty/Julie Christie film, *McCabe and Mrs. Miller,* sparked my interest in the subject of frontier prostitution. Their image of scruffy prostitutes working out of canvas tents amid great snowdrifts struck me as markedly different from the usual beautifully costumed dance hall girls of other films."[69] The politics of academic feminism in the 1970s seek to write women back into history: "Disregarded as social, economic, or political entities, prostitutes are included only for a dash of spice in frontier accounts. It is appropriate that these long neglected women take a more meaningful place in the saga of frontier history."[70] Paula Petrik argues that "the social and economic structure of the nineteenth century, which limited women to the most menial and lowest paying work and made material wealth available to a limited number of them, created an environment conducive to prostitution."[71] The pioneer woman begins to emerge from the labor of new historical research in a wide range of hardworking jobs necessitated by the demands of survival. Recent historians document the strenuous labor of farm women, mothers, boardinghouse keepers, cooks, laundresses, and seamstresses besides their more stereotypical roles as missionaries and teachers. At the bottom of this world of working woman were the prostitutes, what Butler's study calls the "Daughters of Joy, Sisters of Misery." In the words of Elliott West:

> Romantic notions to the contrary the flesh trade was strictly business— and a rough one. Any advantage over the exhausting labor of laundering or running a boarding house was offset by frequent violence, disease, and the debilitation of drink and drugs. From the start life was degraded and improvised for many girls of the line, and when control and profits shifted to male managers, virtually all prostitutes sank into the grim, exploited condition common in every American city. Frequent notices of suicides underscored the brutal long-term consequences for most who chose the crib or whorehouse as their working world.[72]

For many women this choice was a desperate one. A central paradigmatic figure in *McCabe & Mrs. Miller* is the role of Ida (Shelley Duvall). Mail-order brides, lured west by eastern entrepreneurs and western governments alike, answered "Brides Wanted" advertising in church bulletins, magazines, and newspapers all over the country. "Desperate bachelors and pining maidens" found respite in publications like the *Matrimonial News* in Kansas City, "promoting honorable matrimonial engagements and true conjugal facilities."[73] Ida's tremulous arrival initially in the train of that steam tractor as a mail-order bride and the waiting miner Bart's eager greeting dramatizes another route besides the church and education that took many women into the mining frontier. When her new husband dies as the result of a fight, Ida has little choice but to become one of Mrs. Miller's girls. In one of the most telling scenes in the film Mrs. Miller remarks on their similarity, the literal one in physical stature, the other in social situation. Once a wife and now alone, destitute, and anxious, Ida is reassured about her new sexual work:

> *Mrs. Miller:* See the thing is, it don't mean nothing. You never know, you might even get to like it. I mean, you managed it with Bart, didn't you. . . .
> *Ida:* Yeah, but with him I had to. It was my duty.
> *Mrs. Miller:* It weren't your duty, Ida. You did it to pay for your bed and board. Well, you do this to pay for your bed and board too, only you get to keep a little extra for yourself and you don't have to ask nobody for nothing. It's just more honest to my mind.

Richard White writes: "Women's work, in short, usually revolved around serving men. This was true of married women, who at minimum, took care of their husband and often took in boarders, and of unmarried women who worked as waitresses or laundresses. Those women workers who fell out of the ranks of 'good women' and became dance-hall girls or prostitutes even more obviously served men."[74]

In the contests of war it is said that the winners write history and the losers write poetry. Winners also construct museums, and museums about the losers contrast markedly with the celebration of success. For Altman to mount an exhibition about prostitution in the westerns hall is to put on display what in 1971 still awaited fuller historical study. Consequently his displays are sketchy and minimal. The objects and portraits of loss and marginality are scarce, forgotten, hidden away, silent. When mining camps survived the transition into towns and then survived depletion of the mineral vein, reformist energies targeted the saloon, the gambling den, and prostitution for extinction. It is still possible to drink alcohol and gamble throughout the trans-Mississippi United States. Prostitution, however, is illicit practically everywhere. Images then of bordellos and their soiled doves are stigmatized by the reformists' victories of Puritan morality in the late nineteenth century and by their subsequent successors in the Hollywood Production Code. Moreover, the sex trade conjures images of degradation, suffering, and desperation that hardly seem to call for the celebrative recollections of this cinematic museum. Yet the holocaust museums, the famine museums, the slavery museums, the Native American museums, the Confederacy museums, all have come to assert the importance of remembering, of understanding the societal conflict, of putting a face on the victims, of describing human violence. The historiographic project of *McCabe & Mrs. Miller* puts both the life of prostitution and the western genre on display, rendering self-conscious the story of women in western history and in western fiction. The artifacts on display do not revise history and myth but posit terms for the retelling of both. In 1971 the film's prostitution exhibit amounts to a hypothesis about frontier women that historians since have documented and tested. Walking again through its spaces recalls the multiplicity of historic discourse and the diversity of history itself. The film now takes its place amid a larger project of discovery, resurrection, recollection, and perhaps even celebration.

"Prostitution appeared on every mining frontier almost as early as the first gold pans."[75] The women ranged from "crib girls" with just a small space to conduct their business to dance-hall and saloon girls to parlor girls and madams of luxurious bordellos. The film conveys the lowest level in McCabe's initial and amateurish efforts to bring the sex trade to the muddy trails of Presbyterian Church in the three tented shacks for his "ladies on the line": "Two for One Lil," "Almighty Alma," and "Pinto Kate." Limerick describes western prostitution as "a very stratified operation: the adventuress of doubtful morality and the respectable married woman, though in different spheres, were both far removed from the down-and-out cribworker, without even a brothel to call home."[76] McCabe buys the girls in a process like horse-trading in Bearpaw: "Eighty dollars for a chippie?! I can get a goddamn horse for fifty!" The flesh dealer tells him, "You don't know what you're doing, McCabe. You got no experience at this." Mrs. Miller tells him the same thing when she comes to the camp with her proposition for a partnership in "a sporting house with class girls and clean linen and proper hygiene." Mrs. Miller immediately establishes herself as an experienced, direct, and forceful professional; she confronts McCabe in one of the most important speeches of the film:

> What do you do when one girl fancies another? How do know when a girl really has her monthly or she's just taking a few days off? What about when they don't get their monthlies? Cause they don't! What do you do then? . . . What about the customers? Who's gonna skin 'em back and inspect them? You gonna do that? Because if you don't, this town will be clapped out inside of two weeks, if it's not already. And what about when business is slow? You just going to let the girls sit around on

their bums? Because I'll tell you something, Mr. McCabe, when a good whore gets time to sit around and think, four out of five will turn to religion, cause that's what they were born with and when that happens, you'll find yourself filling that bloody church down there instead of your own pockets.

Mrs. Miller offers her experience and expertise as collateral in the partnership for what was not an uncommon relationship of "joint ventures in which women ran the brothel while the men operated an adjoining saloon and gambling hall."[77] She reflects the tough business sense Paula Petrik describes in her extensive analysis of prostitution across forty years in Helena: "Over half of Helena's prostitutes had sound finances; those who were not entrepreneurs in their own right worked under the purview of other women. Prostitution on Last Chance Gulch was women's business grounded in women's property and capital." Like many prostitutes, Mrs. Miller wants most of all to leverage a successful business into escape from the trade altogether. She wants to escape Presbyterian Church for respectability in San Francisco where she hopes to run a "legitimate boarding house." She aspires, in other words, like other frontier capitalists, "to acquire property, to profit, to move up and out into a better social and economic position."[78]

A central aspect of *McCabe & Mrs. Miller* is this desire of Mrs. Miller to flee the desperation that makes her dependent doubly on the sex trade and the capital of a man like John McCabe. In many situations, "working arrangements for these women quickly funneled their earning into the hands of pimps and brothel owners and left the prostitutes only small sums for their living expenses."[79] Occasionally prostitutes made substantial return for their work, sometimes twice as much as the average laboring man,[80] and the film delineates the economics of a very successful trade. McCabe's first girls cost him $67 each, compared to the $50 for a horse. Mrs. Miller's fancy girls charge $1.50 a trick, 50 percent more than McCabe's crib girls, and Constance's rate is $5—both of which are expensive compared to $2 for a bottle of whisky or a weekly wage of $5. If every girl worked only once a day over the whole year, she would earn $548, compared to the $260 earned by the miners in the film.

Mrs. Miller's experience connects her with the network of prostitutes that traveled throughout the west,[81] and she imports five high-class "ladies" from Seattle. With Ida and the three girls McCabe originally bought in

Bearpaw, Mrs. Miller's house has eight working girls, a housekeeper, and herself. If all of them work just once a day for six days a week over the year, the income is $3,744. If Mrs. Miller works just twice a week, the income is $4,264.

Even when the profits are split fifty-fifty with McCabe, the resulting $2,134 would be more than the $1,600 Harrison Shaughnessy pay to buy out all of Sheehan's property. If only two-thirds of the men visit the brothel once a week over the year without seeing Mrs. Miller, the income from McCabe and Mrs. Miller's joint operation would certainly have been at least $6,400, or $3,200 for McCabe's share. He figures his whole worth finally, the brothel, the saloon, and the bathhouse to be worth $6,250. So, conservatively figured, such an income before expenses would represent a profit of over 50 percent of his investment, not counting liquor sales, bath sales, and the house take from gambling. The dollar in 1900 was worth roughly fourteen of today's dollar, so the prostitution end of the partnership with Mrs. Miller could produce about $45,000 annually in today's currency. Limerick observes that "a few madams skilled in a complicated kind of management may have prospered, but most prostitutes did well to keep revenue a fraction ahead of overhead costs."[82] Nevertheless, McCabe and Mrs. Miller have a good thing going here in the film's carefully imagined economies of the prostitution exhibit in Presbyterian Church.

The film displays other significant features of prostitution in the mining frontier, in particular the demographics of the whores. As Elliott West describes them: "The non-Chinese were a mixed lot, usually with a small majority native-born, and others from Ireland, Germany, Latin America, France, and a smattering of other nations."[83] Mrs. Miller's girls are Irish, English, Chinese, and Hispanic, according to their facial characteristics, their names, and their accents. What is especially striking about Altman's hypothesis about the life in Presbyterian Church, however, is not their ethnicity but the community the women form in the bordello. "As public women they faced the problem of creating a private, domestic existence for themselves—precisely the opposite dilemma facing legitimate women who wished to carve out a place in the public sphere."[84] From their entrance in the film, wet, muddy, and bedraggled, these "fine ladies" establish a happy and good-natured relationship more like that of a family than that of depressed sex workers living the dreadful life of selling their bodies to survive. These exhibits may produce only a romantic image of women on the frontier, but historians remark on the importance for women of emotional sustenance derived from other women in the nineteenth century,[85] and these moments in the brothel convey to the viewer images of sensuality, humor, caring, gentleness, and pathos. When Mrs. Miller's girls all climb into one bathtub together with the wind howling outside and sing "Beautiful Dreamer" beside the roaring fire, or when they all gather around a birthday cake that almost fills the screen, the sense of harmony is palpable.

The presence of the brothel and its women extend out into the community as well. The social institution most regularly strengthened by prostitution in the West was the legal system of legislation, law enforcement, and courts that developed around the growing expression of middle-class virtues and morality. But the law has not yet arrived in Presbyterian Church. Mrs. Miller's house rules require a bath before sex, however, so the brothel literally cleans up this western town. At the funeral of Bart, the women provide musical harmony in the hymn "Asleep in Jesus" that contrasts sharply with the discordant hostility of Reverend Elliot. Violence is absent, and sexual interaction in the house—most notably in the scene with Cowboy—is gentle, playful, almost innocent. Indeed, the golden red glow of the parlor as the music box plays "Silent Night" momentarily registers the town as a time and place of religious peace. Significantly, the whores along with the other townspeople at the end of the film fight the fire in the church and celebrate its survival.

Richard White argues that the kind of scene envisioned around Mrs. Miller's bordello in the film could have developed. "Prostitutes might have formed a community among themselves, or a community of sorts might have developed among the prostitutes, their pimps, and their customers."[86] During its heyday in Helena, for instance, Petrik finds that "women owned a large part of the 'half-world,' controlled a good portion of its economy, and established the tone of its social relationships.[87] In Butte, "Parlor Houses . . . were the top of the line; they functioned as social centers as well as brothels."[88] Certainly prostitution and gambling were central to the social life of mining camps and towns, but the nature of the concomitant community engendered by this centrality is questionable. Birthday parties, congenial cowboys and miners, happy girls, and slow dancing to "Silent Night" on the hurdy-gurdy may rather derive from the romantic sentimentality of western myth. The narrative of the film surely knows, however, and historians record, that these moments are transitory.

The life of a prostitute was a desolate one. Anne Butler's gaze here is pointed and unblinking:

> An unending stream of violence and grief brought an aura of physical and psychological misery to the world of prostitution. Immersed in a routine of unmitigated chaos and social rejection, prostitutes had few opportunities to develop into balanced, stable persons.... The personal relationships of prostitutes added to their social segregation, making them unlikely candidates for civic concern. Their behavior, guided by constant personal upheaval and an overt hatred for their fellow workers, retarded the emergence of community awareness sympathetic to the desperate economic and social plight they endured.[89]

Alcoholism and drug addiction were rampant—Mrs. Miller at one point scolds one of her girls for the theft of a bottle of gin—and suicide was the popular way to escape from the sordidness, degradation, and violence of the sex trade. Moreover, if a mine continued to be productive and the community continued to grow, the primitive mining-camp days of prostitution would inevitably end. When mines failed, communities quickly became ghost towns. In both cases, the transient population of gambler and prostitute moved on. "Once the social structures tightened and settled, prostitution became another circumscribed role for women."[90] McCabe's death, the saved church, and the season falling into winter all portend the closing down of this momentary light established in Mrs. Miller's bordello. Its golden glow derives in part from the madam's opium-addicted gaze.

Patricia Limerick argues that the attention of recent western history to the fact, place, and life of the prostitute on the frontier has produced three concomitant "general lessons for Western history at large": It demonstrates that the concept "pioneer woman" is in fact far more diverse than either the older history or the frontier myth recognized. It breaks up the old monolithic notion of the white civilized conquest of wilderness under the "compulsions of Manifest Destiny." It "restores the participants of western history to a gritty, recognizably physical reality." *McCabe & Mrs. Miller* anticipates these effects as it works to restore women to the pages of western narrative so that "the Western drama gains a fully human cast of characters—males and females whose urges, needs, failings, and conflicts we can recognize and even share."[91] American culture at the end of the nineteenth century and western history since had little place for either the ordinary gambler as would-be entrepreneur or the whore as tragic heroine. Films like *McCabe & Mrs. Miller* and historians like Limerick, Butler, Petrik, and others help to open a new space in popular understanding about how history has been and can be told.

FIN-DE-SIÈCLE

In 1900 the Republican Party with the support of big business and big capital held the White House, while William Jennings Bryan and the Democratic populists carried the flag for rural-farming and urban-laboring interests. Teddy Roosevelt—about to become president following the death of McKinley—and Frederick Jackson Turner were writing new historical versions of the American West. They read Indian fighting and pioneering as the twin forces that shaped the American character and that showed the way for the Progressive balance of democratic and capitalistic values. Meanwhile the domestic middle-class woman was moving outside the home to extend the moral values of "true womanhood" into an aggressive reform movement that ultimately would lead to suffrage for women. By the end of the century the concept of the New Woman celebrated individuality, self-reliance, and economic and personal independence. But none of these heroic cultural enterprises of the "strenuous age" had much place for the lives and deeds of ordinary men and women on the western frontier.

Like the continuing revisionist impulse of the classical westerns of the 1940s and 1950s, changing western history and revisionist westerns in the 1970s and 1980s reopened the frontier to new stories. The old stories celebrated the complex and frequently contradictory strength of empire on the cattle range, the value of homesteads on rich farmland, the wealth of bonanzas in the mineral field, or the blessing of community in the hundreds of new towns in the far West. The new stories recount people in places that do not always yield admiration, strength, value, wealth, or community. Indeed, despite lawyer Samuels's assurance to McCabe that he will strike a blow for the little man against the large trusts, McCabe falls victim to the guns of the Harrison Shaughnessy Mining Company. Mrs. Miller falls victim to the loss of her male partner's capital and her opium addiction. Because gambling and prostitution on the mining frontier are not yet prohibited social endeavors, they offer McCabe and Mrs. Miller the opportunity for the self-fulfillment and economic success proclaimed by the myth of the frontier. But the substance of their stories constitutes the trajectories of failure.

Because it ends badly, because prostitutes are the subject, because the film is fogged, because the cinematography is impressionistic, *McCabe & Mrs. Miller* both tells a story and self-consciously asserts its telling. The film enacts a historical time, place, and people, but the growth of "Presbyterian Church" is the growth of a movie set. Its history evokes the historiographic concerns about whose history gets told, who collects the data, why it is told, and who tells it. The western is not history, but *McCabe & Mrs. Miller* asserts that the western is a collection of artifacts and narratives from history. Its exhibits of that Case steam tractor, that Polyphon music box, that lone African American barber and his wife, that cowboy, that church, that photograph of President McKinley, that gambler wearing a derby hat and striding down the street like a gunfighter, that golden picture of prostitutes pressed against the gray, wet, and cold edge of the Pacific Ocean—they are at once familiar and new. We have seen them before but never quite like this. Here is another West, and another effort to remember things about the West for the present, and another way to say that the historiography of the western rests in the pressure of a particular American past that compels retelling.

McCabe & Mrs. Miller enacts two repressions, one in its collection of materials finally not put on display, and the other in the camera placements careful not to expose the film's profilmic space. The screenplay contains a scene left out of the final film:

EXT. PRESBYTERIAN CHURCH   DAY

AN INDIAN FAMILY of some fifteen people—WOMEN, CHILDREN, DOGS, ETC.—all of whom carry their worldly possessions, some leading horses, come down from the woods at the upper end of town. As they pass through town, many of the townspeople come out to watch but NOTHING is said. It is a strange contrast of cultures. Suddenly a cry comes up from the other side of town. The people forget the Indians and run toward the area of McCabe's . . . . They are excited as they look off toward the trail . . . . An enormous steam tractor can be seen turning the bend.[92]

The film significantly represses this scene of forgetting. Indians are a strange and arresting image of the past—quaint, impoverished, sad, and meaningless in the face of a dynamic present screaming its way into this wilderness setting. The postproduction process of the filmmaking (because of actual problems with the film exposure) forgets Indians too. In this story of the mining West, Indians are an absence; the narrative doesn't need them anymore than the people of this mining frontier who are already turning to face another newer reality.

That other reality is the inexorable advance of the East into the western landscape. Pull the cameras of the film back slightly, pan them left or right one degree, and the suburbs of present-day Vancouver surround the film's set. Altman's crew set up shop in the middle of a yet undeveloped suburb of this expanding city of the great Northwest. In order to recreate its image of 1901, in transition between the nineteenth and twentieth century, in between an old and a new western history, in between classic and ironic western storytelling, it represses images of the First Americans and excludes images of modern urbanity. The pristine wilderness has already yielded the tailings of base metal mining and presages the appearance of Industry (big railroads, big mines, big oil) and its shadow Reform (the Ideal Woman). For an idyllic moment in the mythic winning of the West—before the railroad and before the church and before the schoolmarm—this museum displays the new Adam and Eve as partners in the New Garden, where prelapsarian felicity is the very business of selling chance, booze, and sex and where the Fall is inevitable. This Way It Was Museum carefully organizes its exhibits then to show that time of transition when prostitution momentarily provided home in the frontier's gambling on a modern future.

# Revisionist Western

In the middle of *McCabe & Mrs. Miller* the community of Presbyterian Church gathers at a hillside gravesite for the burial of a miner named Bart Coyle. It's an oddly tense moment with the minister's angry and misanthropic eulogy, Mrs. Miller's prostitutes standing among the miners and the two married folk, the new widow stealing glances at the madam, and the group's sincere hymn singing. Burial scenes in westerns frequently provide moments of ritual beyond blessings for the dearly departed. In *Shane* the burial of Stonewall becomes the occasion for Shane to challenge the homesteaders to continue to stand courageously against the cattle ranchers in their efforts to build a home and a future for their families. The death of Doniphon occasions practically the entirety of *The Man Who Shot Liberty Valance* (1962) and its flashback revelations of the legend-fact relationship in westerns. In *The Searchers* (1956) Ethan's angry "Put an amen on it!" closes off the religious rites in order to begin the obsessive quest to find the captured Debbie and avenge the Indians' slaughter of her family. In the western, prayers are not the answer, pistols are.

   This scene visibly brings together for the first time in the film the uncomfortable mix of religion, mining, and prostitution that characterizes progress on the far western frontier. It exposes the minister's view of life as corrupt and sinful. It reveals the tensions that lie beneath the surface between the cult of true womanhood and the soiled doves. It marks the inevitable movement in Ida's life from Coyle's mail-order bride to one of Mrs. Miller's girls. It celebrates ironically in the hymn singing a momentary community of faith. It foreshadows McCabe's own death. It also occasions the arrival of a stranger on horseback. Suddenly the funeral's tense and awkward mix of people and values is displaced by an anxiety over a different threat. The western convention of funeral segues to another dominant convention, the showdown. Fearing the appearance of gunmen from the mining company to enforce the sale of his property, McCabe moves resolutely to a gunfight over the presumed challenge to his property and the town's independence.

The moment is disquieting and uncanny as it foreshadows McCabe's final confrontation at the end of the film with the actual killers from the mining company. Editing and zoom shots build the anticipation of a shootout with a series of shot–reverse shot images of the approaching men. Intercut shots of Mrs. Miller's face capture her dread over the impending conflict. The braggart gambler and businessman, Pudgy McCabe, suddenly becomes the defensive and bold gunfighter, advancing to champion the town. Coyle lies dead behind him, and his own death looms at the end of the story. If it's not showdown now, it anticipates by convention and narrative inevitability the gunfight later. Moreover, almost as though McCabe knows that, as David Lusted describes it, the "implied resolution of the Western involves the common choice forced on the male hero between heterosexual partnership and a fantasy of self sufficiency," McCabe goes forth to battle. In the moment—his fancy eastern fashions cleaned and creased, his stylish derby hat tilted neatly, his gloved right hand held just so and ready beside but just away from the holstered revolver—John is ready, and he looks good. Lusted notes that as McCabe makes fashion an aspect of his own self-conscious display, he also foregrounds how the traditional western "invites sustained looks of admiration."[1] McCabe here also reveals what Lee Mitchell calls the "'fashion leader's self-consciousness' in the western hero's 'preening self-regard,' the vision of himself as an object 'good to look at.'"[2] Uneasiness and anxiety are also part of his appearance here, but they quickly dissipate into humor when the lone stranger proves to be an innocent cowboy lured to the town by the reputation of its prostitutes and looking for a different "piece of ass" than McCabe fears.

The television series *Gunsmoke* famously began every episode with a camera shot at waist height looking over the holstered gun of Marshal Matt Dillon as he faced down some lawless member of the community in the middle of the street. The ritual of the shootout was such a familiar component in the western that Richard Nixon and Nikita Khrushchev turned and silently drew down on each other on Air Force One as they flew over Monument Valley during the Soviet premier's famous state visit in 1959. In the novel *McCabe* Edmund Naughton uses the showdown as a major structural device. It opens with McCabe in the middle of the shootout with the three professional killers sent by the mining company to settle his affairs; it contains the face-off with the cowboy who rides ominously into town yelling and firing his gun; it contains a dreaming flashback to McCabe's confrontation and killing of Bill Roundtree in front of a saloon; it chronicles his rise to business success in town; and it then concludes with the gunfight with the company men.

Here in this moment of the film, however, everything is all wrong. Ernest Hemingway long ago began his short story "The Snows of Kilimanjaro" with an anecdote about the frozen carcass of a leopard at the top of this huge African mountain; he wondered what had brought the leopard to such a height so far from its normal hunting grounds. What brings this gambler and this cowboy to the rainy Northwest territory of mines and lumber? The gunfighter is a saloonkeeper wearing a cravat and a derby. The bad guy is a scared cowboy in a silly oversized ten-gallon hat. McCabe is on foot, at first a tiny figure seen from the other side of the cowboy's horse and then in medium shot framed by a street bordered half by his House of Fortune and half by the mountainside graveyard. The reverse shot frames the cowboy between the cold glare of the sky and the dark shadows of the mountain landscape through which the road runs like a drainage ditch. The space is unbalanced, cacophonous in lighting and graphic mismatches, in conflicting and changing camera perspectives and movements. Moreover, while a confrontation is brewing, the stakes of this showdown are missing. Then suddenly the tension evaporates into the humor of the cowboy's quest for the "fanciest whorehouse in the territory." Jane Tompkins argues that "the women and children cowering in the background of . . . battles between outlaws and posses, good gunmen and bad legitimize the violence men practice in order to protect them."[3] Here, rather than cowering, Mrs. Miller, as she will before the final shootout, just leaves this space of confrontation.

A shorthand synopsis of the film is equally discordant: A traveling gambler parlays his poker winnings in a remote mining camp into significant property, including a saloon, casino, bathhouse, and, in partnership with a madam, a brothel. The depth of the zinc vein and the growth of the town prompt a large mining corporation to buy up the town, and when the gambler refuses to sell his property, they kill him. This western story again chronicles the hero who upholds traditional communal values of society along the American frontier, but here he fights for the values of saloon and brothel. He resists the lawlessness and savagery not of the wilderness but of the corporate powers that send a squad of killers after him. McCabe may not employ his skill as a gunfighter to advance the march of civilization, but when he loads his shotgun and straps on his revolver, he nevertheless goes out to defend what he believes are his constitutional rights. As the town's communal values center around the brothel, as romantic potential between John and Constance is also largely financial, and as its hero is "a failed pimp"[4] who lies dead at the film's conclusion, *McCabe & Mrs. Miller* is clearly a nontraditional western.

Its end is marked both by the death of McCabe and by the opium gaze of Mrs. Miller that at once concludes the film and that establishes the opening narrative point of view to be hers. The plot of the film develops like this showdown with full modernist irony. On the one hand, McCabe's death reflects the loss of faith in the traditional story of the frontier whose hero either in success or sacrifice points the way to a new and better future. McCabe's initial standoff with the cowboy, just like his running gunfight with Butler and his men at the end, is a meaningless gesture. The dandy with the gun, full of empty bravado, McCabe lacks the skill to save himself in a fight whose outcome will hardly change if he wins. The mining company will replace McCabe as the entrepreneur who profits from the town's wealth. This first uneventful showdown self-consciously mirrors the concluding showdown, and it reflects how the film self-consciously looks at this moment of transition so central to the traditional frontier story, when the gunfight marks on a personal level the transition from frontier lawlessness to civilized order. On the other hand, McCabe fights pretty well and succeeds in killing all three of the villains. He may ambush the kid, shoot the half-breed in the back, and use his gambler's concealed derringer to blast Butler between the eyes, but these are guerrilla tactics necessary against a superior enemy. The audience takes pleasure in McCabe's retrospectively earning the reputation ascribed to him at the outset by the townspeople. There is classical satisfaction in his lonely and successful defeat of the foes arrayed against him, one by one, like Marshal Kane's shoot-out in *High Noon* (1952), even if finally McCabe dies tragically and unnoticed in the snow.

McCabe's death negatively and ironically affects Mrs. Miller as well. Unlike the Ringo Kid, who avenges the death of his brother and his wrongful imprisonment and offers a new life for the prostitute Dallas in *Stagecoach* (1939), *McCabe & Mrs. Miller* self-consciously portrays the ineffectual McCabe as unable to liberate Mrs. Miller. In this confrontation, as well as in the scene the night before McCabe's battle with the mining company enforcers, Mrs. Miller abandons the scene of the fearfully waiting woman; she watches neither event. In another way, however, her pervasive point of view establishes the meaninglessness of the showdown with the cowboy as a foreshadowing of the deathly reality of the final fight. She fears not just the loss of a lover, as Marshal Kane's bride Amy, for instance, fears in his meeting with Frank Miller in *High Noon*. Rather, she fears the loss of the man who, like Ethan with Debbie in *The Searchers*, will deliver her from captivity. Mrs. Miller as a prostitute is a sexual captive of masculine desire. Irony resides in the fact that some affection certainly develops for McCabe as a lover, but her dependence upon McCabe's financial partnership is central to the film's understanding of the economies of freedom on the frontier. The happy dissipation of anticipated violence into innocent humor in the discordant encounter between this "fancy dude" and the cowboy reflects the entire middle section of the film and its golden representation of the ugly world of prostitution. These moments reflect not the historic realities of that world but the story's momentary resistance against the cold Northwest frontier, the gray realities of corporate control. They are finally narrative fantasies, like those of the classical western itself, that are generated along with opium dreams in face of its ultimate reality death, what Jane Tompkins calls "West of Everything."

This short scene distills much about how Altman's western works. As Michael Dempsey describes the scene: "Altman casually violates Western conventions, as when McCabe approaches a horseman for the classic fast-draw showdown only to find a gawky kid looking for the whorehouse. Altman's parodies of cliches like this parallel the ways that, in the movie, life destroys illusions as illusions destroy lives."[5]

The film refuses the traditional heroism of the classical western. It disturbs the pro-society happy ending of that form. It develops the narrative as an imaginative alternative to the literal reality of such ends. It elevates the female saloon lady from supportive interest in the hero (Katy Jurado's Helen in *High Noon*, Marlene Dietrich's Frenchy in *Destry Rides Again* [1939], Ruth Roman's Ronda in *The Far Country* [1954]) to the central subject of the story. It reflects a self-cognizant awareness of genre discourse, and it reflexively analyzes the motivations of western fiction itself.

THE REVISED WESTERN

In 1971 *McCabe & Mrs. Miller* appeared some thirty-three years after *Stagecoach* launched the era of the "adult western." In another thirty-three years, the western would effectively be dead. The film stands then at a midpoint on a trajectory of exhaustion and dissolution. But from the perspective of the early 1970s, whether the genre suffered decline or enjoyed revitalization was a premature question. Experimental change in all dominant forms of fictive discourse occurred across the cultural map everywhere at the time, including the alternative fiction of mainstream writers like John Barth, Thomas Pynchon, and Kurt Vonnegut as well as the popular films of postclassical Hollywood. At the end of the 1960s, the evidence of vitality in the western was still strong everywhere, but the incredible number of westerns on television had begun to recede from its high-water mark of twenty-six western shows each week. In the late 1950s, according to *Life* magazine, "one third of nighttime network hours filled with Westerns; the 1957 fall season opened with 28 new Westerns and the 1959 season introduced 32 new ones."[6] Two shows in particular, *Gunsmoke* and *Bonanza*, among the longest-running series in television history, reflected the continuing popularity of the form in their combined runs of thirty-four years. Nevertheless, Hollywood production of westerns diminished significantly. In the first half of the century, 25 percent of all Hollywood films were westerns, but by 1972, westerns represented 12 percent of the Hollywood product. According to Phil Hardy, 44 westerns were released in 1971, including *McCabe & Mrs. Miller*. In 1972 that number dropped to 27, to 16 in 1973, to 9 in 1974. In the bicentennial year 1976, only 12 westerns appeared, including Altman's critically reflexive *Buffalo Bill and the Indians*.[7] The drop in production in the years since then has been so dramatic as to remove the western from the list of major popular narrative genres altogether.

These westerns, however, appear in the midst of the major industrial retooling of Hollywood necessitated by its declining box office popularity in the new television age. The period from 1967, with the appearance of *Bonnie and Clyde*, to 1975, with the release of *Jaws*, witnessed an enormous amount of work devoted to remodeling the popular narrative genres. Part of the changes certainly results from what Rick Altman describes as an inevitable aspect of genre change: "Once a genre is recognized and practiced throughout the industry, individual studios have no further economic interest in practicing it as such . . . , instead, they seek to create new cycles by associating a new type of material or approach with an existing genre, thus initiating a new round of gentrification."[8]

Additionally the incredible energies of work by new and young directors fueled such changes even further. Robert Altman, Sidney Pollack, Arthur Penn, Francis Ford Coppola, John Cassavetes, Mike Nichols, Sam Peckinpah, Woody Allen, and others created an almost decade-long period of innovation routinely designated as the "Hollywood Renaissance" in studies of film history. By 1976, with film-school directors like Steven Spielberg and George Lucas, that energy would congeal into the work and period style quickly recognized as the "New Hollywood Cinema" or "postclassical Hollywood" and dominate film production in the last quarter of the twentieth century. The enormous changes visible in the western both reflect and participate in this time of major transformation in American film history.

The biological fallacy has appeared intermittently in genre criticism from the work of Ferdinand Brunetière in 1870 to Thomas Schatz in 1970. It is difficult to resist the sense that genres are born, like the western, say, in 1823 with the appearance of James Fenimore Cooper's *The Pioneers;* develop into adolescence, like Owen Wister's *The Virginian* in 1902; mature into a classical form, in another medium, with *Stagecoach* in 1939; and devolve into mannerist, baroque, or parodic self-consciousness in the spate of western films appearing in the late sixties. Evolution of the form from innocent experimentation, through romantic celebration, and classical assurance to weary and tired cliché or parody makes a certain sense, until historians remind us that these qualities have existed simultaneously with each other from the outset of the genre. Mark Twain was parodying both Cooper and the western frontier even as Buffalo Bill was enshrining the cowboy-Indian conflict in popular entertainment. While *The Virginian* was teaching the masculine values of regeneration through violence, Stephen Crane in "The Blue Hotel" and "The Bride Comes to Yellow Sky" was self-consciously analyzing the problematic effects of an imaginary West on realistic westerners. As early as the silent era, film producers worried that the parodic elements in the western would "Jack Londonize the Western cowboy—that is, present him as he really is in life." From the earliest decades of the cinema, the history of the movie western recounts numerous parodies—from Buster Keaton in *Paleface* (1922) to Jane Fonda in *Cat Ballou* (1965)—that indicate the vitality as much as the decadence of the form. Even a classical realist film like *Stagecoach* "is a virtual anthology of gags, motifs, conventions, scenes, situations, tricks, and characters drawn from past westerns."[9] Any given era of the literary or cinematic western discloses romance and realism, fantasy and authenticity, tragedy and comedy, evolution and recirculation, innocence and parody, history and myth.

There is little question, however, that the forces of social disruption in the late 1960s also motivated changes in genre style and content. The vastness of the western as a cultural product meant that films like *The Ox-Bow Incident* (1943), *The Gunfighter* (1950), *High Noon* (1952), *Johnny Guitar* (1954), and *Run of the Arrow* (1957) constitute what Jim Kitses describes as "precursors to a counter-tradition that the Western tradition itself generates, a revisionist shadow, a parallel track to the imperial mainstream with all its ideological baggage."[10] By 1970 that filmmaking energy emerges from the shadows in the light of the counterculture. Historians disagree about the effect of revisionist western films. Did films like *McCabe & Mrs. Miller* accelerate the declining power of the western to speak to the American culture with the authority of myth as it had for the first two-thirds of the twentieth century? The widespread social malaise that followed the end of the war in Vietnam and the resignation of Richard Nixon reverberated well into the 1980s. Further changes in the nature of national identification as a result of globalization additionally undermined the white, masculine, imperialistic, violent notions of America promoted by the western. For some cultural critics, then, the basic language, symbolism, and message of the western becomes obsolete, which explains its dissolution and generic decline. For others, the remarkable energy of films in the 1990s like *Dances with Wolves, Unforgiven, The Last of the Mohicans, Geronimo, The Quick and the Dead, The Ballad of Little Jo,* and *Dead Man* indicate that the western is still "gloriously alive."[11]

The genre, its social historians, and its cultural critics construct a vast and diverse and contradictory commentary on the nature of American experience and identity. At the core of this exegetical discourse, however, lie a number of certainties about the "meaning of heroism, the relation of the individual to family and community, the nature of patriotism, the value of freedom, the challenge of making a home, and icons for them in American national identity."[12] The genre's central tenets, as delineated by Steve Neale, are

> that frontier existence and frontier encounters were characteristically marked by opportunity and danger, hardship and bounty, adventure and violence; that the frontier served to cultivate unique national

characteristics, particularly among those who inhabited, crossed or helped extend its borders; that its westward movement served to chart the path of Anglo-American settlement and hence to mark the "Manifest Destiny" and the racial and cultural superiority of Anglo-Americans . . . ; and that contact with the frontier, or at least with the land, the conditions and the ways of life which once marked its existence, was and is a means of personal and national renewal and regeneration.[13]

Honor, restraint, loyalty, justice, veracity, fidelity, and independence are virtues traditionally celebrated in the national imagination of the mythic western frontier. In the romantic telling of its heroic tales, suffering and tragedy on the frontier nurtured democracy and individualism and turned the savage wilderness into the civilization of a vibrant and growing nation.

This was the ideal that by 1970 the winds of psychedelic rock, racial conflict, the Vietnamese war, and political assassinations fed into Bob Dylan's singing "the times they are a-changing." The historian Elliott West describes the western in this radical context as reflecting "a continuing dislocation, environmental calamity, economic exploitation, and individuals who either fail outright or run themselves crazy chasing unattainable goals."[14] The dramatic changes in the genre, where the "Old West comes to embody a lost civilization and the New West a savage modernity,"[15] are everywhere perceived in film history as "modernist" westerns or "revisionist" westerns or "antiwesterns" or even "nonwesterns." The research and development of new filmmaking, whether by the independents or the new Hollywood directors, was variously at work "foregrounding," "confronting," "undermining," "interrogating," "inverting," or "dismantling what was once the quotidian stuff of light entertainment."[16] John Cawelti summarizes what he calls "the four modes of generic transformation" occurring in popular narrative genres at the end of the 1960s: humorous burlesque, evocation of nostalgia, demythologization of generic myth, and the reaffirmation of myth as myth.[17] Despite a striking range of subjects, styles, and historicity, many of the westerns of the period reveal these characteristics: *The Good, the Bad, & the Ugly* (Sergio Leone, 1966); *The Wild Bunch* (Sam Peckinpah, 1969); *Butch Cassidy and the Sundance Kid* (George Roy Hill, 1969); *Little Big Man* (Arthur Penn, 1970); *The Great Northfield Minnesota Raid* (Phillip Kaufman, 1972); *Jeremiah Johnson* (Sidney Pollack, 1972), *High Plains Drifter* (Clint Eastwood, 1973); and *Blazing Saddles* (Mel

Brooks, 1974). *McCabe & Mrs. Miller* is most conventional in its participation in these disruptive rereadings of American forms and values.

Jack Nachbar identifies these modes of a new western in contrast to "the completely conventional product we are all used to." There the "conflict between civilization and the forces of the threatening wilderness is immediately apparent." There we "easily recognize the hero and the violent duty that lies before him."[18] Peckinpah, Penn, Leone, and Altman all make "personal" westerns that interrogate the basic presuppositions of the traditional narratives. They revise their mythic representation of western history. They expose the ideological contradictions endemic to its thematic core. They coruscate its celebration of violence. They denounce its racist and masculinist commitments. They develop the conventions and plots of the western so reflexively, self-consciously, politically, and expressively that for many aficionados of the older narratives they don't make westerns at all. Kitses asserts, however, that "there now seems a strong argument for recognition of the revisionist Western as a discrete, dominant type. Indeed films that in whole or part interrogate aspects of the genre such as its traditional representations of history and myth, heroism and violence, masculinity and minorities, can be seen now to make up the primary focus of the genre." Films like *McCabe & Mrs. Miller* then are among works now seen to "constitute the creative mainstream of the genre,"[19] which is that very same historiographical impulse of the western to revise its take on the past.

Interestingly, contemporary critical reaction to *McCabe & Mrs. Miller* testifies to the fact that Altman's film fits into all these categories. Reviews repeatedly identify the conventionally revisionist impetus of the western. *Playboy* asserted: "Shooting down all the old myths about how the West was won—by fearless lawmen that marched up Main Street and gunned down the bad guys— . . . [the film] shows pioneer life the way it really was."[20] One review proclaimed that Altman and his crew "Make the Western Real."[21] *Newsweek* called the film "an unpretentious morality tale. . . . A tribute to our pioneer forefathers who killed each other over the right to peddle flesh."[22] The original advertising campaign for the film announced its achievement in showing the West as it really was. Altman repeatedly, both at the time of the film's release and subsequently, has asserted his animosity to the unreality of westerns and expressed his concern in *McCabe & Mrs. Miller* for capturing how things really were in the West. He says that "in Paris they referred to *McCabe* as an anti-western and they called it the 'demystification of an era.' That was my reason for getting involved in *McCabe* in the first place because I don't like Westerns. I don't like the obvious lack of truth in them. I see no reason to go back to the reality of it and then tell the story."[23]

Dominant reaction to the film also recognized that the film reads the western against the grain of its traditional narrative, challenging and reworking its assumptions, its forms, and its style. "The film is a 'Western' with a difference, the difference being its whole unorthodox, demythologizing tone."[24] Reviews attacked the film for working against the traditional western's glorification of the American frontier. Many reviews attributed the film's attack on the western to a director with a pessimistic view of social development. The *Christian Century* identified a more modernist impulse: "It is as if *Butch Cassidy and the Sundance Kid*—complete with its understated and contemporary idiom—had been touched up with the surrealistic acid of the early Bunuel."[25]

The former television director of numerous episodes of *Bonanza*, Altman is clearly familiar with both the traditional style and plots of formulaic western storytelling. Reviewers discern these older forms and assert that "the West provides Altman with . . . the very bones of his film."[26] The film interweaves the old with the new for Charles Champlin in the *Los Angeles Times:* "The initial intention . . . seems to have been to prove that you could de-mythologize a certain hunk of the Western past and still entertain. . . . The destruction of myth has been very selective. The shootout preserves the most enduring myth. . . . The teaming of antihero and antiheroine is admittedly recent, if not new, but the ruthless, faceless syndicate, the urbane assassin and his pathological sidekicks have jogged our way before."[27] The cover of the DVD release of the film in 2002 makes the same claim for both continuity and innovation: *McCabe & Mrs. Miller* "stands the mythology of the Old West on its ear. Shot on beautiful Vancouver wilderness locations, it captures the essence of a long-ago time, coupled with [Altman's] edgy modern sensibility."[28]

Other critical reaction claimed that the treatment of the traditional western formats went completely beyond the pale of permissible generic innovation, negatively so for some and positively for others. John Wayne, the major icon of classical westerns at the time, considered the film "corrupt." The film is thus "a failure on the first-level, a lack of appeal for the viewer who is looking forward to a traditional western."[29] Or the film "seems qualitatively different from any Western ever made. It doesn't seem like a Western at all, for it simply does not deal in the usual myths, not even to debunk them."[30] Roger Ebert is unequivocal about both its deviations and its effect: "*McCabe & Mrs. Miller* is like no other Western ever made, and with it, Robert Altman earns his place as one of the best contemporary directors."[31] Similarly for William Pechter, the film's art rests in double commitments: "Seen thus—less as a recreation of the way it was than of a fleeting dream of how one wishes it to have been—the film's naturalism—the artfully cluttered interiors, the flow of movement and hum of conversation heard, half-heard, and almost heard—imparts to it not so much verisimilitude as textual richness, weight, and density."[32] John Cawelti says that finally it is "hard to tell whether he attacks or affirms" the western.[33] Altman's second western, *Buffalo Bill and the Indians* (1976), rightly deserves attention as an aggressive interrogation of one of the western's most influential pioneers. It examines the very terms of western discourse itself at the intersection of myth, history, and the popular entertainment industry. Compared with this self-conscious metawestern, *McCabe & Mrs. Miller* indeed plays in very complex ways among all the perspectives so divergently evoked by critics and reviewers. Altman himself sees a multiplicity of generic impulses in the film: "I don't know how to describe the film. I guess it's a love story, but it's not your average love story, and it's also a traditional Western but it's not exactly that either, and if it's funny at all, it's funny while being incredibly tragic."[34] *Buffalo Bill* is a reflexive, postmodernist investigation of the terms of western storytelling, the authors of its fiction, its distance from historical reality, and the nature of mass-media entertainment. It adapts Arthur Kopit's popular play *Indians*, which both debunked the Wild West hero and arraigned Manifest Destiny for racial genocide in order caustically to reveal that the personal, professional, ideological processes of western mythmaking derive from the values of "the show business."

POPULAR NARRATIVE GENRE

The multiplicity of reviewer responses to *McCabe & Mrs. Miller*, however, reveals a number of important aspects of its power both as a genre film and as a film that actively resists singular generic discourse. Genres always speak from a variety of creative intentions and engage different audiences who use the film in competing ways. As these audiences conduct conflicting readings of the same film, that film becomes a large site not only for negotiation among competing meanings, uses, and values; it also becomes a collective site of commonly recognized modes, means, and purposes of communication. Rick Altman argues, "When the diverse groups using the genre are considered together, genres appear as regulatory schemes facilitating the integration of diverse factions into a single social fabric."[35] In all its revisionist commitments, its narrative deconstructions, and its impressionist style, *McCabe & Mrs. Miller* takes the western story seriously and simultaneously creates multiple and congruent audiences. Part of its individual power then, as well as its place in film history, lies in its very continuation of a traditional and in many ways dominant form of communication so central to the American imagination. For the audience familiar with the generic and cultural codes of the western, the film richly engages with the form, the values, and the history of its tradition.

The seismic shift in practice that characterizes western storytelling in the late sixties is dramatic enough to promote predictions of the demise that has followed, and the film also plays an important role in that late-century transformation. Part of the satisfaction derived from the film, however, results from its continuing demonstration of the western as a tool for rethinking the relationship of the American past to its present. Its interest along with the new western historians in the stories of westerners ignored by the traditional narrative foregrounds the place of prostitutes in the multiethnic contact zones of the grimy mining West. Both John F. Kennedy's proclamation of the "New Frontier" in the sixties and Ronald Reagan's celebration of the western "legacy" in the eighties reflect the continuing vitality of western form and value as a tool for addressing national idealism and will. Part of the film's accomplishment lies further in the cultural continuity it reinforces by the use of familiar rubrics for analyzing the needs and problems of contemporary history.

The Turner Frontier Thesis asserted that history reinterprets the past for the present. This still vital perception energizes the western generally and Altman's tale particularly of the gambler and the madam in the northwestern woods at the very edge of the continent. Hardly a century before Lewis and Clark's Corps of Discovery had exulted in the presence of the Pacific Ocean. Here that ocean, once the symbol of successful western movement, lies like a cold gray slate unnoticed now below the heights of Presbyterian Church, just another symbol of the dead ends that also accompanied human commerce into the American West. For a leftist audience, the environmental scene of an extraction economy and its debilitating effects on land

and lives makes *McCabe & Mrs. Miller* a film allied with the particular political values of the then nascent environmental movement. The film celebrates again the potential along with the costs of some idea of the American Dream, in terms both of success and failure. When McCabe's horse follows the muddy trail into this last remnant of what F. Scott Fitzgerald in *The Great Gatsby* called "the fresh, green breast of the new world," the film also shows us the "foul dust," now the tailings of zinc mines, that has always trailed in the wake of that westering dream.[36] Altman's modernist tale reconstructs the western to illuminate imperial adventure in the midst of another heart of darkness.

Since Aristotle, students of narrative discourse have examined the form and effects of literary genre. The advent of narrative in film one hundred years ago has added the cinema to the field of generic study. Examination of popular narrative genre fiction has in particular established productive ways to understand what it means to produce formulaic stories within formal and historic contexts, the industrial context of classical Hollywood production, and the values milieu of cultural communication. Central to this work is the widespread presupposition in cultural studies generally that a singular discourse is always comprehensible within a larger systemic context. Words are meaningful within a system of connotative and denotative definitions. Sentences are understandable within a system of grammaticality. Arguments are intelligible within a discursive system of intentional—and perceived—form, logic, and value.

Rick Altman distinguishes among semantics, syntax, and pragmatics in the analysis of classical Hollywood genre film. Semantics are the "shared building blocks" of a genre, its "common topics, shared plots, key scenes, character types, familiar objects, recognizable shots and sounds."[37] Semantics of the stage musical, for instance, include the characters of writers, musicians, dancers, and producers, and frequently as well particular star personae, like Fred Astaire or Cyd Charisse or Gene Kelly. Musical semantics also include generic icons, such as top hat and tails, chorus lines, and musical venues. Its conventions include the invention process, musical numbers, choreography of dance routines, rehearsals, and the proscenium arches that literally or metaphorically separate the space of audience and performers. Its stylistic aspects include dynamic, choreographed camera movements and expressive, rhythmic editing.

Generic syntax, in contrast, focuses on how "a group of texts organizes those building blocks in a similar manner," including such "shared aspects as plot structure, character relationships, or image and sound montage."[38] Again, for example, the syntax of the musical involves the coalescing of invention and production, the dynamics of boy meets girl, and the mobilizing of a parallel structure of performers who struggle to produce and put on the show and the lovers who work to consummate their romantic relationship. Narrative intentionality and reception derive from an expectation that the story will involve what Thomas Schatz calls the establishment, the animation/intensification, and the resolution of the basic thematic oppositions that are central to each genre: "A genre's basic cultural oppositions or inherent dramatic conflicts represent its most basic determining feature. Also the sustained popularity of any genre indicates the essentially irresolvable, irreconcilable nature of those oppositions."[39] In the musical, that static nucleus involves the tension between dramatic story and musical production numbers, between courtship rituals and entertainment, between social reality and utopian fantasy.

The process of communication, the dynamics of comprehension, and the experience of enjoyment in generic discourse all derive from the cognitive relationship among story, its generic repertoire of vocabulary and structure, its cultural codes of social referentiality, and audience familiarity with all of these. Thus, for instance, the meaning and power of Baz Luhrmann's musical *Moulin Rouge!* (2001) derive from the way the dreaming writer Christian, the lonely prostitute-performer Satine, and the rich duke uniquely in the film and routinely in the genre interact in the simultaneous stories of the production of the show, Christian's and Satine's romance, the duke's jealously, and the ultimate defeat of love because of the heroine's tragic illness. Reflexive confusion of performance, retrospective narration, film story and style, and multiple audience positions draw on the generic self-consciousness of the classical film musical that is always about itself as entertainment even as it replicates the process of entertaining. Luhrmann's modernist take on the genre leads melodramatically to the unhappy conclusion of the romance despite the success of the show. His pastiche of musical numbers and performances from both the Bohemian Paris of Toulouse-Lautrec and contemporary popular music, his unexpected use of Nicole Kidman and Ewan McGregor as singers, and his flamboyant cinematic style not only call attention to themselves but do so in a way that reanimates the musical's complex play of fantasy and actuality. The film is readable by itself, but its play with the semantics and syntax of the musical deepens the richness of its discourse and enhances the level of appreciation in the audience familiar with its conventions.

Similarly, *McCabe & Mrs. Miller* mobilizes many of the resources of the western in telling its unique story. Like *Moulin Rouge!* its power lies in part in its similarity to generic convention and its variation on those conventions in both expected and unusual ways. For example, McCabe is the iconographic lone rider at the beginning of the film, as he emerges from the wilderness. From the outset, however, the film employs western vocabulary askew. Compare McCabe's entry to the traditional single cowboy rider of Louis L'Amour, who authored hundreds of popular western stories:

> He rolled the cigarette in his lips, liking the taste of the tobacco, squinting his eyes against the sun glare. His buckskin shirt, seasoned by sun, rain, and sweat, smelled stale and old. His jeans had long since faded to a neutral color that lost itself against the desert.
>
> He was a big man, wide-shouldered with the lean, hard-boned face of the desert rider. There was no softness in him. His toughness was ingrained and deep, without cruelty, yet quick, hard, and dangerous.[40]

A lone rider swallowed up inside a heavy, full-length bearskin coat replaces this familiar opening movement of L'Amour novels in the film. The bedroll is replaced by a carpetbag that hangs from the saddle of his packhorse along with a hatbox. An effete dandy who mutters incomprehensively to himself replaces the tough and dangerous rider. When McCabe stops to take off the coat, he displays not Shane's buckskin shirt and Indian-tooled belt or Hondo's sweat-stained workshirt but the well-tailored frock coat and black tie of the classical western gambler—Oakhurst in "The Luck of Roaring Camp," Hatfield in *Stagecoach,* or Bart Maverick in *Maverick*. He is "the shady gambler resignedly moving on."[41] And when McCabe removes his derby from the hatbox and fixes it to his head at a rakish angle, he is the fashionable easterner who seems very much out of place in this mining camp. Thus the film opens unconventionally on the convention of the lone rider emerging from the wilderness like Shane coming down from the mountains into the valley of civilization.

The wilderness itself is another major semantic element in the western, geographical space being a major marker of the genre. In the mid-nineteenth century the Rocky Mountains captured the painterly imagination of the American West, especially in the majestic paintings of Albert

Bierstadt. Edward Buscombe points out, "From the earliest Westerns located in the Rockies of Colorado to the classics of the 1950s and 1960s, mountain scenery has been used to authenticate 'westernness.'"[42] This classical landscape of the western in many ways is summed up by the lush valley of *Shane,* a "fruited plain" stretching below "purple mountain majesty." But the predominant use of landscape to signal the generic West came typically to be the barren, arid desert of Monument Valley, Utah. An overwhelming number of western narratives emerge from the landscapes of the desert Southwest. Given the dominance of the journey motif in the genre, such landscape has thematic significance: "landscape then becomes an obstacle, which has to be overcome. Its beauty is incidental to its function as a test of the protagonists' character.... The conquest of the terrain is emblematic of the achievement of the individual in overcoming personal trials and is analogous to the wider victory of capital in subjugating nature."[43] Tompkins characterizes the space further: "The land revealed on the opening pages or in the opening shot of a Western is a land defined by absence: of trees, of greenery, of houses, of the signs of civilization, above all, absence of water and shade.... Fertility, abundance, softness, fluidity, many-layeredness are at a discount here.... When a man walks or rides into a forest, he is lost among the trees, can't see ahead, doesn't know what might be lurking there."[44]

In *McCabe & Mrs. Miller* the wilderness is the uncharacteristic mountainscapes of the far Northwest, heavily forested, a looming green and gray omnipresence, sodden with an ever-present rain, cold with the descent of winter. This forest surrounds the mining camp, and while the muddy yield from the earth shapes the camp initially as an ugly and chaotic mess, the rapidly developing town quickly mines the forests for the construction of its new buildings. This wilderness is ambivalently lush and fertile at the beginning and buried beneath a snowy blizzard at the end. It offers the means for mining and logging success at the beginning but by the end becomes the site of defeat.

The mining camp presents two other ubiquitous icons of the western. Surprisingly, it already has a church. This iconic structure usually appears toward the end of the narrative, as in *My Darling Clementine* (1946) or *Stars in My Crown* (1950), indicating the advance of the civilizing forces of religion. Its initial appearance here and its emptiness at the end challenge this traditional connotation. The film's other significant structure is the saloon, generally located centrally in the middle of the frontier town, even of the half-streeted embryo of a town in *Shane*. Sheehan's saloon is strangely accessible by a rope bridge and seems to be constructed in the middle of a pond. Inside it is cramped, dark, cluttered, and shot with tight framing that conveys a dismal sense of claustrophobia. As the town is constructed across the time of the film, it replicates this initial sense of disorder, and as it is constructed from the redwood trees that surround it, the town takes on a reddish glow as though the wilderness were literally bleeding into the civilization.

But there are no Indians, no cavalry, no pioneers, no wagon trains, and very few horses in this film. And no sheriff and jail, no bank and banker, no settlers and homes. There is one cowboy, but no cattle and no ranch. The generic mix, however, of townspeople, villain, and hero remain. Altman peoples his town with miners and merchants, the colorless, nondescript, defenseless lot typical of the western. The striking addition to the cast is the group of prostitutes whom the film individualizes both by name and by appearance—the young scared teenager, the older Irish woman, the self-confidant "Chinese princess," the toothless Indian woman, the tall skinny ex-wife, the fat housekeeper, the cockney madam. As Lusted observes, "A defining strategy of revisionist Westerns is to provide the central 'active and independent' roles for women otherwise lacking in the genre."[45] The film expands the iconic Frenchy in *Destry Rides Again*, the supportive Miss Kitty of *Gunsmoke*, the knowing Helen Ramírez from *High Noon*, and the assertive dance-hall girl Feathers in *Rio Bravo* (1959) into a community of working women who fill the middle space of narrative interest. Part of Altman's "real story" lies in this expansion of the Production Code's innocent saloon girl into a role that is diverse, human, and sexual.

The actual villain in *McCabe & Mrs. Miller* is the Harrison Shaughnessy Mining Company, represented by two levels of the company. The stereotypical three villains are a familiar motley lot of killers—the young hot-headed kid out to prove his cold-blooded brutality, the somber and silent half-breed, and the gigantic English hunter with an equally huge rifle—"Natural-born bushwhackers," says the novel.[46] The surprising representation of villainy comes in the figure of Sears and Hollander, whose eastern fashions outshine McCabe's and whose professional demeanor belies their own indifference and the ruthlessness of the mining company. They are respectable businessmen.

And so is John McCabe. The hero of Edmund Naughton's novel, like Altman's McCabe, is a saloonkeeper, a professional gambler, the owner of a brothel, and a dandy in creased brown-striped trousers, red vest decorated with gold nuggets, big and fashionable mustache, Spanish boots. In the novel, he is indeed the killer of Bill Roundtree and a gunman: "He was a sidearms shot... and most of the shooting he had ever seen had been quick, and in saloons, or on streets at short range." His pistol has no trigger: "McCabe had the trigger removed a long time before, and the mechanism filed and adjusted so that he could fire the gun in one motion on the draw."[47] Warren Beatty's McCabe, however, is only rumored to have shot Roundtree; he wears his gun holstered low with a bravado that Butler immediately sees through: "That man never shot anybody." He calls himself a businessman, and his success as a gambler fuels his developing business. The first episode of the film introduces him to the camp and establishes his game. The second shows him in Bearpaw purchasing three prostitutes. The third shows his return to a town where men under his employ are already building his House of Fortune. McCabe mines the men of their wages and mines the local garden of redwood trees to build his warmly glowing saloon and red light house. The town and McCabe's holdings grow apace together.

WESTERN HEROES

Tales of heroes fill the pages of world literature. Their larger-than-life characters undertake monumental tasks, undergo arduous journeys, and overcome fearsome obstacles. In achieving their goals they found national identities; they articulate religious values; they establish legal and moral institutions; they express ideal characteristics of the human persona. These stories regularly employ traditional patterns of mission-obstacle-success such that their familiar repetition amounts to a ritualistic celebration both of the values required to succeed and of the estimation secured with triumph. Cultural historians define the hero's ubiquitous tale of struggle and triumph as a worldwide monomyth. John Cawelti further specifies the heroic function:

> The central fantasy of the adventure story is that of the hero... overcoming obstacles and dangers and accomplishing some important and moral mission.... The true focus of interest in the adventure story is the character of the hero and the nature of the obstacles he has to overcome. Perhaps the most basic moral fantasy implicit in this type of story is that of victory over death, though there are also all kinds of subsidiary

triumphs ... the triumph over injustice and the threat of lawlessness in the western.[48]

As a special avatar of this figure, the western genre has produced a wide range of iconic heroes over the almost two hundred years of its development of a frontier myth. From James Fenimore Cooper's Natty Bumppo to Owen Wister's Virginian, from Louis L'Amour's Sackett, to Larry McMurtry's Call and McRae in western fiction, from William S. "Two-Gun" Hart to John Wayne in western film, the concept of the western hero develops especially as a function of individual persona.

Some scholars identify the western hero's role and skills in terms of the particular historic stage of civilization being depicted against challenges of the wilderness landscape. The frontiersman is the epic hero involved in the establishment of fundamental political laws; the federal marshal is the romance hero who establishes the civil laws that make the new city livable; the town sheriff is the melodramatic hero who maintains the criminal law determining relations of disobedience and punishment; the outlaw is the satiric hero who counters public opinion, morals, and customs to distinguish them from foundational laws.[49] Others characterize the hero in terms of his alignment with particular social values. Natty Bumppo is the Daniel Boone frontiersman, hunter, and Indian fighter—"the man who made the wilderness safe for democracy."[50] He epitomizes the hero of Frederick Jackson Turner's perspective on the frontier—the man who knows Indians, who shares their skill, who vanquishes them with natural nobility. The Virginian and Buffalo Bill are the Rooseveltian Rough Riders who pit themselves against the threats and lawlessness of the wilderness, submerse themselves in racialist violence, and emerge victoriously purged of debilitation and purified for the social advancement of civilization.

The qualities of the western hero are ubiquitously rehearsed in the story's thousands of retellings: moral integrity, physical strength and endurance, superior ability with revolver and rifle, restraint, steadfastness, loyalty, courage, independence, concern for the underdog, even indeed godliness: "The coming of the Western hero is a kind of Second Coming of Christ."[51] Particularly relevant to an understanding of *McCabe & Mrs. Miller* is its parallel to one of L'Amour's archetypal westerns, *Comstock Lode*. The novel is significant because in addition to developing one of his exemplary portraits of the mythic, western hero, its settings and action reside in the environs of Virginia City, Nevada. The action of the novel is set at the height of this famous mining town's transition, like that of Presbyterian Church, from mining camp to booming frontier metropolis, without, in L'Amour's world, the assistance of prostitution. Val Travallion's journey from the orphan of frontier violence and lawlessness to the successful avenger of his parents' murder to become the worthy owner of Comstock wealth defines the western American dream of achievement. Like Willie Loman's uncle who walked into the Alaska wilderness and walked out a millionaire, Travallion gains riches, respect, romance, and power by the end of L'Amour's classic tale. But McCabe is like Willie, whose tragic death is lamented by his son, "He had to dream; it comes with the territory." *McCabe & Mrs. Miller* is the very inverse of *Comstock Lode*, and McCabe the ironic shadow of the western hero venerated in Travallion. In the first place McCabe is a gambler. The role carries with it a whole load of negative images. Smooth, fast-talking, sneaky, and untrustworthy, gamblers more often fill the villain slot in western syntax than the hero function. Lee Mitchell wonders why Bret Harte cast the gambler in the leading role of his best stories and concludes that the requirements of poker "dictate the importance of the gambler's character, which clearly resembles the model of self-restraint that Cooper had popularized in the figure of Natty Bumppo." The gambler's self-possession, "his smooth self-composure in confronting the dictates of fate alone,"[52] even presage the gunfighter hero. The fact remains, however, that the gambler figure seldom merits the role of hero in the western frontier narrative. The cardsharp's field of action is the saloon card table, and usually his skill amounts to luck and the ability to keep a poker face. His winnings derive from the losers who take a chance at his table. The mining frontier in particular provides a ready environment for the game, but the gambler's skill hardly derives from the struggle to survive in a harsh wilderness.

Part of *McCabe & Mrs. Miller*'s revision of the western lies in its elevation of such a character to a role of centrality in the narrative. Altman's portrait, however, is complex in its mobilization of traditional motifs with an untraditional hero. McCabe rides into town as the loner from the wilderness. He brings with him a "big rep" as a gunfighter. He is a proud, independent, and ultimately courageous man who finally confronts the villains in a showdown that concludes the story. He is also the gregarious, wisecracking professional. McCabe calls himself a businessman, and his business is the sale of fortune, booze, and sex, those trades so central to the classic western's resistance to the Victorian Cult of True Womanhood. The success of Altman's hero in these ventures appears in his ability to attract players, acquire land, contract workers, construct buildings, and outfit fancy houses of pleasure. Others easily pierce his cocksure facade, however. The prostitute owner in Bearpaw scoffs at his attempt to bargain for the three girls early in the film: "You don't know nothin' about it." Mrs. Miller disdainfully puts him down initially as "another frontier wit." The representatives of the mining company coldly dismiss him in his blustering arrogance as a "damn fool." The company's hired gun laughingly rejects his reputation as a gunfighter. The camera, too, punctures his bravado when it zooms in on his face to suggest an insecurity that underlies all his action and behavior. The teenage prostitute's poignant assertion, "I have to go to the pot, and I don't think I can hold it," confronts McCabe for the first time in the film with a series of situations beyond the scope of his expectations and abilities. McCabe appears then not as the rugged individualist, the taciturn gunman who knows and masters the wilderness, the town, and himself. He is finally a conceited and fatuous gambler; an amateur trader in sex; a likeable, childish, and confused lover; and a proud, foolish, but finally courageous—if inefficacious—champion of his right to his own property.

Patricia Limerick writes that "the encounter of innocence with complexity is a recurrent theme in American culture, and Western history may well be the most dramatic and sustained case of high expectations and naiveté meeting a frustrating and intractable reality."[53] The film personifies that frustration for McCabe in another transformation of the conventional western cast of characters. While Bret Harte occasionally presented gamblers and whores as major characters in his fiction, dominant western practice in the twentieth century portrayed them as minor characters. The prostitute figures routinely as a friend, confidante, and potential lover of the gunfighter or sheriff in numerous westerns. Nevertheless, according to Tompkins, even if these women are present, they are, like the Indians, there but repressed because "Westerns pay practically no attention to women's experience."[54] In particular, these stories generally suppress the fact of prostitution itself. Altman's film, then, revises traditional semantics in the western not only by elevating a stereotypically minor role to central billing but by constructing the experience of women and prostitution as pivotal to his focus.

Still, McCabe is the classic independent western hero in that he wants no partners: "Partners is what I come up here to get away from." Lee Mitchell, Jane Tompkins, and other scholars of the genre assert that westerns "insist on the ... importance of manhood as an ideal."[55] They trace the development of the genre in terms of its historic response to moments of stress in masculine identity. Susan Johnson, for instance, writes: "The construction of a masculine West was part of a larger late-nineteenth century 'crisis of manliness' in the United States—a crisis in which older definitions of white, middle-class manhood that emphasized restraint and respectability (manly men) gave way to new meanings that focused on vigor and raw virility (masculine men)."[56] Westerns constantly engage the question of "what it means to be a man."[57] Feminist critics have consequently criticized the genre because the frontier, especially as new western historians have aggressively demonstrated, accommodated a far greater number of women in positions and work little imagined in the homosocial narratives of the western, which "still exists as a kind of happy hunting ground of Anglo virility."[58] While some critics argue that the western is "one of the finest places for women characters in all of cinema,"[59] most deplore "the impoverished range of female stereotypes on offer (mother, schoolteacher, prostitute, saloon girl, rancher, Indian squaw, bandit)."[60]

In many ways Altman focuses this issue directly by bringing Constance Miller into Presbyterian Church and by making her McCabe's aggressive business partner. The issue of romantic and sexual desire is subordinate and definitely marginal to the challenge Constance Miller presents to the "hero" of this western story. In broad psychological terms, in realms beyond the western, she is the stereotypical female figure who both attracts and threatens the male. In this film she threatens before she attracts, and perhaps the attraction is the threat. In the middle of the film, Cowboy stands in the parlor of the brothel wearing his long johns and ten-gallon hat and announcing his desire for another girl. Two of the prostitutes whisper between themselves; one holds up her fingers to indicate shortness, and the two giggle. In what constitutes a comic, almost throwaway moment, the film self-consciously addresses one of the most central fantasies of the cowboy story—masculine adequacy. The two prostitutes laugh at the male's shortness. The prostitute's laugh at the customer's "teensy little pecker" can lead to violence, as later in Clint Eastwood's *Unforgiven* it motivates the vicious slashing of the prostitute's face.

Mrs. Miller does not laugh. McCabe's prowess is important to her escape from this backwoods camp. When she challenges him to perform, she marks both her desire for freedom and her dependency on his success. The genre, and a central concern with masculinity, depends upon that success as well. Masculine efficacy constitutes the terms of female security—an old syndrome of patriarchal culture. Its challenge remains as the core critique this film presents to the traditional frontier myth. One of McCabe's idiosyncratic behaviors is to crack a raw egg into a glass of whiskey and then to drink it down at once. This unusual act seems designed to impress as a kind of macho gesture. The men at the saloon are amazed, but the company negotiators dismiss it along with all of McCabe's expansive affectations. Mrs. Miller's own voracious consumption of a large meal of stew, eggs, and tea just overwhelms McCabe's egg-whiskey with the kind of aggressive energy that challenges McCabe throughout the film.

It begins directly and immediately. As McCabe self-consciously brushes at his fashionable derby, Mrs. Miller leans over and says, "If you want to make out you're such a fancy dude, you ought to wear something besides that cheap jockey club cologne." Her alert awareness of his self-regard and her assertive confrontation produces a look of consternation that characterizes McCabe's discomfort with Mrs. Miller throughout the film. She pitches her offer of partnership with him on the basis of his ignorance about operating a brothel. After her insistence he could double his profits with a proper whorehouse, he asks, "What makes you think I ain't thought of all that already?" Because, Mrs. Miller suspects, he's "too dumb to see a good proposition when it's put to him." As her partner, then, the narrative depicts McCabe's subordination to her direction. In one telling scene, the workers ask him when the prostitutes from Seattle are coming. He responds in his typically swaggering manner that "them girls'll come up here when I goddamn tell 'em to come!" He goes then to Mrs. Miller's room to ask her the same question, but in the golden warmth of her room she reads and ignores his questions as well as entreaties to let him in. He stumbles off drunkenly into the windy cold dark, muttering to himself that she constantly costs him "Money. Money and pain. Pain, pain, pain." The shot of McCabe immediately following the scene of her proposal of partnership slowly zooms out to capture the titular male character sitting alone in his room, drunk, trying with difficulty to close and put away his pocket watch, fumbling over his whiskey bottle, burping, farting, and muttering to himself about the affront she has given him—altogether a very unglamorous portrait of the western male hero.

This central confrontation on the story depicts the brash, articulate, knowledgeable, and experienced Mrs. Miller and her braggart, untutored, and fatuous partner. One of the most significant challenges to his competence comes the evening in McCabe's new saloon when she starts to look over his books and realizes "No wonder you don't know how much money you got. You've got your credit column on a different page from your debit." When she quizzes him on simple arithmetic, he grabs a whiskey bottle and stomps out in hostile embarrassment. Constance Miller is just a cockney whore, but she is also an educated businesswoman whose competence discloses his own inadequacies. Whatever McCabe thinks or feels, her concern is clear: "I don't want no small timer screwing up me business." She constantly watches, goads, and judges McCabe. From the outset she challenges his ability to manage "a proper sportin' house," to manage the girls, to take care of his investment. Indeed her ability to establish the brothel as a community of warmth against the cold, wet Northwest woods strikingly contrasts with the images of McCabe, alone, drunk, and mumbling about his separation from that warmth. She pointedly derides his ability to keep the books. She makes him pay for sex with her and in her bed treats him like a child. When he mistakenly thinks he has won the upper hand in negotiations with the mining company, her better business sense and knowledge of the mining company bemoan his arrogant blindness. When the mining company enforcers come to town to kill him, she despairs not for his life but her own future. Ultimately, for Constance Miller John McCabe is an "amateur" who is "screwing up me business."

McCabe is equally an amateur in his dealing with the two representatives of the mining company. They have little sympathy for his arrogant and exaggerated sense of his worth and are insulted by his inebriated attempt to foist them onto the girls of the brothel. The older man of the company men angrily insists to his colleague that they give McCabe up as a lost cause that the company can deal with in more aggressive and terminal ways: Let the enforcers handle it. Mrs. Miller understands his mistake right away: "You know who they are? . . . They'd as soon put a bullet in your back than look at you." From the narrative perspective the die is cast here, and she sees its inevitable outcome: "They're gonna get you, McCabe!" McCabe reaches Bearpaw too late to renegotiate with Sears and Hollander; his attempt to get legal protection from lawyer Samuels ends in political bombast; his effort to bargain with the company's hired gunman encounters Butler's dismissive, "Oh, I don't make deals." The western's commitment to the appropriate forms of masculinity collapse in this portrait of the abject male whose foolish and drunken behavior puts his life at risk and the tough prostitute who understands all too well the power relationships in play on this far-western frontier. McCabe articulates the sense of humiliation that underlies the last half of the film when he asserts that partnership with a woman must inevitably mean a loss of the woman's respect. He misunderstands, however. Constance Miller is his best and strongest ally, but his, the culture's, the western's patriarchal devaluation of woman's ability in the public world facilitates the tragic conclusion of the story. Robert Warshow in his famous essay, "The Westerner," asserts that "in Western movies, men have the deeper wisdom and the women are children."[61] *McCabe & Mrs. Miller* reverses this characterization.

The film revises in the end yet another conventional feature of the classic western narrative, the showdown and shootout. Frequently at this juncture in the narrative conflict, the generic forces of wilderness and civilization devolve onto the personal actions of individual westerners. Individual gunfighters routinely here resolve the larger social issues at stake in western mythology. The iconic image of two armed men facing each other in the middle of the frontier town has recurred endlessly in the western. The classic shootout ritually resolves the story's conflict between good and evil and thus becomes the single moment when the tensions of the genre's thematic core appear in stark clarity. John Cawelti describes the forces at play:

> Geographically, the frontier settlement represents a group of civilizers or pioneers on the edge of a wilderness, tenuously linked to the civilized society behind them in the East by the thinnest lines of communication.... Historically, the western represents a moment when the forces of civilization and wilderness life are in balance, the epic moment at which the old life and the new confront each other and individual actions may tip the balance one way or another.[62]

Jim Kitses's famous delineation of the central opposing forces in the western between wilderness and civilization conveys the complex ambiguity embedded in the genre's thematic core. In lining up concepts associated in westerns with these two phenomena, he finds parallels for "The Wilderness" among individuality, freedom, nature, pragmatism, savagery, and equality. In "Civilization" he locates the community, restriction, culture, idealism, refinement, and democracy. He sees the West contradictorily as, on the one hand, "a Garden of natural dignity and innocence offering refuge from the decadence of civilization" and, on the other, as "a treacherous Desert stubbornly resisting the gradual sweep of intellectual life in the nineteenth century." The community too offers conflicting values, as either "a positive force, a movement of refinement, order and local democracy into the wilds or as a harbinger of corruption in the form of Eastern values which threaten frontier ways."[63]

This core set of ambiguous values stands at the heart of various syntactical structures evident in the western genre over the course of its history. Frank Gruber, author of dozens of western novels, films, and television series, distinguishes some seven inevitable western plots, including journey narratives, ranch stories, stories of empire, and law and order stories.[64] Sociologist Will Wright rigorously describes the syntactic structures of classical, revenge, transitional, and professional plots.[65] Historically, the logic with which these different patterns animate and resolve the irreconcilable tensions between society and freedom, civilization and violence have changed. Cawelti writes:

> This epic confrontation of forces calls forth the hero, who, whether Leatherstocking, cowboy, gunfighter, or marshal, is defined by the way he is caught between contrasting ways of life. Most commonly, the hero is a man of the wilderness who comes out of the old "lawless" ways of life to which he is deeply attached both by personal inclination and by his relationship to male comrades who have shared that life with him.... But, despite his separation from the pioneers and his association with the old wilderness life, the hero finds himself cast in the role of defender of the pioneers.[66]

What narrative structure then shapes the experience of *McCabe & Mrs. Miller*? What conflicting values mobilize the tensions among hero, villain, and society in Presbyterian Church? What resolution of the wilderness-civilization conflict does the narrative achieve? Wright describes the classical western plot, the "prototype of all Westerns.... It is the story of the lone stranger who rides into a troubled town and cleans it up, winning the respect of the townsfolk and the love of the school marm."[67] The archetypal example of this plot is *Shane*. In some surprising ways, *McCabe & Mrs. Miller* fits this pattern, and its differences highlight key ways Altman's film revises traditional western syntax.

McCabe is clearly at first the lone stranger with the exceptional ability of gambling that sets him apart from the miners; he is given a special status because of his reputation as a gunman. His entrepreneurial ability further sets him apart from the community; as a successful businessman, he contributes significantly to the rapidly growing mining town. *McCabe & Mrs.*

Miller works some telling variations on the middle functions in this plot. Rather than rejecting McCabe, the mining community embraces the gambler, saloonkeeper, and brothel owner. The strong relationship that frequently links classical hero and villains who threaten the townspeople emerges ironically in this film. McCabe and the mining company share a common pursuit; they are both in the extraction business—Harrison Shaughnessy taking zinc from the mountains, McCabe taking the miners' pay at the poker table, the bar, and the prostitute's bed. Thus the conflict of interests that routinely arises between the villains and the society here arises between McCabe and traditional moral values of community that could condemn all of his operations as sinful. In the traditional plot, the strength of the villains threatens the weak society that requires the hero's strength to confront the villains.

Multiple ironies shape Altman's configuration of these elements and their syntactical structure. The threat to the town of sex, booze, and gambling from a moral point of view is actually perceived as welcome entertainment and central to its economic health. The community at this stage in its development hardly perceives itself as threatened and, indeed, is unaware of the threat posed by the mining company to McCabe's interests and thus their own. The novel makes that threat clear as well as the hero's knowledge of it. McCabe fears

> all the things he knew would come to Presbyterian Church with the Mining Company.... The owners of the mine lived in the East and they would get the ore and their money out of the hillsides and the town as fast as they could.... Everything would be efficient.... The company might even build the town its own smelter,... And the smelter would kill all the vegetation on the mountainsides near the town and the company would dirty the creek with its waste, and the smell of its efficiency would keep the wild game from ever wandering into town again. It would possess all the dwellings and sell all the hardware, all the clothing and all the food. It would set the prices and pay everyone in company scrip, and keep the men so deep in debt they'd have to have company permission any time they wanted to leave town....
>
> The knowledge that stood by the front door of McCabe's thoughts was that the company would never tolerate no gambling house it didn't own.... Then, the Bearpaw men would have to have his whore house... they would have to have it all.[68]

The film eliminates this threat to the town and, more important, McCabe's awareness of how the company operates. In the novel, McCabe is a gunfighter as well as a gambler who has acquired a classic sense of responsibility for the town. The film reduces the motivation for his confrontation with the company to his foolish arrogance about his "holdings" and a shallow sense of "standing up for the little guy." Still, McCabe's bathhouse has literally cleaned up the town, and Mrs. Miller's brothel actually constitutes a force for community. Thus, ironically, McCabe's showdown with the hired killers, while apparently just a fight for his business and his life, is also a fight for the community he has helped to build. His victory or defeat will not stop the inevitable movement of the mining company whose presence depends simply on the continuing richness of the zinc deposits. The showdown between McCabe and Harrison Shaughnessy pits not good and evil but two different entrepreneurial forces against each other. Ironically, were he to win, McCabe's business would eventually run afoul of more traditional moral values that would seek to close the brothel and prohibit alcohol. For the moment, however, McCabe's struggle with the mining company for his rights is morally superior to corporate greed.

Certainly in terms of classical narrative functions the film follows the generic script: the hero fights and defeats the villains. However, like the abortive showdown earlier between McCabe and Cowboy, nothing is generically right about the shootout that concludes the film. Classically, the showdown occurs on the main street, in the middle of town, high noon, combatants facing with holstered revolvers. Here, in the first place, the showdown amounts to a kind of extended cat-and-mouse sequence rather than any face-to-face confrontation between adversaries. McCabe scurries around town hiding from the killers whom he ultimately defeats by surprise and deception rather than any particular skill as a gunfighter. His prowess entails ambush, back shooting, and a hidden pistol. Moreover, that skill derives not from the necessities of survival in the wilderness but survival around civilization's games of chance. The gambler's devious derringer rather that the shootist's six-gun finally dispatches the last killer. And the ironies only mount. The killers are dead, but the powerful mining company will continue. McCabe sets out bravely "to stick his hand into the fire and see what he's made out of," but in his drunken arrogance he has brought this fight upon himself. McCabe is victorious, killing all three of his opponents, but then unbeknownst to anyone dies in the snow from his wounds. Indeed, the community hardly knows the showdown is occurring because throughout its length the townspeople fight to extinguish the fire started in the church when Butler kills the minister. They save the building, literally an empty shell, which they have hitherto ignored and which metaphorically represents the absence of religion in the life of the community for which it is named. The town is hardly safer from this series of events. The hero certainly gives up his special status, but he dies alone, without efficacy. Only Mrs. Miller laments his leaving this lonesome valley.

Lost in this analysis of the film's adherence to the classical plot is the conflict suggested in the title. Roger Ebert asserts: "Study the title. 'McCabe & Mrs. Miller.' Not 'and,' as in a couple, but '&,' as in a corporation. It is a business arrangement. Everything is business with her."[69] "McCabe & Mrs. Miller" indicates the partnership, the corporate relationship, not the romance, between the two principals, but it also points to a tension between them. Two major stories course throughout the narrative structure of the film. The conflict between McCabe and the mining company is an important struggle among the men over economic interests and control. In the novel, named only after the man, Sheehan more aggressively resents McCabe's success in the developing town and actively resists his authority by colluding with the agents of the mining company. McCabe, as his influence grows, paternalistically starts to assume a nurturing concern for the town and is uncomfortably mindful of its growing moral resistance to his business interests. In the film, this conflict is displaced by the weight of the second name in the title. The conflict between wilderness and civilization becomes the partner's struggle against big business. The corporate world by 1901 has spread its power from sea to dull gray sea. McCabe considers himself the small business man looking for an opportunity to make his own way in this financial milieu. The company's commissioning of his killing in the wilds of northwest Washington parody the notion of some western regeneration through violence that will ensure a progressive era for the nation. McCabe's struggles with the mining company dimly echo the struggles of a populist and agrarian resistance to the robber barons and corporate trusts. These are the central energies of McCabe's story.

Constance Miller's story more centrally engages the thematic core of the western. The business interests of mining create a wilderness where immigrants and miners, saloonkeepers and prostitutes exist outside the law, on the border of loneliness and need, at the mercy of international forces that drive them from home to work. If the ore continues, the town will grow and merchants will come and families will replace single miners; churches and schools will be built. And the whorehouses will be closed. Civilization and respectability and social responsibility will make its place where the crude mining camp once wallowed on the dirty frontier. Or, alternatively, the lode-bearing veins will run empty, and the mining company will pull out; the camp will disappear and its inhabitants scurry to find sustenance in some economic elsewhere. For a moment, on the cusp between boom and bust, between possibility and negation, the frontier enacts the tension of wilderness and civilization. The western hero is the figure who mediates between these contending forces. McCabe, however, is, on the one hand, a man of civilization, a businessman, and, on the other, a man complicit in the villainy of the captivity narrative. Constance Miller is the cockney whore who lives in the wilderness and is its captive. Her story begins and ends this film. It motivates the middle of the film. It both extends the oldest tradition in the western and critiques the impetus of western storytelling.

THE CAPTIVITY NARRATIVE

National narratives are the dominant stories in particular cultural histories that organize a sense of the past, social identity, collective desire, and the psychic pressures of repressed cultural trauma. They represent the ways a culture informs its individual members about the legal, civic, religious, economic, and psychic possibilities of social interaction. They designate appropriate realms of desire, and they delimit fields of anxiety. They characterize and then exorcise fears of natural and national and neighboring others; they personalize and celebrate the terms of conflict and victory, national struggles and local heroes. Lauren Berlant identifies this discourse as part of "National Fantasy," one of the "conditions under which national identity takes shape." It organizes the nature of cultural subjectivity—the "images, narratives, monuments, and sites that circulate through personal/collective consciousness." She describes national narratives as the "National Symbolic":

> Its traditional icons, its metaphors, its heroes, its rituals, and its narratives provide an alphabet for a collective consciousness or national subjectivity; through the National Symbolic the historical nation aspires to achieve the inevitability of the status of natural law, a birthright. This pseudogenetic condition not only affects profoundly the citizen's sub-

jective experience of his/her political rights, but also of civil life, private life, the life of the body itself.[70]

Thus, for instance, one of England's national narratives flows through the fields of Runnymede where King John was forced to sign the Magna Carta; it recounts the masterful organization of Europe's first national state under Queen Elizabeth I; it hesitates in front of the bloody civil war between Catholic royalists and Protestant parliamentarians, averting its eyes from the beheading of the king and celebrating the Glorious Rebellion that restored the monarchy with the Parliament's blessing. It culminates ironically with the declaration that "all men are created equal," then stands against the treason of the American Revolution and the fearsome excess of liberty, equality, and fraternity in the French Revolution. The British Empire signals the inevitable authority of a Christian and democratic nation dedicated conservatively to liberty but purchased on the cost of military might and what Joseph Conrad called the "colonial squeeze."

Across the Irish Sea runs another, more fraught national narrative. Its four-hundred-year tale recounts Catholic Irish resistance against Protestant England: military defeat, colonial dispossession of language and sovereignty, armed rebellion in every generation, deportation and emigration, Catholic emancipation, and ultimately what William Butler Yeats called the "terrible beauty" of revolution and national independence. The Irish national narrative contains the Great Famine not as just historical fact but as symbolic of imperial genocide, colonial dependency, and personal insufficiency. It stands emblematically for the sense of insecurity that runs through the Irish imaginary.

The western may be called America's national narrative: the story of the European immigrant's religious and mercantile journey into the wilderness—the struggle to reclaim and convert the savage wilderness; the quest for religious redemption and political freedom; the desire for wealth, to strike it rich; the manifest destiny to take possession of this continent. It's a story like England's with national heroes in the quest for land and liberty, empire builders with vision, thirst, and power. The sense of the West and national American identity gets narrativized by Frederick Turner, Theodore Roosevelt, William F. Cody, and countless other authors as the relationship between frontier and democracy. This national narrative has its dark side, particularly in its anxiety about First Americans, and part of the repressed, the unspeakable in this story is the genocide of Native Americans as white

Europeans conquered the continent from coast to coast. The westerner is also a killer. Moses is the oft-cited antecedent to this tale: the anointed leader of the people to the Promised Land whose sin makes him unworthy of its holy freedom.

Within this context, the captivity narrative may be the quintessential incarnation of the national narrative. Richard Slotkin in *Regeneration through Violence* details the characteristics of two major narratives that dominate American discourse: the hunter/woodsman stories epitomized by the figure of Daniel Boone and captivity narratives. Of the latter he says, "The great and continuing popularity of these narratives, the uses to which they were put, and the nature of the symbolism employed in them are evidence that the captivity narratives constitute the first coherent myth-literature developed in America for American audiences." He further defines the form:

> In it a single individual, usually a woman, stands passively under the strokes of evil, awaiting rescue by the grace of God. The sufferer represents the whole, chastened body of Puritan society; and the temporary bondage of the captive to the Indian is dual paradigm—of the bondage of the soul to the flesh and the temptations arising from original sin, and of the self-exile of the English Israel from England.... The ordeal is at once threatful of pain and evil and promising of ultimate salvation. Through the captive's proxy, the promise of a similar salvation could be offered to the faithful among the reading public, while the captive's torments remained to harrow the hearts of those not yet awakened to their fallen nature.[71]

The fraught voyage of discovery into the wilderness, the contingency of survival there, as well as the uncertainty of one's salvation and the efficacy of religious faith appear dramatically in the representation of the Indians. In the captivity narrative, all the fear of the savage other is enacted in the kidnapping of its more treasured possessions: hearth, home, faith—all collected in the image of the woman.

These stories encapsulate all the anxieties about safety, about survival, about worth and redemption. The woman is simultaneously a representation of desire for purity and a fear of its loss. In a culture that designates men as guardians of women, the abduction of women must constitute both an attack on and challenge to the adequacy of masculine identity as well. The captivity narratives then serve as a call for bravery, rescue, and retaliation against threatening savagery. The journey is here reified as the desperate search for and courageous struggle with the alien to restore the sacred object, and it becomes a test of moral, religious, and physical courage and steadfastness. What is unspeakable in such narratives is the fear of descending into the very savagery, of becoming the alien other that must be vanquished in the quest.

Lee Mitchell writes: "Based upon a residual belief that other cultures represent forms of psychic entrapment, the captivity narrative could not help but become self-conscious about the idea of culture itself, with the prevalence of a 'captivity plot' in recent Hollywood films suggesting this narrative legacy remains a persistent anxiety."[72] In film history, *The Searchers* epitomizes this captivity story, but as an archetypal revenge western, it examines not the captive, Debbie, but the avenger of her family and ultimately her rescuer. The fear and desire concomitant with the image of the woman as victim in the captivity novel appear symbolically in the hair of Marty's mother. Now a scalp in Chief Scar's lodge, the lustrous red hair is at once an object of beauty and an object of revulsion. The same is true of Debbie—the figure of childish innocence and family now horribly shattered and doubly threatened by the loss of her virginity as she matures in captivity. John Wayne's portrayal of Ethan captures the duality of the classical western hero astride the values of civilization and wilderness. The pathology of his obsession to rescue Debbie by killing her emerges from his own subversive love for his brother's wife, and as his search continues, his resemblance to the savage Scar becomes increasingly disturbing. The film's famous final exclusion of Ethan from the settler's home reflects the unspeakable at work in these narratives. The greatest anxiety is that the savage other resides in ourselves.

The captivity narrative has been perceived as an ongoing instrument for the analysis of a variety of conflicting ethnic and gender roles in modern as well as past American culture. Even in the past, where the "community" westerns generated stories about the fear of its challenges, its impossibility, and its loss, literary historians come to read the captivity stories that dramatize some "real or imagined helplessness in the face of a savage Other" as "essentially a response to a frontier situation, stories generated to engage and resolve one culture or group's precarious existence in the face of a hostile enemy threatening from the opposite side of some border (geographic, racial, cultural)."[73] "Where there were once always Indians in Westerns to occupy the place of the Other . . . in the twentieth-century literary West heterosexuality becomes the structure of difference, and often men are 'other' to women who are imagining their own destiny."[74] Captivity narratives focus the themes of what Christopher Castiglia calls "confinement and community"[75]—confinement that is doubled in the space of captivity and of home, community that develops in the place of containment among captives, captors, and other women, both at home and in the readership of the narratives.

The widespread feminist criticism that began to develop at the time of *McCabe & Mrs. Miller's* release has urged a close examination of the ways culture situates women, in particular women's roles, social position, and exchange value. Prostitution is a condition that especially speaks to women's place in culture. At the end of the nineteenth century, prostitution, like the western genre itself, represented a threat to the values of "religion, motherhood, home, and family," identified by Tompkins as the central commitments of the popular domestic fiction of Victorian America.[76] All across the continent at the end of the nineteenth century, a "generalized scare about prostitution" and middle-class anxiety about the sexuality of the lower classes mobilized the "Purity Crusade," "anxious to revive traditional sexual morality through public means."[77] Like the captivity narratives, prostitution constitutes border crossings that generally foreground issues of female identity. It is transgressive and threatening and especially illuminating as it defines boundaries particularly between upper and lower class, between proper and scandalous, honorable and abhorrent, legal and criminal, repressed and ostentatious sexuality, indeed between women and nonwomen. One Montana law distinguished between "women" on the one hand and, on the other, "lewd and dissolute female persons."[78] An effect of red-light districts in American towns was to "mark off boundaries of women's social space,"[79] and that space marked the fallen woman.

Captivity narratives and prostitution then significantly engage questions about the nature of gendered identity; captivity and prostitution represent social conditions of women. In captivity narratives, the threat to women's purity and identity resides in the savage male other, its salvation in the power of white masculinity. If stories of captivity are hegemonic narratives designed to maintain masculine and feminine social identities and to regulate anxieties about their stabilities, prostitution marks their failure. The Indian male other here becomes the white man. In prostitution the white male is both the literal abductor and the potential savior. To be the subject of female deliverance then requires the recognition of the confluence in the male of desire, misogyny, and imperialism. The woman's body, like the land, becomes the site not just of purity and ideality, of gold, but of commerce, materialism, physicality, of base metals like zinc; the woman becomes the object of exchange that validates or calls into crisis the identity of the male.

The captivity narrative exposes masculine subjectivity by questioning its efficacy. In prostitution, when the social male becomes de facto the captor, then his masculinity is exposed as the menacing savage other. Now the woman is threatened not by the Indian but by the white man, the pimp, the procurer, the buyer and seller of women, and the home is threatened not by external savagery but by patriarchy. Castiglia writes: "Rather than call return to white society 'freedom,' captives repeatedly expand the parameters of their texts to show their continuing imprisonment, even after their return from captivity, within the subordinating, infantilizing, and immobilizing gender ideologies of white America."[80]

McCabe & Mrs. Miller engages the terms of this captivity. After McCabe, the only immigrants into Presbyterian Church are the black couple and the stream of women captive in the so-called oldest profession. Altman rings changes not only on the quintessential western but also on the central narrative of the National Symbolic. To fall into prostitution is to fall into the lowest form of social degradation, outcast by civil society and enthralled to an inexorable masculine economy. McCabe rides into town carrying all the generic baggage of western heroism, but he quickly assumes in his buying and selling of women the role of the captivity-narrative Indian. Thus simultaneously and impossibly he must be captor and liberator. The western frontier further becomes the fringe of an economic enterprise where all laborers—miners, gamblers, and whores—compete and struggle among themselves as the mutual captives of a larger and more savage capitalistic other. McCabe gambles and struggles and loses. Mrs. Miller remains in captivity.

There are no Indians in *McCabe & Mrs. Miller* and, at the beginning, no women, only working-class white miners and menial Chinese. Early in the film, McCabe sees a business opportunity and imports the first women into town as prostitutes. Two of these three women are older and experienced and joke and laugh among themselves, but the third is a young teenager whose fear and abjection and then her attack on a client with a knife make their status clear. The inversions of the classical western are already dramatically apparent: their situation of captivity in the sex trade predetermined before the beginning of the story, the women are chattel, bought and haggled over like animals. Living in tents on the muddy street of Presbyterian Church, they are "crib cows," who have come not to make a home but to service the men sexually. There are only three married women in the film. Mrs. Dunn hovers in the background, clerking and cooking for the men who frequent Sheehan's Saloon. Another of the three is Ida, the mail-order bride whose husband's death occasions her descent into prostitution. And there is "Mrs." Miller herself, who specifically asserts the similarity between marriage and prostitution. In marriage or in prostitution, the women are all ultimately dependent upon the men.

The white man as captor comes ironically to fill the roles of both the Indian and the rescuer, but McCabe is no rescuer; rather he buys the women from Bearpaw and Mrs. Miller's ladies from Seattle into the continuing captivity of his newly built brothel. Instead of paralleling some savage other as Ethan mirrors Scar in *The Searchers,* the closeness between Ethan and Scar has merged into a singular identity. McCabe is the kidnapper. As he rides into town with his string of prisoners in a freezing rain, Leonard Cohen's music on the soundtrack ironically identifies the women as "sisters of mercy," thus suggesting as in the earlier captivity narratives a redemptive religious dimension to their trials. But in the world of Altman's film, all the characters are prisoners. Unlike the economically inexplicable ability of Ethan and Marty to roam the Southwest for years in search of Debbie, the characters in *McCabe & Mrs. Miller* struggle to survive in the grim conditions of frontier life. Both McCabe and Mrs. Miller are captives of a system of big business and land exploitation beyond their ken and their control. The nature of their plight is marked in Cohen's song when he sings:

> Yes, you who must leave everything
> that you cannot control.
> It begins with your family,
> But soon it comes around to your soul.

The women McCabe buys reveal this condition—large and heavy "Two-for-One Lil," the snaggle-toothed half-breed "Pinto Kate," and the young teenager—three abject "nuns" captive to male sexuality and McCabe's "investment" in his struggle up the ladder of business success. McCabe is the "Indian" who takes these women into captivity, but for him to rescue them, he has to defeat the larger enemy, the savage and cannibalistic other that has captured both of them, the eastern mining trust. The tragic fact of the film chronicles no escape here for Mrs. Miller and her girls because they are all prisoners of the same entrepreneurial patriarchy, whether it's McCabe or the mining company. Part of McCabe's authority ironically results from the power over the women whom he is also powerless to rescue. Certainly his relationship with Mrs. Miller is a partnership, but she bring no money to the arrangement; rather, she is able to secure this elevation in her captivity through her experience in the trade.

Mrs. Miller's is a particular kind of captivity. She recalls earlier survivors of captivity stories who persist through their ordeals not just by physical endurance but also by intelligence and by manipulation of her captors. Like numerous women in both real and fictional captivity narratives, she makes an arrangement with her captor that, failing the possibility of deliverance, permits some form of empowerment even in captivity. McCabe ultimately is a man only marginally in control of his own circumstances and is constantly out of his depth. Constance Miller proposes a partnership with him as part of her scheme for freedom, her plan to buy her way out of the frontier and to return to the civilization of San Francisco. She is stronger, smarter, and more knowledgeable than the senior partner in their prostitution business, but she is nevertheless dependent upon the success of his business sense. The film employs this discerning dependency in part to reveal McCabe's insecurities and inadequacies. But it is also informed by a developing awareness of the power of the patriarchy.

In the dominant captivity narrative, the heroine emerges in the nobility of resistance and the power of deliverance, supported by the heroism of masculine search and rescue. In *The Searchers* Ethan's reaction to Debbie's abduction is a relentless mission of revenge. His own guilty complicity in the subtext of savage desire results in his brooding anger, which finally helps procure Debbie's return even as it bars him from entry to the hearth of "civilization." In Altman's captivity story, however, McCabe participates in the abduction. He assures its existence as a function of his own survival. He accepts its inevitability. The central male figure is insecure, vain, vulnerable, and inept, and when he dies alone, unnoticed, meaninglessly in a blinding snowstorm, Mrs. Miller is still a captive, not just to the opium but to sexual and economic necessity. The film aggressively revises the role of the masculine hero not only by reducing him to a sadly ineffective gambler but also by making him complicit in the continuing abduction of the feminine into prostitution.

Lee Mitchell pointedly analyzes how the "persistent anxiety" about gender roles in the captivity narrative emerges in the American culture contemporaneously with both the time of this story and the publication of Wister's *The Virginian* (1902). Fears at the time about white slavery led to vice commission reports that "detailed how innocent girls became prostitutes not because of low wages but because of a powerful, all-encompassing conspiracy controlled by foreigners. Again, the genre clearly drew on the Indian captivity narrative, with rural women abducted to urban wildernesses and held sexually against their wills." Mitchell points out too how Zane Grey's famous *Riders of the Purple Sage* (1912) develops "three separate plots of women abducted, enslaved, or under threat." The novel "organizes materials according to the conventional captivity plot, with Mormons and outlaws replacing the traditional villainous Indians as the alien Other."[81] The savage other feared in the wilderness returns again in this film, but now as a result of white male weakness and desire. *McCabe & Mrs. Miller* tells another tale of western captivity that situates ineffectual masculinity at the heart of darkness. Western individuality is severely limited by the power of the business world already on the frontier "ahead of the rest." The savage is not the red man but the white, and this "savagery" shapes a condition of weakness, of insecurity, and powerlessness.

A recurrent image in the film is the hooded female leaving the scene of violence. One of its most troubling and ambiguous occurrences suggests this status of the enslaved dependency of the woman. Sumner Washington, the black barber, and his wife appear several times in the film—upon their arrival, at the funeral of Coyle, and finally in the crowd of people putting out the church fire. When the fire is extinguished and the townspeople celebrate exuberantly, Washington and his wife flee the scene, she with her head shrouded in a scarf and he looking back anxiously as he also shields her with his arm. The image is reminiscent of images of Orpheus and Eurydice, when the two in similar poses flee hell from which Orpheus has rescued his love. The image is also another of Altman's remarkably dense representations of the African American gaze on the white community. An implication here is that in the presence of Bart's death and of the unexplained fire, the community is likely to blame the black for its cause. The woman runs in fear and dependency on the man for her safety.

The same image of flight in the context of both Mrs. Miller's fear and her dependency on the male occurs two other times in the film. Hooded each time in a veil, she leaves the scene when her partner McCabe heads for that apparent shootout with the cowboy, and she walks away into the snowy dark on the night before McCabe must go to meet the killers. When

Ida arrives as a mail-order bride from Bearpaw, she is dressed in black and sits on the back of the wagon similarly shrouded in a black hood and anxiety as she enters this western frontier to be the bride of the crippled Coyle. Both scenes depict the anxiety of the female in a culture of violence and dependency. The black couple, Ida, Mrs. Miller in the face of violence flee, shrouded, abject, fearful, ashamed, hiding, knowing—captives of the white male world. Dependency itself yields anxiety, and anxiety is realized as fact: white people, men will fight among themselves; blacks and women will suffer. As Slotkin summarizes,

> the cycle of the myth never really ends.... Rescue from dark events is never complete. Physical combat with and captivity to the dark forces (whether they are really dark or only imagined to be so) infects the mind itself with darkness.... The struggle turns inward: Indians are discovered lurking in subversive forces within society itself, in the independence and aspirations of one's own children, in the recesses of one's own mind.[82]

McCabe & Mrs. Miller ends with the long zoom in on Constance Miller lying in an opiated stupor; the zoom goes all the way into her eye and then cuts to the extreme close-up of the surface of a ceramic vase she is contemplating. The relationship with McCabe is gone with the death she feared would happen. The partnership that might provide her means of escape from this wilderness also disappears. She seeks refuge from the captivity in this place through drugs. Her captive consciousness pervades the narrative, and the film self-consciously captures her plight as the motive for the western itself. Even as the camera pans across the cold northwestern landscape in the opening shot, Leonard Cohen's "Stranger Song" fills the soundtrack in retrospection. The point of view in the song conveys the woman watching and waiting in resignation for rescue that never comes. As the camera watches the enshrouded McCabe wind his way into Presbyterian Church, the narrative is shaped by awareness of the woman's perspective:

> I know that kind of man
> It's hard to hold the hand of anyone
> who is reaching for the sky just to surrender.

This opening portends the sad conclusion of the film. McCabe's story develops along a trajectory of success-confrontation-death; its tragic ending emerges ultimately as a function of McCabe's boastful ignorance and inadequacy, and even though the narrative unfolds implicitly, its structural path is clear. But another story, Mrs. Miller's, crosses this text as well. It appears in miniature in the story of Bart and Ida: The woman sold into marriage with a cripple whose death pushes her into prostitution. It's told again in the innocent hope that the cowboy stranger brings Ida in the whorehouse and that dies with his callous murder. Those narrative ends are already in the film's beginning:

> Ah you hate to see another tired man
> lay down his hand
> like he was giving up the holy game of poker.

The film is suffused with the sad knowing that entails McCabe's fruitless death, Mrs. Miller's continuing prostitution, and their mutual entrapment in the hand of forces beyond their ability to control. Cohen's song at the very beginning of the film establishes both an identity with the woman and a sense of futility deriving from dependency on inadequate men. The opening shots amount to the reverse angle of Mrs. Miller's opium gaze at the end of the narrative. The narrative identifies with the male's struggle and final defeat, but the events and situations and moods of the film are shaped by the melancholy awareness of their inescapability:

> And while he talks his dreams to sleep
> you notice there's a highway
> that is curling up like smoke above his shoulder.

The middle of the film is then motivated not just to explain the movement of McCabe from arrival to death but also to depict the nature of imagination in the face of negation.

Mrs. Miller dreams of partnership and escape. That hope disappears into the cold wind of nature that blows across the entirety of the film, but the trauma of its loss shapes its recollection by the narrative. The middle of this film explains McCabe's "reaching for the sky just to surrender," as in "The Stranger Song" earlier, but it also reflects Constance Miller's "smoke, and gold, and breathing," in "Winter Lady" at the end. The fact of the end, the fear of impending death and continuing captivity motivate the representations of community that grow momentarily with the growth of Presbyterian Church. That partnership, "my beautiful ladies," the warm and melodious bathhouse, the rich furnishings of the madonna-blue house, those quiet nights of reading in bed, vacuum cleaners and mechanical music boxes, golden hearts full of money, birthday parties with the girls—images "stored against my ruin."

Cawelti distinguishes the formulaic quality of genre fiction from the mimetic qualities of serious literature "on the grounds that the latter tend toward some kind of encounter with our sense of the limitations of reality while formulas embody moral fantasies of a world more exciting, more fulfilling, or more benevolent than the one we inhabit."[83] The pressures of the messy, violent, uncertain, ambiguous world produce the ideal world, the land of heart's desire. In the real world, prostitute Dallas and ex-con Ringo flee across the border in the middle of the night, free from the blessings of civilization. Huck Finn, mindful that the widow intends to civilize him, determines to light out for the territory ahead of the rest. Shane rides away from the peace in the valley, because as Marshal Thibido tells the Shootist, "We don't want your kind in this town."

Mrs. Miller's brothel is a place of fantasy. Historians record the awful reality of the life of frontier prostitution where few lived to thirty and where drugs and suicide were the usual means of escape. We see that whore at the end, and we hear her song in the beginning, but the middle depicts a haven, as Bob Dylan sings in exhortation to imagine "a place where it's always safe and warm":

"Come in," she said,
"I'll give you shelter from the storm."

McCabe's story derives from the harsh realities of the world of corporate power, where men buy women and where the company owns both. Mrs. Miller's community of prostitutes confronts "Sisters of Misery" with "Sisters of Mercy." Its inner warmth and golden red hearth provide shelter from the cold, gray, howling frontier outside. In the 1930s, William S. Hart's recorded preface for the sound version in his momentous silent western *Tumbleweeds* talks nostalgically about the early days of making westerns and recalls how, after all the dust and sweat of a scene concluded with the director's cut, "that dust became a golden haze." Desire in the western motivates the sentimentality; need motivates images of community; failure motivates stories of success.

McCabe & Mrs. Miller entwines the mimetic with the formulaic, and to the extent that it examines how the mimetic motivates the formulaic, Altman's western becomes reflexive and self-conscious. Ernest Hemingway's famous story "Big Two-Hearted River" describes the fisherman, a shell-shocked soldier returned from the burned-over past of the Great War and fearing the treacherous water ahead, who builds a camp here and now, "a clean, well lighted place," as a brief respite from that past and that future. The story constitutes a major paradigm of modernist literature. The aesthetic work of literary modernism provides what Robert Frost called "a momentary stay against confusion."[84] Mrs. Miller's red light in a madonna-blue house in the middle of that wilderness marks the delicate moment between frontier camp and mining town when the visionary gleam of the western hovers between the "green breast of the new world" and the "foul dust" of civilization that follows. Mrs. Miller's story is that same modernist fantasy, and as such it develops a reflexive sense of how the western comes to be produced. Spurgeon remarks: "Myths are what we wished history had been—a compressed, simplified, sometimes outright false vision of the past but a vision intended to serve a specific purpose in the present and, just as importantly, to bequeath a specific shape to the future."[85] Knowledge of the gray dust, of death in the streets, of hopeless captivity generates the desire for escape across the border. Weakness and failure motivate fantasies of strength and heroism and success. The grim, gray reality of frontier prostitution motivates golden images of refuge, warmth, and community.

A revisionist impulse underlies all genre narratives. Every retelling of the formulaic story requires invention for freshness and vigor. The western in particular with its grounding in a specific time and place revises its depiction of history in part because all histories of the past derive from a sense of the present. Cawelti writes: "The most significant aspect of the western is its representation of the relationship between the hero and the contending forces of civilization and wilderness, for it is in the changing treatment of this conflict, so basic to American thought and feeling, that the western most clearly reflects the attitudes of its creators and audiences at different periods."[86]

Certainly in the revolutionary winds of the late 1960s revisionism was in the air, not only for westerns and other genres, but also for Hollywood itself. Paul Arthur, reviewing the 2002 DVD reissue of *McCabe & Mrs. Miller,* asserts that when it appeared "genre revisionism was among the hottest ideas in European and American moviemaking."[87] Altman's entire career may be described as a filmmaking process that, as Adrian Danks asserts, creates a "revisionist form which interrogates, critiques and pays homage to the genres and archetypes of classical Hollywood cinema"[88]—from the combat film *MASH* (1970), to the musical *Nashville* (1975), the film noir

Gingerbread Man (1998), to the murder mystery *Gosford Park* (2001). Then and now, literary historians see titles like *McCabe & Mrs. Miller, The Wild Bunch, Monte Walsh* (1970), *Hannie Caulder* (1971), *Blazing Saddles, Butch Cassidy and the Sundance Kid,* and *Little Big Man* at the beginning of the seventies as a radical break from conventional western discourse that signaled its dramatic decline in film and literature. Nevertheless, the so-called classical period of the film western in the 1940s and 1950s represents a continuing movement away from the resolution of the western's thematic opposition between wilderness and civilization in favor of society. Films like *Johnny Guitar* and *High Noon* are revisionist certainly in their anti-McCarthy rhetoric. But even John Ford, the major figure in western narratives during these years, makes a string of films from 1939 to 1964 that are variously ambivalent (*Stagecoach, My Darling Clementine*), pessimistic (*The Searchers, The Man Who Shot Liberty Valence*), and unsympathetic (*Cheyenne Autumn* [1964]) to the notion of the advance of civilization along the American frontier.

An interesting aspect of the western is its compulsive return to a historical period of American history committed to establishing a (mostly masculine) sense of individualism and of moral and social justice. The western is not historical but about history, about the ways Americans read, discover, shape, and know themselves. The western is a cultural tool of construction and acceptance. Its compulsive retelling is, like the mythic West, a place of opportunity to get it right, to assert the values of social right and wrong, to establish a hierarchy among competing and conflicting values. Robert Frost in "Death of the Hired Man" celebrates home as "the place where, when you have to go there, / They have to take you in."[89] The western demonstrates how to stand and how to walk away when there is no home here. Gamblers and prostitutes reflect the gendered ways of being in the West—would-be winners at the games of life and slaves to the human sex drive. Not rugged individualists whose skillful shooting shapes destiny or attractive partners whose personal caring facilitates romantic bonding, but marginal figures sadly missing their goals and revealing the value of fantasy in their failures.

Richard Slotkin concludes his study of the *Regeneration through Violence* by asserting that

> our heroes and their narratives are an index to our character and conception of our role in the universe.... Under the aspect of mythology

and historical distance, the acts and motives of the woodchopper, the whale and bear hunter, the Indian fighter, and the deer slayer have an air of simplicity and purity that makes them seem finely heroic expressions of an admirable quality of the human spirit. They seem to stand on a commanding ridge, while we are still tangled in the complexities of the world and the wilderness."[90]

Pudgy McCabe and Constance Miller inhabit that wilderness as well. And their revised western stories remind us of the value of vision and the fact of failure. The movement from Wilderness to Civilization is not natural and foreordained (a "manifest destiny") by the struggle of individual heroes in a fertile garden, but an inexorable movement of capitalism in a place of brutality, betrayal, selfishness, and passivity. The hero is not the powerful, knowledgeable, alert, skilled frontiersman but an incompetent gambler and businessman who is forced to act on his phony reputation as a gunfighter. "Pudgy" McCabe is not the desirable masculine hero but a bragging, wisecracking, foolish, and childlike character who is prone to tell stupid stories and mouth conventional, sentimental clichés.

Constance Miller does not fill the romantic, domesticating role or even that of the "prostitute with the heart of gold"; rather, she is an opium-addicted, hard-eyed, intelligent prostitute who would transform experience into freedom. Romantic possibilities are not depicted in terms of growing trust and sympathy between the man and the woman but as the effect of a business relationship in the drugs, sex, and gambling trade. The individual is not the triumphant representative of community, order, and justice but a figure of defeat and powerlessness. Community is itself not a reflection of coherence, shared values, and social order but, rather, a reflection of fragmented desire, aimlessness, and superficial values. The film evolves through a series of tensions between a style of gentle lyricism and a story of blighted romance and impossible love, between actions aimed at building a future and forces that defeat those actions, between conventional generic expectations about the story and what actually happens in the film and in the world. The visionary gleam of possibility that flickers past the darkness of the film remains in its title, in the sign of their partnership: "McCabe & Mrs. Miller."

Warren Beatty
as John McCabe.

Julie Christie as
Constance Miller.

McCabe rides into the mining settlement of Presbyterian Church.

McCabe dealing cards in a game of poker at Paddy Sheehan's saloon.

McCabe returns from Bearpaw with several prostitutes.

McCabe and the prostitutes Kate, Alma, and Lily.

Mrs. Miller takes in the mining-camp realities of Presbyterian Church.

Mrs. Miller introduces herself to McCabe.

McCabe introduces Mrs. Miller to the camp.

Mrs. Miller proposes a deal to McCabe.

Madame Miller in her brothel chambers.

Sears and Hollander arrive by horse and buggy to make a deal with McCabe.

Butler (center) and another gunman confront McCabe at Sheehan's bar.

A skeptical Mrs. Miller hears McCabe's bragging self-confidence.

While gunmen stalk McCabe, residents try to save their burning church.

McCabe stumbles in the snow during his showdown with the gunmen.

A wounded McCabe plots his next move.

Mrs. Miller takes refuge in a Chinese opium den.

Warren Beatty, cinematographer Vilmos Zsigmond, and director Robert Altman

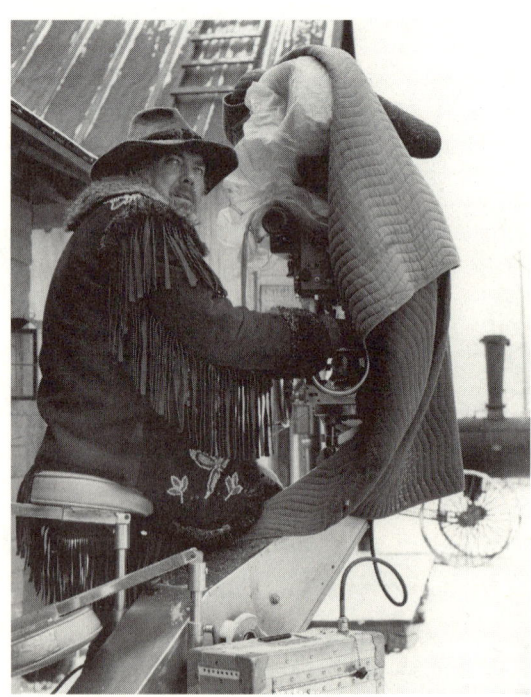

Robert Altman directing *McCabe & Mrs. Miller*.

Countercultural Contexts

Studies of the western inevitably begin with a commentary on genre narrative form or meditation on the relationship between the mythic and the historic West. *McCabe & Mrs. Miller* anticipates this approach because it has itself already undertaken a contemplation of these matters. Appearing at the height of the Hollywood renaissance and in the midst of the countercultural resistance to traditional aspects of American society, the film actively participates in the revisionist thinking of both movements. Historical research dresses the film in the western's obligatory periodicity and self-consciously depicts turn-of-the-century fashions and artifacts. The mythical gunfighter is rearrayed against a wilderness evolving into civilization. Narrative complexity deflects classical narrative discourse and conflates poetry with storytelling. Its blending of McCabe's with Mrs. Miller's narrative perspectives queries the gendered nature of the western gaze. Set halfway between the classical days of the genre and its collapse, it develops the mythic with the historic western in ways that contemplate both the continuing and diminishing future for the form. In particular, it also engages contemporary social issues, particularly the western's traditional representation of generally masculine gender roles.

In 1971 the editors of the *Saturday Review* proclaimed that the "new American revolution has begun."[1] For almost a decade Bob Dylan had served as the poet laureate of disaffection, anguish, and rebellion among young Americans. According to Frank Davey, Dylan's vision detailed a world where the unemployed ... are allowed by their fellow countrymen to starve ..., where civil rights workers are murdered ..., where prisoners are abused by sadistic guards ..., a world of embittered immigrants ..., of frivolous and materialistic women.... It is a world where white Americans systematically destroy entire tribes of Indians, where each warring nation and faction imagines smugly that God is on its side ..., where the "masters of war" hide in their mansions "as young people's blood/flows out of their bodies/and is buried in the mud" ..., where poor whites are taught by the rich to hate negroes ..., and the country where mine and factory are opened and closed with little thought to the welfare of the worker.... To the young, in Dylan's eyes, the United States is an absurd, surrealistic place.[2]

The cultural rebellion against such an American society, according to one historian, came to "a crescendo in 1972":[3]

I met a young woman whose body was burning,
I met a young girl, she gave me a rainbow,
I met one man who was wounded in love,
I met another man who was wounded with hatred,
And it's a hard, it's a hard, it's a hard, it's a hard,
It's a hard rain's a-gonna fall.
    (Bob Dylan, "A Hard Rain's A-Gonna Fall," 1963)

As one historian describes the times: "The 1960s had set the social, cultural, and political forces in motion, and the sixties era not only carried over into the 1970s, but reached its crescendo, creating a nation in 1972 that was vastly different from 1960, 1965, even 1968. A legion of activists demanded liberation and empowerment, confronting the establishment on almost every level and at almost every institution."[4] The voice of *McCabe & Mrs. Miller* is part of that crescendo. In rich, provocative, and illuminating ways, at a time when the whole country experienced the traumas of cultural and political transformation, Altman's film both reveals and employs the western as a way that Americans conjure national identity. The film actively participates in the discourse of resistance and change everywhere apparent in American culture at the beginning of the 1970s.

Popular narratives always develop within the context of events and values of the contemporary culture. As time passes, *McCabe & Mrs. Miller*'s sharing in the multiple energies of the late 1960s counterculture is forgotten. But a large part of Altman's early success with young audiences in *MASH* (1970), *Brewster McCloud* (1970), and *McCabe & Mrs. Miller* derived from the exuberant energies and chaotic resistance to the "Establishment" these films display. These first film successes not only reflect the social distress and crises of the late sixties, they also share the period's cultural irreverence and its enthusiasm for innovation and experimentation. They also enact the problematic interplay of historical tradition and contemporary necessity. Along with the back-to-the-land movement and the commune movement, they continue the mythic sense of nature as a site of hope and possibility. They illustrate the loss of civic faith that accompanies hostility to the Establishment. The film reveals the "deep well of cynicism about national politics"[5] that developed first during the presidency of Lyndon Johnson and then especially during the terms of Richard Nixon between 1968 and 1974. *McCabe & Mrs. Miller* at once shares the romantic idealism of the counterculture and the despair of the antiwar movement. The film is yet another historic text that now evidences a time of great national upheaval but that then, through its participation in the rebellious New Hollywood Cinema, contributed to that turmoil.

The historian Bruce Schulman describes much of the cultural production in the early seventies as "knowing, jaded, and circumspect" and argues that it "produced a tough-minded confrontation with the dark forces of a new age."[6] This energy is especially apparent in the negative visions of the revisionist westerns of the period like *The Wild Bunch* (1969), *Little Big Man* (1970), *High Plains Drifter* (1973), and *Blazing Saddles* (1974). Some western analysts have said of *McCabe & Mrs. Miller* that despite its dreamy poetic evocation of the traditional story, Altman's bleak social vision blunts its message,[7] but in many ways this social vision is indeed itself the message. Historians of the genre routinely assert that the thematic outlook of the western had already increasingly dimmed during its classical period after World War II. The large spate of B westerns that filled American theaters during the 1920s and 1930s inevitably resolve the genre's core opposition of wilderness and civilization in favor of the Turneresque view that the wild West inexorably gave way to the democratizing ways of individuals bringing civilization from the East. Altman, then, makes another contribution to a genre that after World War II steadily articulated a growing disaffection with contemporary political and social values.

A MIRROR TO ITS WORLD

With the advent of the serious, adult westerns at the end of the 1930s, generally grounded in John Ford's *Stagecoach* (1939), the western entered into a thirty-year period of remarkable aesthetic achievements. Its array of successful directors, popular stars, and industry approval sometimes masks the generally pessimistic themes that underlay much of its dominance as a Hollywood product. Whether prostitute Dallas and ex-con Ringo heading for the border away from civilization, or Marshal Kane throwing his badge into the street, or Marshal Thibido ordering the shootist John Books to leave his civilized western town—these westerns generally find it difficult simply to resolve plots in favor of civilization. They variously illuminate social forces that are restrictive, corrupt, destructive of individualism, influenced by corporate greed, and subject to political compromise. As the West becomes civilized, no place remains for the hero and his skill with weapons. Genre historians of the western routinely chart the increasingly bleak vision of the form as a measure of shifting and contradictory contemporary social values as American culture made its way to the Vietnam War and the counterculture.

The structural genius of the western has always resided in the two-way potential for its resolution of the wilderness-civilization conflict. Indeed, part of its continuing appeal involves the ambiguous potential for any given film to resolve its plot in divergent directions, thus providing endless variations on the theme that worked in part to provide fresh entertainment for the dedicated audience of the form but generally to indicate shifts in American beliefs and values. John Lenihan in his study *Showdown: Confronting Modern America in the Western Film* argues that examination of evolution in the western reveals "how a particular form is modified in accordance with the constantly changing concerns and attitudes of a society."[8] The conflicting treatment of the hero Buffalo Bill, for instance, or the outlaw Jesse James gang or the military hero George Armstrong Custer during the years between World War II and the Vietnam War easily reveals the conflicting issues and values engaged by the divergent concepts wilderness and civilization. Lenihan points out, for instance, that "Jesse James' change from exploited farmer in 1939 to troubled juvenile in 1957 and ragged nonconformist in 1972 makes abundant sense when put into the context of those particular years."[9] Similarly, Errol Flynn's Custer in *They Died with Their Boots On* (1941) on the eve of World War II paints the famous cavalry hero as a rebellious but successful and popular hero. His death at Little Big Horn helps the army defeat the Indians but ultimately appears as the self-sacrifice necessary to convince a deceived Congress of the bad faith and unscrupulous dealings of the government-subsidized Western Railroad Land & Trading Company. In 1970, with the United States deeply engaged in the increasingly unpopular Vietnam War and historians beginning to describe the colonial conquest of Indians as genocide, Arthur Penn's commercially successful *Little Big Man* revises the heroic, procivilization image of Custer to depict him as a vain, egotistical, mentally unstable leader of Indian massacres.

To identify films like *McCabe & Mrs. Miller* as simply reflecting the anti-Establishment mood of the late 1960s is to ignore the ongoing participation of the western in the complex tension between American ideals and practice. The revisionist western is thematically different only in degree, not kind. Because the cultural conflicts in the late 1960s escalate so dramatically, however, that degree itself marks the highly volatile social world into which the film was released and to which it significantly contributed. Like so many westerns across the history of westerns, *McCabe & Mrs. Miller* engages many of the issues of 1970 that have continually been characterized as revolutionary. Literally, narratively, and metaphorically, the film depicts the construction of social space in a vacuum from, in opposition to, and in defiance of the East, the Establishment, Hollywood, and corporate America. Wilderness in the film becomes a space of opportunity for the redefinition of cultural identity, and this opportunity resided in the very production of the film itself. Large numbers of the production crew had fled to Vancouver and established a commune in the Canadian woods. Its set builders are indistinguishable in long hair, beads, and faux Indian garb from the hippie draft dodgers who similarly had constructed over three thousand alternative ashrams and communes all over the United States and Canada by 1971. Most of the film's carpenters lived in the very sets they were constructing for the six months of the production. Widely published images from the shooting of the film showed Altman himself in large cowboy hat, full beard and fringed leather jacket. At forty-five, he was the aging hippie who presided every evening over parties of scotch and marijuana to watch the dailies with the entire production company.

The efforts of the counterculture to transform "Amerika" coincided with Altman's efforts to remake his own career. After a decade of directing adventure series for mainstream television and repeatedly running afoul of their stories, their styles, and their production process, Altman's fledging movie career as a Hollywood rebel drew vital energy from the rebellious times. The counterculture movement and Altman's personal and professional resistance to traditional modes of cinematic discourse perfectly suited each other, and his iconoclastic films in turn fed the period's energy of defiance. He directs eight revisionist movies between 1969 and 1974—a productivity as amazing in its number as in its liberatory drive. The experimental and iconoclastic qualities of *That Cold Day in the Park* (1969), *MASH*, *Brewster McCloud*, *The Long Goodbye* (1973), *Images* (1972), *Thieves like Us* (1974), and *California Split* (1974), in addition to *McCabe & Mrs. Miller*, built a large following for Altman among a disaffected audience of young viewers widely perceived at the time as a movie generation. *McCabe & Mrs. Miller* in particular supported their delight in experimental film as well as their anti-Establishment sentiments and their growing pessimism about the country that would only deepen within the year when the country reelected Richard Nixon by the largest plurality in American history.

At the same time, out of the counterculture, the civil rights movement, and the antiwar movement of the 1960s, another major revolutionary energy developed into the second wave of feminism (the first culminating in suffrage for women). In 1970 the women's movement burst upon the scene, and more than any other contemporary social force, it shaped much of the film's thematic and narrative commitments. The power of *McCabe & Mrs. Miller* derives in large part from its anticipation of what would be a vital interest of the new western history—the role of women, especially prostitutes, in the development of the West. It derives from the narrative expansion of the western myth to include its historic outsiders, *Gunsmoke*'s Miss Kitty brought to life. It also derives from the transformation of the classical narrative form that dominates the western into the aesthetics of modernism. Under the impulse to convey two competing points of view that compound McCabe's narrative with Mrs. Miller's, *McCabe & Mrs. Miller* works toward the complex discourse of the New American Cinema. These energies develop both from Altman's political, temperamental, and artistic resistance to the norms of the Hollywood Establishment and from a sympathetic recognition of women's oppression in contemporary American culture.

THE COUNTERCULTURE

Bob Dylan's rhythms and lyrics capture and express much of the ethos of the times:

Come mothers and fathers
Throughout the land
And don't criticize
What you can't understand
Your sons and your daughters
Are beyond your command
Your old road is
Rapidly agin'.
Please get out of the new one
If you can't lend your hand
For the times they are a-changin'.
   (Bob Dylan, "The Times They Are A-Changin'," 1964)

The film both jokingly and dismissively has been described as a "hippie western." The counterculture scene of drugs, sex, and rock and roll seemed particularly in evidence on an Altman shoot. The apparent spontaneity and improvisatory quality of the filmmaking, the regular ensemble of actors and production staff, the communal gatherings to party and watch the dailies, the freedom of all the company to provide ideas for the project—these seemed to personify the carefree and rebellious mood of the time, and they culminate for many in his best film, the iconoclastic, pessimistic, and innovative *Nashville* (1975). In the Canadian Northwest, the *McCabe & Mrs. Miller* shoot became another hippie commune, its inhabitants dodging the draft, living on the land, building a new culture. The casual representations of nudity in the film attracted *Playboy*'s interest for its "Sex in the Movies" features, but even more it reflected the rebellious attitude toward clothes in general and the acceptance of nakedness so widespread in Woodstock Nation. One historian describes the new "acceptability of explicit sexual detail" in popular culture as one of the "signs of a new celebration of the human body."[10] The display of the naked bodies of Mrs. Miller's prostitutes is casual, offhand, matter-of-fact. In this liberated atmosphere the movies began to develop an openness to show nudity and to discuss sex. Indeed, to make prostitution itself a subject is just another way to participate in the developing sexual revolution.

Despite its grounding in the historic conditions of life on the frontier, especially among prostitutes, Mrs. Miller's opium smoking further references the omnipresence of marijuana, LSD, and other drugs in the youth culture of the sixties and seventies. Like many of the youth generation, she keeps a "stash" in her closet along with her smoking "paraphernalia." Head shops abounded in towns across the country, and marijuana seemed to be everywhere the youth culture congregated. Much of the new awareness about all facets of the "straight" world in the period derived for many in the counterculture from "stoned thinking," that is, a kind of illuminated discovery of both life's beauty and its ugliness and an appreciation for their interrelated connectedness. While LSD provided a hallucinatory view of the world, its effects also motivated language that described the youth rebellion in terms of an "altered consciousness." When the Beatles turned away from the soft rock that made them famous in the mid sixties to the electronically enhanced sounds of *Sgt. Pepper's Lonely Hearts Club Band* in the late sixties, audiences largely assumed that songs like "Lucy in the Sky with Diamonds" referred to LSD. The music along with the new electronic sounds of the Grateful Dead, the Doors, Janis Joplin, and Jimi Hendrix represented a whole new genre of "acid" or "psychedelic" rock. When McCabe asks Sheehan about the availability of "mud" at the beginning of the film or when Mrs. Miller casually brings out her smoking supplies, the film repeats and reinforces the casual prevalence of drugs in the counterculture. These associations have evaporated with the fading of "the Revolution," and now the historical understanding of the desperate association of prostitution and alcohol, laudanum, and opium seem more vivid an understanding of the narrative core of the film. Nevertheless, when the film appeared, Mrs. Miller's casual and then finally desperate use of opium in complex ways reflects the countercultural mantra "turn on, tune in, and drop out." Schulman notes, "The counterculture embraced salient features: dope, as an entry way to expanded or altered consciousness, heightened awareness, and communal experience; freer sexual mores and living arrangements; a new relationship to nature; distinctive dress and foodways; and a commitment to communal living."[11]

The use of Leonard Cohen's music further references the popular folk-music culture of the time. In the early seventies, Cohen enjoyed popularity second only to Dylan; thus his singing literally indicates the way the film at once reflects the spirit of the times and contains it. In Davey's analysis, "Dylan seeks the destruction of what is to him an inhumanly competitive, exploitive, classifying, and confining society," while Cohen's music "presents a threatening, devouring world and men desperate to delay their doom" where "love serves most obviously as a panacea for society's demand that one control, discipline, and enslave one's environment and fellow man."[12] Cohen's music like Dylan's provided the soundtrack for the revolution. The three songs in the film come from Cohen's immensely successful album of 1968, *The Songs of Leonard Cohen*. The songs are full of mystery and magic and discovery, sung with Cohen's sense of tired longing that seemed to promise opportunity and loss simultaneously. The lyrics and tempos of its major hit "Suzanne" as much as the bardic "Hard Rain" of Dylan distill the emotions of an era:

> there are children in the morning
> they are leaning out for love
> they will lean that way forever
> while Suzanne holds the mirror
> And you want to travel with her
> you want to travel blind
> and you know that you can trust her
> for she's touched your perfect body with her mind.

Suzanne, like the Beatles' Lucy, links love as an escape with the female and the hallucinogenic. Altman asserts that he finally used Cohen's music on the soundtrack of *McCabe & Mrs. Miller* because it both shaped the mood and energy of the production process and recapitulates the emotional energy of the story. Much like the music of Simon and Garfunkel in *The Graduate* (1967), Cohen's popular music reflected and characterized contemporary feelings of longing, magical fulfillment, and loss. Using the songs on the soundtrack imports those emotions into the film, and in turn the film's story and style give vibrant life to those emotions.

ANTIWAR, ANTI-ESTABLISHMENT

In 1971 the politics surrounding the Vietnam War split the country and underlay the striking "generation gap" that coursed through every dimension of popular culture at the time. The violent atrocities of the My Lai massacre in 1968 significantly fueled the antiwar movement and the youth rebellion. In a speech later in 1969, when Nixon evoked support for his policies by the "great silent majority," he decried this strife with its "drugs, crime, campus revolts, racial discord, draft resistance" and asserted that "on every hand we find old standards violated, old values discarded, old principles ignored."[13] In that same year the antiwar demonstrations around the country and government reactions against them culminated in the tragic killing of students by National Guard troops at Kent State University and at Jackson State University, confirming the worst fears of the youth about the fascist direction of the country. In the fall of 1969 a declared "Moratorium against the War" led to the first national strike of American students against the government. In 1970 after the U.S. military "incursion" into Cambodia, the May Day march on Washington brought a half million demonstrators to the Capitol, led to over ten thousand arrests, and further increased the hostility of the president toward the youth culture. In 1972, the Democratic Party's presidential nominating convention in Miami unveiled all the democratic reforms initiated after the violent rioting at the 1968 convention in Chicago. Black delegates increased to 15 percent of the delegates after minimal numbers in that disastrous convention, women delegates increased to 38 percent, and delegates under thirty increased from 3 to 23 percent.[14] As they mingled with traditional Democratic party faithful, the resulting clash of hawk and dove, old and young, national and southern sympathies splintered the party and ensured Nixon's mobilization of the silent majority in opposition to what he demonized as communist-inspired, traitorous, debauched, and sex-crazed youth.

But the post–World War II generation of baby boomers had been raised on a strange combination of economic expansion, Cold War paranoia, fear of the Bomb, violence, and the social optimism symbolized for many in John F. Kennedy's inaugural charge to ask "what you can do for your country." One historian observes, "Perhaps because this postwar generation had matured in an idealistic world of infinite possibility, perhaps because it possessed a special sensitivity to the terror of extinction, the antiwar youth experienced deep feelings of revulsion and disaffection from the politics of the national leadership."[15] The bloody demonstrations for civil rights in the early and mid-sixties gave way to racial rioting in several American cities. Popular leaders Martin Luther King, Jr., Malcolm X, Bobby Kennedy, and even the country's president John F. Kennedy were all very publicly assassinated. The movies become saturated with the gun violence of the era. *Bonnie and Clyde* (1967), *The Wild Bunch, Little Big Man, Mean Streets* (1973), and *McCabe & Mrs. Miller* all resonate with this violence.

This baby-boom generation, however, had also been raised in part on the values of the traditional western, where cowboy heroes stood for self-reliance, fair play, and restraint, the regenerative power of the wilderness, concern for the underdog, and resistance to the oligarchic forces of civilization. Radio, movie, and television cowboy series, in the words of Patricia

Limerick, "provided young baby boomers with unconfusing heroes and a clear sense of right and wrong."[16] Indeed, she traces a direct road from the Code of the West to the Port Huron Statement. To read values promulgated by "The Lone Ranger Creed," Gene Autry's "Cowboy Code of Honor," Hopalong Cassidy's "Creed for American Boys and Girls," and Roy Rogers' Riders Club "Rules To Live By" is to discover both the moral and rhetorical roots of the idealistic manifestos like the Port Huron Statement of the student New Left in the 1960s. The Lone Ranger Creed asserts that "all men are created equal and that everyone has within himself the power to make this a better world" and believes "in being prepared physically, mentally, and morally to fight when necessary for that which is right."[17] Seeing its inheritance as "human capitalism, functioning at three-fourths capacity while one-third of America and two-thirds of the world goes needy, domination of politics and the economy by fantastically rich elites, accommodation and limited effectiveness by the labor movement, hard-core poverty and unemployment, automation confirming the dark ascension of machine over man instead of shared abundance, technological change being introduced into the economy by the criteria of profitability," the Students for a Democratic Society proclaimed that "we would replace power and personal uniqueness rooted in possession, privilege, or circumstance by power and uniqueness rooted in love, reflectiveness, reason, and creativity."[18] Annette Kolodny specifically asserts the connection between the youth movement and the western: "Their ranks were swollen with those inspired by the democratic vistas associated with the wilderness, the frontier, and the West—and by other intimations of liberty that Thoreau described as 'American mythology.' They acted on those fictions. They believed in the myths of liberty, equality, autonomy, and democracy. Their America was a spacious theater of freedom and unpredictability."[19]

For such an audience, Altman's western *McCabe & Mrs. Miller* engaged the more traditional popular genre for thinking again about American identity and values. It reveals an anti-Establishment mentality in the scene between McCabe and lawyer Clement Samuels. Punning obviously on the famous literary artist Mark Twain, the film stages a Twain-like satire of the windy, hypocritical politician played by William Devane (recognizable for his portrayal later of John F. Kennedy in the made-for-television film, *The Missiles of October* [1974]). In the novel *McCabe* the lawyer in Bearpaw to whom McCabe goes for legal assistance in his impending encounter with the Harrison Shaughnessy Mining Company is a gaunt, embittered old man, a ghostly veteran of ongoing struggles against the corrupt power of big business. Cynical about the law's delay, he wants McCabe to document his situation so that upon his death he will leave behind just another scrap of evidence in the indictment against big business that perhaps in some future court will cause justice to prevail.

Altman's lawyer, however, is a slick, fancy-dressed young politician campaigning to be the next senator from the state of Washington. At the time of the film's release credibility for lawyers in the United States had sunk to 12 percent: "The loss of faith in doctors and lawyers, the skepticism about corporate leaders, the omnipresent distrust of politicians—all produced a spreading disillusionment about the competence of the dominant institutions of society."[20] Samuels epitomizes this attitude; he is a parody of the glib politician who bamboozles McCabe with empty, bombastic rhetoric and assures him that the courts will protect his interests. "The laws here protect the little guy like yourself, McCabe." He promises to make McCabe a hero of the "little man" whom the system is designed to protect, although along with the big guy too: "I'm here to tell you that this free enterprise system of ours works and that working within it we can protect the small businessman and the large businessman as well." To McCabe's fears that the mining company may kill him, Lawyer Samuels offers meaningless slogans: "Until people stop dying for freedom they ain't going to be free." A popular poster of the antiwar movement proclaimed: "Fighting for peace is like screwing for chastity." The activist audience would have recognized the Establishment's similarly empty logic in Samuels's speech. Moreover, he ironically champions the political optimism of the western that the film depicts as bankrupt: "When a man goes into the wilderness and with his bare hands gives birth to a small enterprise, nourishes it, and tends it while it grows, well, I'm here to tell you no dirty sons-o-bitches are going to take it away from him." The thrust of the scene is to depict the politician as superficial and phony and condescending. His depiction echoes the Left's perspective of "tricky Dick," the manipulative and duplicitous president who claimed to speak for the "silent majority" while continuing to wage a bankrupt war against anticolonialist Vietnamese in Southeast Asia for American freedom. He buys McCabe's approval with flattery, empty platitudes, and grand promises but gives him no real assistance.

Politicians like Clement Samuels, like Richard Nixon, motivate the era's hostility toward national politics. The parody here is broad and aggressive, much like the street theater productions of the time that played out politics of resistance to big government and by the "over thirty" Establishment responsible for the great span of social wrongs castigated by the counterculture. Less obvious is the critique of the hero himself in this narrative. Rather than a cowboy, or gunman, or sheriff, John McCabe is an itinerant entrepreneur and, ironically, as a small business man, part of the 1970s Republican Party faithful, one of Richard Nixon's "great silent majority," the bane of his political existence for reelection in 1972. McCabe becomes the most prominent man in Presbyterian Church across the temporal movement of the film, and the source of his capital is gambling. He builds the town on the extraction of wealth from the miners, exploiting their desire for entertainment and parlaying the odds of their losses at his card tables. McCabe is "the House" that exploits labor for his own ends. The selfless individual gunman or cowboy or sheriff who defends the powerless townspeople against the forces of evil has become the antihero. Killers, outlaws, dropouts in this time of great national resistance have become the heroes of disaffection, the representatives of revolution, the central characters in narratives of futility. In a time of distrust, despair, and descent, the man who would go to Congress is a self-seeking blowhard, and the man who straps on the gun to defend the good is a tinhorn gambler.

Another aspect of this antiheroic stance is the film's representation of masculinity itself. An antimachismo mood is everywhere in revisionist representations of the male hero in late sixties and early seventies stories. In many ways Dustin Hoffman in *The Graduate, Little Big Man,* and *Midnight Cowboy* (1969) epitomizes this figure. Short, nonmuscular, nasal, and plain, Hoffman in his very physique speaks resistance to the images cut by John Wayne, Charlton Heston, Gary Cooper, and Gregory Peck. He would break that image barrier altogether in the cross-dressing role of Michael/ Dorothy in *Tootsie* some ten years later. His roles in these films too—the disaffected college graduate, the alternatively white and Indian westerner, the homosexual drug addict—indicate the depth of antisocial values in mainstream movies contemporary with *McCabe & Mrs. Miller.* Similarly, Warren Beatty imports the aura of the charming but sexually dysfunctional and murderous Clyde Barrow from *Bonnie and Clyde* and the pretty boy hairdresser of *Shampoo* (1975) to the role of Pudgy McCabe. His boyish good looks covered by a bushy beard, his attempted bravado crossed by his inane witticism, his dandyish attention to his clothes, his bouts of drinking, his muttering self-absorption, his thwarted desire for Mrs. Miller— all combine to create a portrait at once sympathetic and pathetic. Warren

Beatty's portrayal of McCabe carries with it the bravado of the male playing at the role of gunman, the ineffectual victim of the male bully played so arrogantly by the huge actor, 6-foot, 7-inch tall Hugh Millais. This hired thug sees through McCabe's plaintive bluster, which Altman's screenplay substitutes for the novel's sharpshooting gambler. Hollander from the mining company echoes the older generation's putdown of the ineffectual younger generation when he tells McCabe, "Actually you're not unlike my son"—hotheaded, impractical, self-deluded, and immature is the implicit evaluation. Altman's perception of McCabe as a "two-bit kind of guy" who is "over his head," is more explicit. "He reminds me of myself. He's a fool. I always liked fools."[21] McCabe is firm and confidant, gentle and unsure, engaging and assertive, shallow and ineffective. In 1971 he is less a heroic figure larger than life than an ordinary man with a complex mix of strengths and weaknesses.

RELIGION AND BUSINESS

This figure then attempts to establish his gambling and prostitution enterprise between two major forces in American culture, the Christian church and big business. The mining frontier absolutely depended upon eastern capital to dig the ore and build the railroads to ship the tonnage to company mills and to extract the wealth from the ground. The missionary drive of Christianity further fueled much of the westering process. The church and the corporation are omnipresent in westerns, but their presence in the revisions of the counterculture undergoes significant transformation. "Frustrated by the failure of orthodox religions, Americans pursued alternative spiritualities."[22] In particular, the youth culture of the 1960s and 1970s displays a remarkable quest for the spiritual—from the pantheism of Native American culture to the insights of oriental mysticism. Drugs, humanist psychology, Zen Buddhism, Transcendental Meditation, Silva Mind Control, even Kurt Vonnegut's fictional religion Bokononism in *Cat's Cradle*—the search for mind expansion and inner peace took many forms during the era. The traditional church appeared in this light as part of the enemy. Widely perceived as resistant to the civil rights movement, the sexual revolution, the women's movement, the human potential movement, and the antiwar movement, the Christian church stood in many ways for the reactionary voice of the Establishment, characterized by one historian as the "failed, bankrupt religious traditions of Western culture."[23]

Altman's hostility to the church underlies much of the satiric force of *MASH*—particularly in the destruction of the pious Major Burns and in the last supper and resurrection (re-erection) of Painless. The varieties of Christian worship ironically fill the middle space of the debilitating materialism of *Nashville*. In *McCabe & Mrs. Miller* the minister's construction of the church runs like a negative counterpoint to all the communal values associated with McCabe's House of Fortune and Mrs. Miller's brothel. Their bathhouse becomes more central than the church, literally becoming the force for cleansing the town, whose physical layout isolates and turns its back on the structure that names the community. The black-clad minister walks through the narrative spaces on several occasions in the film, his glowering scowl, his hunched back and elevated shoulders reflecting hostility and withdrawal from the activities of the community. When Coyle fights for his wife's honor and lies bleeding and unconscious in the muddy, dark streets, the minister walks "on the other side" and flees from the dying miner. His subsequent eulogy for Coyle is a grim evocation of the horrors of hell in the context of the town's veil of sin. Finally, when McCabe seeks refuge in the church from the murderous intent of Harrison Shaughnessy's killers, the minister refuses him sanctuary and orders him out under the threat of his own shotgun.

The church has dominated the physical landscape of the film from the moment it appears as McCabe's destination in the opening scene. It shapes one of the most ironically beautiful images of the film when the minister places the cross atop its steeple against a fiery red and gold sunset. Altman juxtaposes this striking and symbolic moment with the arrival in town of the first prostitutes and Cohen's song "The Sisters of Mercy." Redemption resides, not in the church, but in the brothel, where prostitute and miner dance to the Christmas hymn "Silent Night." Indeed, this complex mixture of Christmas hymn, mass-mediated music, dancing, and prostitution encapsulates countercultural energies. In stark contrast to the warmth of Mrs. Miller's brothel, the inside of the church appears on McCabe's entry a place of unfinished construction, as chaotic within as the minister is mean-spirited, self-righteous, and misanthropic without. The film's crowning irony then in the last scene, where the bartender profanely exclaims, "Jesus Christ, the church is on fire!" depicts the townspeople's finally successful effort to extinguish that fire. They celebrate at the end of the film the salvation of a building with the dead body of the minister that they have ignored throughout the story and that is merely an empty shell of the values it symbolizes.

Lenihan observes, "The church will remain a part of the town's future but, like everything else, as an adjunct to the ruling corporation."[24]

While much attention is devoted to the shoot-out between McCabe and the company assassins, the penultimate shoot-out (of four such confrontations in the film) occurs significantly between Butler and the minister. The giant gunman creeps up the stairs in anticipation that McCabe hides in the church, and when the door swings open, the gunman and the preacher face each other with rifle and shotgun. Butler's blast kills the preacher and sets the church on fire. Emblematically this showdown sets the forces of religion against the forces of big business. But the film characterizes both misanthropic preacher and murderous corporate gunmen negatively. The image of Dustin Hoffman is again relevant in this context. *The Graduate* in 1967 set the tone and captured the revolutionary energy of the counterculture. At the end of the film, the Hoffman character violates the religious ritual that would celebrate the marriage of Elaine when he steals her away from the altar in her wedding dress and uses a large cross to barricade the angry families in the church. At the very beginning of the film, one of his dad's business associates famously counsels Benjamin on his future: "Just one word: plastics!" In the parlance of the counterculture, "If you're not part of the solution, you're part of the problem." The church and big business become part of the problem to many in this period.

The major expression of this perspective occurs in the characterization of the conflict between McCabe and the Harrison Shaughnessy Mining Company. In many ways the antiwar movement critiqued the Vietnam War as a continuation of the imperialist policies of the French, who were driven out of "French Indochina" after the fall of their fort at Dien Bien Phu in 1955. The answer to the ubiquitous question "Why are we in Vietnam?" was Texaco, US Rubber, Dow Chemical, and Boeing. As historian Terry Anderson puts it, the counterculture was variously resisting "Harvard, Selective Service, General Motors, IBM, A&P, IRS, CBS, DDT, USA."[25] If McCabe as "businessman" is its small-town avatar, the lesson of the film teaches the costs of competition with big business. The mining company steps in to acquire property in the town, apparently because the zinc deposits warrant continuing operations in Presbyterian Church. The only mining clearly visible in the film, however, is the lumbering that takes place in order to construct the town. Whereas the novel explicitly describes the inexorable growth of the company, in the film, the only apparent increase in worth is the development of McCabe's property. The appearance of Eugene Sears and Ernie Hollander seems then motivated by McCabe's success; the mining camp grows into a small town, and the company reaches out to own it. This process reveals the Janus-faced quality of the company's public persona—the smooth representatives of corporate reason on one side, and the grim muscle, the armed enforcers of corporate policy on the other.

The first representatives of the company are well-dressed purchasing agents who arrive in a fancy, chauffeured horse-drawn carriage to buy up the town businesses. After reaching an agreement with Sheehan, they attempt to negotiate with McCabe but quickly tire of his drunken demeanor and exaggerated sense of his net worth. Their unwillingness to spend a second day bargaining over a sale price for his saloon, bathhouse, and brothel results from Hollander's impatience with McCabe: "Here we are ready to give you a substantial gain in capital, an offer from one of the most solid companies in the United States, and you say no. Well, frankly I don't understand." After all his years with the company, he also resents their sending him on this field trip in the first place: "After seventeen years I think I deserve something better than being sent out on some goddamn snipe hunt like this." He despairs about making a deal because McCabe is "impossible," "he hasn't the brains. I want to turn it over to Jake." On the other hand, McCabe's business associate thinks, "You handled them beautifully. They knew they weren't dealing with no tinhorn!" McCabe is uninformed and naïve, however, when it comes to the powerful company, and Mrs. Miller astutely recognizes his plight: "They're going to get you, McCabe. They'll do something terrible to you." As he runs to Bearpaw after the agents, as he attempts subsequently to negotiate with the hired killers, and as he confronts them in the ultimate showdown, the rest of the narrative traces McCabe's sad efforts to defend his position away from the eyes of the town, his masculinity in the eyes of Mrs. Miller, and ultimately his "holdings." The little guy has no chance against their ruthless power. Bluntly put, big business kills him for his property. Big business is the enemy, and the people have little chance against its murderous force.

In terms of human geography, a central conflict in *McCabe & Mrs. Miller* involves differing conceptions of space. For McCabe and Mrs. Miller, Presbyterian Church is a real place where the spatial potential of success drives their partnership. For Harrison Shaughnessy, Presbyterian Church is an abstract place within a space of corporate expansion. For the mining company, the space of corporate power dictates the ownership of this little mining town and the displacement, one way or another, of its local owners.

The lived space of individual potential clashes with the abstract space of corporate control. In the novel *McCabe,* Ed Naughton describes the conflicting spatial imaginaries that would shape the ways Presbyterian Church develops as a frontier place. The narrator ascribes to McCabe sufficient frontier experience to know how the mining company would shape this place: "The company would never tolerate no gambling house it didn't own. It wouldn't have no game running, but it would have to say the way it would be run. . . . He knew the company's reputation."[26]

WOMEN'S LIBERATION MOVEMENT

Altman's film, however, adds another spatial imaginary to this confrontation. When he adds "& Mrs. Miller" to Naughton's title, he indicates the film's participation in another major cultural development in the early 1970s, the Women's Liberation Movement. Sandra Schackel writes, that the "biting social commentary" of westerns in the 1960s and 1970s emerges from "the anti-war resistance, the civil rights struggles, and campus unrest, but especially too from the re-emerging women's movement. In this era a change occurred in women's movie images that reflected society's growing awareness of female capabilities."[27] The end of the 1960s and the early 1970s witnessed the flowering of the second wave of feminism in the United States. In August 1970, the national Women's Strike for Equality was "the first major feminist demonstration in a half century" since the demonstrations of the suffragette movement at the beginning of the century. Betty Friedan's *The Feminine Mystique* in 1964, the establishment of the National Organization for Women in 1965, the protest against the Miss America Pageant in 1968 were but a few of the growing public expressions of women's resistance to their social repression. The Port Huron Statement in 1962 tellingly defines the oppressions of men by men and fails to recognize women's secondary role in American culture. Within the next decade, however, young women especially began radically to rethink their relationship to the newly perceived coercions of American patriarchy. "Feminists with roots in the civil rights movement, Students for a Democratic Society (SDS), and antiwar groups began to protest against male domination and sexual discrimination within the radical movement."[28]

Energized also by the countercultural values of empowerment and liberation, women began aggressively to protest their exclusion from the professions, their unequal pay, their imprisonment by domesticity, the absence of their voice in politics. Numerous books and magazines examined the inferior role of women in American culture everywhere. In 1972, Congress recognized this new political energy when it passed the Equal Rights Amendment, intended to prohibit discrimination against women. One historian writes that between 1970 and 1972 "no issue received as much national attention as women's liberation."[29] Increasing numbers of women entered the academic world, where they encouraged the development of feminist perspectives across the professional disciplines. According to Terry Anderson, this period inaugurated feminists' challenge to "the traditional system of education and brought about more sensitivity in the classroom and in text books, and they inspired female writers who flooded the nation with new, exciting literature and scholarship"[30]—including investigation into the roles of women in the West, in the movies, and in literary history. In the influential publication by a collective of Boston women, *Our Bodies, Ourselves,* the authors asserted one of the manifestos of the movement: "We are women, and we are proud of being women. What we want to do is to reclaim the human qualities culturally labeled 'male' and integrate them with the human qualities that have been labeled 'female' so we can all be fuller human people."[31]

McCabe & Mrs. Miller emerges precisely in the middle of all this social foment and lends it voice to the energies of resistance. Free to depict nudity, to use vulgar language, to represent the casual use of drugs, to castigate business and religion, the film is equally free to portray its male hero in ways that reflect feminists' challenge to the macho male. Feminist liberation also meant liberation for men to recognize and accept the feminine aspect of the masculine self. The film's fool is "a fancy dude" in dress and hairdo, soft, increasingly sad in his empty boasting, childlike in his last sleep with Constance Miller, a man who asserts self-reflexively as he straps on his pistol for the last showdown that he has "poetry in me." He hardly shares the traditional strengths of macho hero, but he reflects an emerging social acceptance of the interweaving of the feminine and the masculine in all gendered identity. The poignancy of the last image of the dying McCabe covered in snow is captured in Leonard Cohen's lyrics that lament, "I know I'm not your lover." The film is here far from the ritual celebration of the triumphant male whose physical and firearm skills close the traditional western narrative. It is not, however, far from the effect of the Women's Liberation Movement on the successful 1970s male who "possessed the traits that earlier sociological surveys had labeled stereotypically female:

interest in their own appearance, aware of the feelings of others, gentle, talkative."[32] In his bedroom scene prior to the final shootout, McCabe delivers a lengthy soliloquy that is both revealing of his inner thoughts and emotions, as well as touching in what is a final confession of love to his absent lady. McCabe loses the western confrontation of good male against bad, but he wins the gender war against the taciturn western male hero. Epitomized by the central character over a hundred years previously in Owen Wister's novel *The Virginian,* then by Gary Cooper's famous performance of the Virginian in 1929, and again by Joel McCrea in 1946, this strong, quiet macho hero is destined always to vanquish and silence the female.

Among the changes wrought by the feminist movement of the sixties and seventies was the reexamination of American history that reveals women's stories in western fact and that Altman's film delineates in western fiction. The feminist intervention in American literature also opened the pages of neglected writing by and about western women, which in turn illuminates retrospectively the nature of Altman's narrative commitments. The interpretative circle here begins with the second wave of the feminist movement, which, like the film, grows out of contemporary resistance politics and which subsequently motivates a widespread rereading of the American cinematic, literary, and historical past. Academic work in these fields—in the search for neglected texts, in theory, and in practical analysis of both old and newly recovered writing by women—broadly establishes and authenticates feminist research. Susan Johnson sums up the significance of this endeavor: "The new work on western women that began to appear in the late 1970s opened up whole social and political worlds to views that had long been obscured by the stultifying maleness of the West as it had been represented in both academia and popular culture."[33] The insights and excavations of this work have in turn enabled the present understanding of the vital ways that *McCabe & Mrs. Miller* participated in and reinforced that movement as it developed.

McCabe & Mrs. Miller imports onto the screen space of the classical myth of the American West the presence and the voice of a strong woman. Helene Keyssar notes that "the title of Altman's film might signify partnership to the reader, but attention will then be called to the rarity of a partnership between a man and a woman."[34] When it adds her name to the title, it simultaneously asserts her story parallel to, in struggle against, and captive to his story. Consequently the film enacts the struggle between the gendered spatial imaginaries of the traditional masculine story of the West and the female conception of that same wilderness territory. On the one hand, analysts of the western routinely remark upon the confrontation between wilderness and civilization as the conflict that shapes and characterizes the American masculine identity. On the other hand, Annette Kolodny's studies, among other feminist analyses of western women's writings, have in particular revealed the extent to which women conceived the wilderness in dramatically different spatial metaphors than the masculine image of space to be conquered and resources to be capitalized. Women's writing reveals a fear and anxiety generated by the forested space of the Allegheny and Appalachian West so congenial to the mastering exploits of Daniel Boone and Natty Bumppo. The unfolding natural vistas of the Midwest and Southwest, however, led to the burgeoning feminist perception of the West as a garden, not dominated but domesticated. A fear of trees in representations of the Mohawk Valley and the Alleghenies yields to a desire for open, cultivated spaces with glowing perspectives of panoramic nature: "When settled in, women would have set about transforming the wilderness not into portable wealth but in to what one Nebraska newcomer called a 'sanctuary of domestic happiness.' . . . Men sought sexual and filial gratification from the land, while women sought more the gratification of home and family relations."[35]

Equally important in the understanding of these metaphoric distinctions are the very revelations by feminist literary scholars that discover and characterize these voices in women's imaginary representations of the West, from Mary Rowlandson's captivity narrative in the 1680s to the present. This scholarship gives place and voice and character to women in the West. Robert Altman's narrative about John McCabe and Constance Miller similarly works to articulate a western woman's voice, her gaze, her desire as it is emergent from and spoken against the culturally familiar and dominantly male-oriented values of traditional western discourse. Thus the film's importance in relation to the women's movement resides at once in its effort to give weight to the woman's role in 1971, in the impetus such weight lent to the subsequent development of feminist cultural analysis, and in the value such criticism brings in turn to an understanding of the film's feminist work.

In the novel *McCabe,* Constance Miller emerges generally as the object of McCabe's gaze, of his characterizations, of his generally distant and frustrated desire for her. From his third-person point of view, Mrs. Miller plays a traditionally subservient role to him. She is a tough and angry prostitute who nevertheless apparently loves him and who, in the last paragraph, waits with McCabe's shotgun to kill Sheehan for his complicity in McCabe's death. Altman's story reinforces the traits of independence and, more significantly, makes Mrs. Miller even more self-reliant in her relationship with McCabe. "You John McCabe?" she bluntly interrogates upon her arrival in Presbyterian Church to propose the gambling-prostitution partnership. She asserts her appetite forcefully: "Got anythin' to eat around here? I'm bloody starvin'!" The gusto with which she eats both mocks his showy and affected practice of drinking a raw egg in a glass of whisky for his meals and disconcerts him. She quickly and certainly assesses his operations, his assets, and his need for her expertise. The speech in which she aggressively details her proposal and argues its sense is one of the most important in the movie. McCabe's reaction in the novel makes her effect on him clear: "She annoyed McCabe; she made every sentence a crisis: she made everything a challenge." The book then summarizes early the easy relationship that develops between them and that then serves primarily as a backdrop to his encounters with the mining company:

> There wasn't any doubt that he and Mrs. Miller were the focus of the town's attention.
> And he liked it. He had never really been a big man anywhere before. He kept saying he would sell out and go back East, and Mrs. Miller said she was saving to go to San Francisco. But they never left.[36]

The visual and dramatic development of Mrs. Miller by Julie Christie, however, effectively removes her character from the narrative control of McCabe's point of view. Keyssar describes the effect: "From the first instant of her arrival to the last frame of the film, Mrs. Miller is in command of our attention and of the attention of all who come in contact with her.... But while the presence of Mrs. Miller in some sense does justify the existence of *McCabe & Mrs. Miller,* the film generates attention to her through gestures that consistently defy our expectations of the treatment of women on film."[37] Her brash speech, her unabashed manner, her self-confident body language, her easy command of the space of the bordello and the space of the narrative certainly display the qualities of performance that earned Christie an Academy Award nomination as best actress. Even more important is the extent to which her performance elevates both the physical and metaphorical significance of the woman's role in this western. Naughton's novel essentially characterizes and contains their relationship within one early chapter of his eighteen-chapter novel. Altman extends that relationship to the full length of his film and gives the tension of gender roles as much, if not more, importance as the conflict between the little guy and the big corporation.

If the genre promises some sort of romantic relationship between this hero and heroine, the film delivers another story. McCabe by film's end asserts explicitly his desire and the nature of his love for her. But Mrs. Miller's need is for the partnership. Prostitution is still captivity, and a successful business provides the means for her escape. The pattern of her relations with McCabe across the film signals her personal distance from him. She ignores his early efforts at entrance to her room; she derides his business skills after their operations begin; she attacks his ignorance of the mining company's power; she berates him for missing the birthday celebration of one of her girls; she gets stoned before sex with him and then makes him pay for the sex. In the last scene between the two of them, she takes him into her bed with sympathy for his fear of the morrow's armed confrontation and holds him to her breast like a child. Again Keyssar summarizes the significance: "The story of McCabe and Mrs. Miller tells us not of a union of two souls but of a tenuous partnership . . . , and the precariousness and final severance of this partnership has everything to do with Constance Miller's refusals to forge the expected romantic bond . . . . We may regret the failure of connection between these two, but it is precisely that failure that allows Mrs. Miller to survive and that frees the image of woman in the film from the usual servility."[38] If he laments that he "never was a percentage man" when it comes to love, her experience with men has been even more debilitating. "Oh, you've seen that kind of man before," the Cohen lyrics at the beginning of the film intone, "reaching for the sky just to surrender." The film opens from the perspective at the end of the film of her loss not of love but of escape.

In the middle of the film, Mrs. Miller constructs, in the words of Virginia Woolf that have become so symbolically important to the women's movement, "a room of one's own." Her bedroom is not just a place to conduct the business of her trade, but a private space as well. McCabe seeks admission to assert his rights as the partner with money, and she ignores him in a scene that contrasts his standing in the blue and windy cold with her happily massaging her feet and reading a book with delight in the golden warmth of her personal inner sanctum. Tellingly, her one word in this scene is "No!" Likewise, through the middle of the film she develops the brothel dramatically as a domestic space against that cold wilderness outside. The brothel connotes home as well as trade. Its parlor with sofas and curtains and carpets and paintings, its kitchen of baking and celebration, its warm golden lights signify the clean, well-lighted space of human sanctuary.

When she greets the prostitutes she has called up from Seattle, she stands in a cold, gray rain looking at their wet and bedraggled appearance and then welcomes "my beautiful ladies" into the warmth of her parlor and of her care. Her manner as madam is brusque, forceful, and business-like with the men, but with her girls she becomes the mother. The music of Bob Dylan echoes here from the cultural context of the film: "'Come in,' she said, / 'I'll give you shelter from the storm.'" The women bathe and sing in the steamy comfort of the bathhouse as the wind howls outside. At a time when the feminist movement was declaring that "sisterhood is powerful," the film depicts Mrs. Miller's house as a community of sisters, as a shelter, as a place of nurturing. Here is peace, laughter, games, and ritual celebration of the turns of life.

Krista Comer argues that what is significant about this notion of shelter from the storm is the very gendered suggestion to the identity of place itself: "Place, like western nature, enters contemporary representation in a female form. Western places, like women and nature, take care of people, feed them, nurture them when they are hungry, tired, or hopeless. They instruct the needy about how to tolerate that which cannot be changed. They heal; they nurse; they listen; they reassure; they care; somehow they love. Places point the way to new beginnings. Through it all, another day can be faced. Life is worth living."[39] This relation is especially marked in the little narrative about Ida Coyle. Brought west as a mail-order bride, left without material support by the violent death of her husband, Ida has nowhere to turn. Mrs. Miller recognizes her need and takes her in. Dressing her in her own clothes, Mrs. Miller compares the two of them, again with literal and metaphoric weight: "You're little like me." She further consoles her upon entering the sex trade with advice about sexual encounters with men. When Ida protests that it was her duty to have sex with her husband, Mrs. Miller remonstrates, "It weren't your duty." Mrs. Miller assures Ida that prostitution will be little different from marriage, with the added benefit of "a little something for yourself." Under the care and shelter of Mrs. Miller, Shelley Duvall performs Ida as blossoming from a withdrawn and unsmiling wife to a happy and girlish prostitute. Unrealistically, nonhistorically, the middle narrative of the film presents a fantasy world of Mrs. Miller's "Little Women." This moment is as transient as it is unreal. Robert Kolker reminds that "this is a film in which warmth and security are shown to be delusions and snares and community a fraud."[40] But in this middle passage, Leonard Cohen's "Sisters of Mercy" captures a sense of the prostitutes and the brothel in the metaphor of the monastery, sanctuary, open to "you who must leave everything / that you cannot control," with the promise of comfort, confession, and renewal.

Within the cultural revolution in the early seventies, radical feminists disavowed the need for men, some proclaiming "until we all become lesbian we will not be free."[41] The film hardly motivates such a radical perspective, but its gender politics actively display a feminist sensitivity only beginning to develop in American culture at the time of the film's production. Much of the narrative follows Mrs. Miller's effects on others in the film, McCabe in particular. The agents from the mining company dismiss McCabe's drunken, cocky bravado: "He's a smartass is what he is." And Constance Miller regularly emerges as the governing figure in their interactions, laughing at his affectations, belittling his business sense, castigating his lack of sensitivity, despairing over his ignorance about the power of Harrison Shaughnessy. He routinely retreats before her authority. The story of McCabe versus the mining company as well as the story of McCabe and Mrs. Miller come coterminously to an end together. The conflict with Harrison Shaughnessy makes him try to express and finally to defend his principles. In the end as he straps on his pistol for the showdown, he is resolute and prepared for the job a man's gotta do. But Altman transfers the description of his feelings from early in the novel to the end of the film. The western male hero, head turned from the camera, soliloquizes about his inner feelings toward his partner and the poetry he's discovered inside. Read one way, she is the castrating female: partnering with a woman will get you killed. Read otherwise, he succeeds through their partnership, draws strength from the relationship, and even if he cannot prevail against the force of big business, he can load his pistol in the light of her presence. The film chronicles Mrs. Miller's effect on McCabe.

Similarly, the film's prostitutes emerge from mere "chippies" and "crib cows" to domesticating woman cleaning their parlor, to cooks in the kitchen, to bookkeepers managing the business. If they are ladies of the night, they are also in Mrs. Miller's house and business purposive women of the day as well. The brothel may be only a momentary stay against the cold windy dark outside, but the very visual structure of the film is about the construction of woman's space as both private and domestic, public and corporate. Paula Petrik significantly entitles her historical study of prostitutes in Helena, Montana, "Capitalists with Rooms."[42] The parlor is also the office of the brothel. Mrs. Miller first appears as one of the retinue of prostitutes owed by the flesh dealer in Bearpaw, but by the film's climax, she commands the well-lit space of her brothel, of McCabe's saloon, and indeed her own room. Standing stalwartly upright in hooded cape, Mrs. Miller transcends Julie Christie's diminutive height. The tragedy of the film's end is remarkable in contrast to her expansive control of the narrative's middle.

THIRD SPACE

The narrative, too, becomes part of the contemporary struggle in 1971 over gendered spatial imaginaries of American culture. Comer argues that the "the story of the western . . . as the nation's founding myth" undergoes significant transformation in the 1970s: "No longer will popular symbols of westernness lend themselves so handily to the maintenance of nationalist empire. Courtesy of the antiwar, gay, feminist, and civil rights movements, the assault on the notion of a unified nation and its national subject . . . is well underway by the early 1970s." Her concern in *Landscapes of the New West* is to examine the new writings of a feminist West that reflect a contestation of the masculinist perceptions of the mythic western story in efforts to "remap the masculinism of western spaces." She further recognizes the distinctions between a western sense of *place* that is feminized and a masculine *space* that contains it. New feminist western fiction challenges these distinctions as a simplistic and false dichotomy between a masculine public or global space and feminine private, or local, places by insisting upon "the *web* of social relations that is operative across *all* social scales."[43] *McCabe & Mrs. Miller* is meaningful in this critical context as the representation of competing spaces and the difficulties of transcending them.

Comer and other social geographers use the terms "place" and "space" in ways productive for understanding how the film reflects feminist thought. *Space* is an abstract arena of potentiality, circumscribed by ideological concepts and imagination rather than by actual boundary lines and borders. *Place* is a literal terrain of lived locations, an actuality enacted out of spatial possibility. The film posits Presbyterian Church not just as a *place*—fixed and local and contained, known and familiar—but as a *space*—full of explorable potential, a region of possibility, new, unfixed, exciting, dangerous—indeed, like an ideal conception of wilderness itself, commensurate with some human power of wonder. Both heroes come to this mining camp with the baggage of their gendered identities, a gambler dependent on the odds of chance and the resources of others, and the prostitute dependent on the economic exchange value of her sexuality. The film puts into play the interchange of their gendered imaginaries within a context of not just local but national politics. If her possibilities are ultimately dependent upon his, both are shaped by the determinant forces of a global and imperial imaginary of extraction, wherein the wealth of the local fuels an international, impersonal, and capitalist economy and leaves the tailings of human and ecological ruin.

Recent western historians talk about the frontier as a "zone of cultural interpenetration between two previously distinct societies,"[44] where spatial imaginaries motivate human behavior and interaction. The town of Presbyterian Church develops under the competing pressure of divergent goals and desires. The visual structures of the film graphically reveal the number of conflicting masculine intentions and desires. The opening sequence in Sheehan's saloon dramatizes this competition for space. McCabe enters, surveys the interior, and claims part of it by spreading a red felt cloth on one table, staking out the space of gambling. Immediately, the off-shift miners jostle with each other over seats around the table, staking out in turn their claims around the potential lode of luck. Sheehan marks his ownership of the saloon by lighting the lamp over the table. McCabe and Sheehan then negotiate their share of the profits from booze and cards. Later Sheehan proposes a partnership agreement with McCabe that would control the entrance of other saloons into the town. This kind of masculine competition over frontier locales develops from particular expectations about the possibility of the West.

Equally competitive is the control of space by the church, essentially the first and the last image of intrusion into this Pacific mountain wilderness. Its phallic energy thrusts upward over the valley as McCabe enters the camp. It looms over McCabe as he dismounts and prepares his own conquest of the valley. Its steepled silhouette against a fiery sunset seems to assert natural authority against McCabe's second entrance into the camp with three prostitutes in tow. At the end, only partially damaged by the fire, it seems to reassert the importance of its claim to ownership of the place it names. The church has grown around the minister's purposeful organization of space, majestic and distinct on the exterior, yet chaotic and empty on the interior, and finally a casket for a misanthropic religion that dominates the valley but ignores its people.

Mining, too, has already entered and shaped the little valley as the film opens. The muddy street that flows through its middle, the ramshackle dwellings of its residents, the grubby and gray miners along its length, all reflect the place shaped by the masculine and mining sense of space. Value here lies in the zinc below ground, and the mining camp above is the ugly consequence of its removal. The transformation of the wilderness into a civilization recalls Joseph Conrad's sense of a "fantastic invasion." Kolodny's feminist perspective captures it exactly: "The success of settlement depended on the ability to master the land, transforming the virgin territories into something else—a farm, a village, a road, a canal, a railroad, a mine, a factory, a city and finally, an urban nation."[45] The corporate mission into the wilderness is too busy extracting wealth from the land to bother with social necessities. Sheehan's Saloon and Hotel seems to grow organically out of this muddy waste. It shapes a space of dark, crowded, cramped, leaky, divided, mean social compartments. McCabe imagines a larger possibility than "that hole on the other side of the creek." His spatial imaginary immediately recognizes the potential for profit from another kind of conquest. Presbyterian Church becomes a place under his impetus aggressively and continually in development. Initially a construction site, messy, full of building materials, walls open to the outdoors, busy with carpenters, his buildings also transform the natural resources of the surrounding forests into lumber for his growing enterprise. The completed saloon contrasts significantly with Sheehan's graying and dilapidated construction, shining with new wood, ultimately clean and gracefully modern. Compared to Sheehan's dark and grungy interiors, McCabe's House of Fortune is lit with a glossy uniformity, its space sparsely furnished and warmed by the intrusive bulk of a space heater that looks like an industrial boiler.

In contrast, Mrs. Miller's spatial imaginary motivates an entirely different sense of place that works dramatically against the place conceived by the town's leading male citizens. This contrast is dramatically realized in the scene where the Seattle prostitutes recover from their journey. These shots alternate with shots of men playing poker in McCabe's new saloon. A more formal atmosphere prevails than in that initial game; the men are better dressed and more restrained in manner. They talk in wonder about the erotic and mysterious nature of women's bodies. McCabe's entertainment business has effectively organized this male place and male behavior and capitalized on male desire. Alternatively, the naked women in the bathhouse climb together into one large wash tub and sing together a song of romantic celebration, to each other and to themselves: "Beautiful dreamer, awake unto me." Their place is one of shared comfort, a warm and steamy site of cleansing, harmony, and community. The brothel, too, evocates this same sense of feminine space, one that motivates a domestic place of nurture and refuge. The contrasts among these spaces clearly delineate the gendered imaginations encouraged by the fact and the possibility of life on the American frontier. As a mining settlement, Presbyterian Church designates the frontier as a borderland, a place of contestation between forces aggressively shaped and clarified by the discord of the sixties and seventies—between the small business man and the large corporation, between business and nature, between camps and towns, between men and women. The masculine conquest of frontier confronts the feminine settlement of frontier. The town itself externally develops with the same contradictory, competitive, and contrary sense of space organized by these interiors.

But the feminist space driving the setting of this story goes further than the elaboration of a feminine imaginary in contrast to the more traditional masculinist delineation of conquest and control. The film depicts the way the chaotic masculine town encloses the female. Prostitutes after all displace wilderness and Indians as land to be mined and people to be conquered. Part of the film's feminist project is to reveal the dimensions of this containment, to explore the ways that masculinist notions of territory contain and shape women's lives. But the role of Mrs. Miller works further to assert the place of women in the masculine space as well. "McCabe, the trouble with you is you think too small." Mrs. Miller is not just a prostitute and madam; she is a businesswoman, hardheaded, expert, productive. When McCabe complains about how much "money and pain" her visions are costing him, her response is to place a heart-shaped box of "whorehouse money" on his bar. She imagines a place as energetically mobilized by the profit motive as McCabe's, with the added incentive of liberation from the male—a room, a building, a business of her own in San Francisco. Her theme is summed up in that assertion: "I don't want no small-timer screwing up me business." Both McCabe and Mrs. Miller are ultimately defeated by the power that fuels the spatial imaginary of big business.

McCabe enters a wilderness of possibility at the beginning of that film. The middle of the film displays the dynamic realization of competing masculine and feminine spaces, but at the end McCabe lies dead in the frozen landscape, dispossessed of all his material constructions, and Mrs. Miller's clean, well-lighted space has shrunk to the space of an opium glow. The male story and the female story fall before the forces of eastern capital on the western frontier.

These conflicts in the story further reflect contemporary concepts in cultural analysis that examine the zone of interaction between differing and colliding cultures. Rather than just Turner's sense of a unique frontier experience that gave rise to the ideology of American "exceptionalism," the frontier of western myth and history provides numerous case studies in this interaction. The familiar conflict among Native Americans and white Europeans in particular replicates scenarios repeated everywhere around the world as a function of the colonial enterprise from the days of Roman conquest to the beginning of the twentieth century. In these myriad "contact zones," as Mary Louise Pratt describes them, or "borderlands" as Gloria Anzaldúa describes them, there occurs not just a subordination of the weaker by the stronger social group but an interpenetration between these groups as well.[46] Social geographers have come to call this space of interaction "third space," what Homi Bhabha defines as a hybrid space "that is established by an interaction between two social groups in one site." The concept varies among different scholars, but all refer to a space "in-between" an imagined space and a real place, between a colonizer and a colonized, a dominant and a minority culture. Bhabha argues that the encounter between two culturally different individuals or groups "is bound to set up a new space of communication that manages to keep both perspectives in some field of vision in order to make it possible for either side to translate the other perspective."[47]

A particular power of *McCabe & Mrs. Miller* is its representation of several third-space interactions. There are no Native Americans here, but McCabe is a gambling outsider to the miners, and Mrs. Miller and her prostitutes constitute another challenge to the mining camp. The contact zone between the McCabe & Miller partnership and the Harrison Shaughnessy company represents the most determinant third space in the narrative. But the business partnership itself, between gambler and prostitute, between male and female, may well constitute the most significant borderland of the film. The confrontations here are many; they contrast the dominant masculinist imaginary of western conquest and the minority imaginary of feminine domestication. They contrast the historic gender roles of the late nineteenth century and the emergent ideals of the 1970s. They contrast the power of big business and the labor of individuals. The partnership of the title is the most dramatic third space of the film. Here, as Bhabha says, is that "hybrid, contradictory, ambivalent" interaction which may permit a "third perspective [to] grow in the margins of dominant ways of seeing."[48]

In the world of the western, "civilization" is a practical *place*, where the rules and regulations, the infrastructure and the financing, the courts and the banks shape the daily routines of social existence. The "wilderness" is an alternative *space* that affords the developing social frontier the opportunity of imagining some new, some different place, some elsewhere. The frontier mining camp, or ranch, or stagecoach becomes then an experiment in society, a "third space" where the clash of alternative imaginaries struggle for expression, for dominance, and for identity, where an actual place grows out of potential space. In all of its various articulations of countercultural resistance, *McCabe & Mrs. Miller*'s representation of a feminist perspective may be the most important. The possibility of a strong woman's voice, the possibility of an assertive businesswoman, the possibility of a woman smarter and more astute than the man, the possibility of a partnership—not marriage or even sexual union—between this gambling man and this prostituted woman—these shape the central ways the film participates in the 1970s' critique of the patriarchy's repression of women. Writes Bhabha: "It is that Third Space, though unrepresentable in itself, which constitutes the discursive conditions of enunciation that ensure that meaning and symbols of culture have no primordial order or fixity; that even the same signs can be appropriated, translated, rehistoricized, and read anew."[49] The film then constitutes such a space that renegotiates the cultural representation of women. As Keyssar argues, "We have every reason to respect Mrs. Miller at the end of the film: she has treated well the women she employs, she has made a successful enterprise out of a disorganized business, and she has given McCabe what she could, including warnings against his self-destructive romanticism. And she refused to be a martyr to a hopeless cause in which she had no way of intervening."[50]

The sixties and the early seventies were a time of rereading American culture and national identity. The tremendous flux in values motivated descriptions of numerous spatial endscapes, and revolutionary rhetoric and practice seemed to proclaim the end of institutional representation everywhere. New music, new architecture, new religion, new literature, new social relations—"This is the dawning of the Age of Aquarius," proclaimed the hit song from *Hair*, the youth-cult Broadway musical of the 1960s. But not new politics. Nixon is reelected in 1972. The Vietnam War continues till 1975. Revolutionary dissent declines into the scandals of Watergate, impeachment, and the resignation of an American president. For one shining moment, from the windows of that illusory Camelot a decade before was glimpsed the possibility of a presidentially sanctioned "new frontier." The counterculture's sense of another way of life slowly faded in the light of intransigent and intractable mainstream values. In the 1970s national identity was suspended in a struggle of thwarted possibility and muted idealism. As the decade progressed, "the eager optimism of the women's liberation movement" slowly changed into the "realization that the dominant structure of society would not easily accommodate fundamental changes in sexual relations."[51] The popular culture could experience the end of *McCabe & Mrs. Miller* as an inevitable consequence of a widespread sense of the difficulties and traumas involved in cultural transformation: in the words of the Dylan song, "Everybody must get stoned."

The cultural revolution of the late 1960s and early 1970s emerged dramatically in the arts. According to historian Bruce Schulman,

> The same distrust of the powers that undermined traditional sources of authority and fractured public life also spurred creative, personal, highly charged art that addressed that discontent. The decade's most potent and memorable cultural products raised an upturned middle finger at conventional sources of authority—be they the White House, record companies, or the Hollywood studios . . . [and] produced a tough-minded confrontation with the dark powers of a new age. . . . They reshaped the cultural landscape with a blend of outrage and resignation, passion and black humor, and forged a new sensibility, a distinctly skeptical style.[52]

These energies appear everywhere in the revisionist genre films of the period. Few actively examine the roles of women in the culture, but *Cat Ballou* (1965), *Hannie Caulder* (1971), and *Zandy's Bride* (1974), among westerns, create sympathetic women heroes in films that challenge and critique genre assumptions. Notably *Klute* (1971) takes on the representation of the human side of prostitution where Jane Fonda becomes famous for her realistic personalization of the struggles of workers in the sex trade. *Bonnie and Clyde*—in its pairing of the outlaw couple, its depicting a strong and equal woman, and its portraying in Warren Beatty's Clyde a likable but sexually dysfunctional male—encapsulated many of the values of countercultural resistance.

Altman established his career as the misanthropic director whose revisionist films between 1969 and 1975 aggressively join in shaping this period style. *MASH,* though set in the Korean War, was clearly taken to be a film against the Vietnam War; its huge success (the largest box-office success of Altman's career) derived from its hostility to military authority, its chaotic structure, its irreverence toward religion, and its black humor about death and dying. Between 1967 and 1970, films like *The Graduate, Bonnie and Clyde, The Wild Bunch,* and *MASH* did not simply reflect the counterculture; they actively expressed and gave social meaning to the terms of countercultural, antiwar resistance to the Establishment. In films like *MASH, McCabe & Mrs. Miller, The Long Goodbye, Thieves Like Us, California Split,* and especially *Brewster McCloud,* Altman made eight movies between 1970 and 1975 that situated him as one of the major rebels against the established order in American popular art and made him one of the most popular directors among America's disaffected youth.

Within the feminist movement of the early 1970s, however, Robert Altman early gained a reputation as a misogynist, largely for the sexist sexual humor and the derogatory representation of the character "Hotlips" Houlihan in *MASH.* The advertising campaign that sold the film with Sally Kellerman's legs and the shower scene designed to publicly humiliate her character were only part of the evidence adduced in Altman's arraignment by feminists. Most American men were sexists in the early 1970s, but second-wave feminism taught many of them what women's liberation meant. Two different attitudes toward gender and social power slowly emerge across the subsequent thirty-five years of his Hollywood career. Altman repeatedly depicts the nature and efficacy of weak, immature, and debilitated men: the rebellious Daedalus figure of *Brewster McCloud;* the gambling addicts in *California Split;* the befuddled star in *Buffalo Bill and the Indians* (1976); a suicidal Nixon in *Secret Honor* (1984); the failed presidential candidate in *Tanner '88* (1988); the hotshot lawyer in *The Gingerbread Man* (1998); the congenial gynecologist in *Dr. T & the Women* (2000); the bumbling detective, among others, in *Gosford Park* (2001). He systematically demotes the usually dominant male from the center of his innovative narratives, and he ascribes to them character traits that further diminish the place of masculine authority in contemporary culture. In *McCabe & Mrs. Miller* the narrative fantasy develops in the context of parallel, problematic, and vulnerable couples: Bartley and Ida, the Cowboy and Ida, McCabe and Mrs. Miller. In the violent world of masculine confrontation, the death of the male reveals the debilitating dependency of the surviving female. This same sympathy to unattractive, quirky, vulnerable couples appears again in *Thieves Like Us, A Perfect Couple* (1979), and *Popeye* (1980). More strikingly, however, from the beginning to the end of his film career—particularly in *Images* (1972), *3 Women* (1977), *Come Back to the 5 & Dime, Jimmy Dean, Jimmy Dean* (1982), *Kansas City* (1996), *Cookie's Fortune* (1999), *Gosford Park* (2001), and *Tanner on Tanner* (2004)—Altman tells stories with women as the central characters. He examines the cultural conditions of the patriarchy that entrap them, and he characterizes their struggle to escape these conditions. In 1971 *McCabe & Mrs. Miller* expresses the discontent of the counterculture, and it posits a dynamic male-female relationship in the struggle against the destructive energies of corporate power.

4 Altman's Art

In 1970 the renowned cinematographer Vilmos Zsigmond was a recent immigrant from Hungary with only one film to his credit. The opportunity to work on *McCabe & Mrs. Miller* allowed him the opportunity to pioneer a technique that would become ubiquitous in subsequent Hollywood filmmaking. Altman told Zsigmond he wanted a yellow-gold look to the film in order to capture a sense of antiquity as reflected in the yellowing of old photographs; he remembers: "I was doing everything I could to destroy the clarity of the film, including using a heavy number three fog filter. I wanted it to have that antique, historical look." And Zsigmond knew what to do: Altman "explained to me he would like it to look like old faded pictures, with saturated colors. The movie should look as if it were shot in 1890, when there was no camera and no film. But if there was a camera and film, that's how it would look today. It was very clear what he wanted. And it just happened that I was already involved in testing flashing."[1] Originated by Fred Young on the Sidney Lumet thriller *The Deadly Affair* (1966), but not much developed thereafter, the stylistic potential of flashing first appears in *McCabe & Mrs. Miller*. Zsigmond describes the process: "You pre-expose the film in a controlled way and alter the contrast to get a softer look. Flashing is the process of exposing the film stock prior to using it to shoot the film's various scenes." Altman and Zsigmond experimented extensively with different levels of pre-exposure, from 10 to 25 percent, to achieve the particular coloration that uniformly bathes each shot of the film in a kind of golden haze. He recalls the work and their motivation:

While I was shooting *McCabe & Mrs. Miller,* executives at the studio were watching dailies in Los Angeles. They hated the way the movie looked because we flashed the film and pushed it so it was grainy. For them it was terrible. For us, it was art. Robert knew that if he admitted what we were doing, they would shut us down and probably re-shoot everything we had done, so he lied to them. He said, don't worry about the negative. It's perfect. This lab up here doesn't know how to make dailies, and they believed him. It was my really first big movie, but I felt very at home even though I had never done anything like it before.[2]

The extraordinary artistry of Zsigmond—who would go on to make award-winning films like *Deliverance* (1972), *Close Encounters of the Third Kind* (1977), and *The Deer Hunter* (1978)—constructs the film as a tour de force of cinematic ways of seeing. It mixes a number of extravagant low and high angles with painterly long shots and extreme close-ups that mirror the film's multiple frames of reference and modes of representation. Telephoto lens at the same time flatten the planes of reference and compress dramatic depth of field. Sharply focused shots contrast with grainy, underlit shots; medium-lens shots contrast with filtered long-lens shots. In what will be identified as central to the Altman signature, the camera pans with human action; it follows animal movement; it pans along inanimate landscapes. In every scene the camera is constantly in motion, probing, curious, attentive. As the human figures speak in oblique and ambiguous ways, as Leonard Cohen sings haunting lyrics about the "secret heart" of this matter, as the narrative builds to an idealistic center driven by a hopeless past, the camera listens with a zoom lens that traverses space and breaks narrative flow, that looks past the dramatic to the peripheral, that expands minute particulars into human tragedy. Zsigmond's camera zooms into the spatial fields of the film in ways that simultaneously link events and motives and desires of the narrative logic and sublimate logical connections to the stasis and imagery of poetry. The cinematography at once displays the reality of this imaginary western world and lyrically paints the reality of its myth.

Widely noted at the time by reviewers and continually praised by film critics since, the flashed looked of the film achieves numerous important effects: it establishes a look that not only colors the film literally but colors the story in a way that alters classical reading strategies. As the viewer strives to follow the story of McCabe and Mrs. Miller, the cinematography motivates questions about the kind of "pastness" this western presents: the story unfolds in the present of the screening, but the flashed golden hues distance it as a nostalgic or dreamy or mournful past—recollected through an aging genre or retold through the lens of sadness that at the very outset derives from the knowledge of its end. The cinematography establishes a lyrical voice that shapes the narrative trajectories of characters and actions. Moreover, it raises questions about the relationship between the story's realism and its expressive telling. Clearly much time and effort underlay the recreation of this 1900 space, its props, its buildings, and its costumes. Actors create actual human beings moving in real places and interacting in socially recognizable patterns. Thus, like traditional classical cinema, the film is committed on the one hand to a distinct realism that is, on the other hand, compounded by a lyrical and painterly cinematography. The look of the film asks to be understood not literally but metaphorically; it ceases merely to ground the reality of the story with a photographic realism and serves less as a literal presentation than it serves as a figurative representation of its significance.

Zsigmond notes that as the film progressed the degree of flashing steadily decreased until the gunfight scene is shot with no flashing at all. Here then is a rhythmic development of the visual field that reflects Altman's conscious decisions about the look of the film. He is quite specific about his practice here and his self-conscious concern to determine with the cameraman what the camera philosophy will be for the film: "I deal with the cameraman mostly *before* we start shooting. . . . What's our color philosophy gonna be? What's our lens-length philosophy? . . . Is it gonna be a point-of-view film? Is it gonna be a look-through-the-windows film? Where are we gonna place the audience? And we do lots and lots of tests and try different things. Then once we start shooting that's set up."[3]

Concomitantly then with the play of the color palette in Leon Ericksen's set design and its capture of a particular season of the year, the cinematography comes to the fore as a signifier of consequence independent of the narrative. As it does so, calling attention to itself against traditional uses of film stock, the flashing also becomes reflexive. It collaborates with other elements of style—notoriously overlapping and indistinguishable sound and constant camera and lens movement—as visibly experimental filmmaking. As it makes palpable the surface that at once presents the story and separates the story from its reception, it also asserts that the history of the western story is historiographically a construction.

The power of *McCabe & Mrs. Miller* relates significantly to its reflection on the emergent perspectives of developing western history. It derives from the film's interrogation of classical generic western form and myth. It conveys the voices of cultural dissent during the era of the Vietnam War. Apart from these dynamic qualities, however, the power of the film also resides in its simultaneous definition of the American Art Cinema and its aesthetic amalgamation of the formal possibilities of that cinema. The experience of the film is a moving engagement with complex narrative construction, attractive and tragic lives, lyrical cinematic style, and contemplative reflexivity. While the film is not just revisionist history or alternative western or counterculture, it all the more strikingly conveys these matters because of its achievements first of all as cinematic art. Out of revision, resistance, and reformation, *McCabe & Mrs. Miller* emerges as a voice of the Hollywood Renaissance and remains as a powerful manifestation of movie magic. At the beginning, the mournful wind and the cold gray rain seem to motivate the reflective lyrics of Leonard Cohen, which in turn seem to conjure the fur-shrouded rider from a desolate and verdant mountain wilderness. At the end, the film vanishes into the eyes of the woman whose drugged contemplation of the golden surface of a tiny ceramic urn becomes the screen of the movie's vision.

Altman's resistance to dominant institutional practices begins with the classical Hollywood cinema. Virtually all of his fifteen films in the 1970s challenge the narrative and stylistic dimensions of traditional cinematic storytelling. *McCabe & Mrs. Miller* in particular reveals the experimental energies that fueled the development of an American Art Cinema. Between 1967 and 1976, the Hollywood film industry underwent a dramatic shift in the economics of production, in the nature of its storytelling, and in the expectations of its audiences. The innovative practices of filmmakers like Robert Altman, John Cassavetes, and Stanley Kubrick actively challenged the parameters of funding, of narrative, and of success in American cinema. They found a young film-going audience aware and appreciative of the international art cinema of directors like Ingmar Bergman, Federico Fellini, Luis Buñuel, François Truffaut, Jean-Luc Godard, Akira Kurosawa, and others. Indeed, as a function of both the films and the criticism of young French filmmakers, the "politique des auteurs" developed as an assertion that the director was the author, the major creative force behind a film. The popularity of the Auteur Theory located the artistry of the cinema in a pantheon of great film artists and looked critically at the developing work of new, young directors. Zsigmond recalls:

> In the sixties and seventies, we had this era that all these new, young filmmakers wanted to create a totally new direction in movies. That's where I grew up as a hired hand, on movies like *McCabe and Mrs. Miller,* all the Robert Altman movies, and the Jerry Schatzberg movies like *Scarecrow,* and then Steven Spielberg. This was an era where we had a revolution in American filmmaking. Our movies looked totally different than any of the movies Hollywood had made. Our movies looked European, and then they began to look better than the European movies because these also had to be sold to the audience.[4]

These directors, both international and American, emerged as "auteurs," the new authors of film, its new stars. Thomas Bohn and Richard Stromgren write of this period: "The 'discovery' of the director as star [represented] . . . a reassessment and shift in audience attitudes, industry policy, and perhaps most importantly, critical evaluation. . . . Helped by the decline of the studio system, the director *as an individual* with ideas he wanted to express in film became a significant force in the American film of the Sixties and Seventies."[5] Their films moreover constitute for many film historians a "Hollywood Renaissance." Glenn Man succinctly describes the developing style of this new American cinema:

> It combines in an eclectic way the codes of expressionism and realism, fusing new wave and neorealistic techniques: on the one hand, disjunctive editing, ellipses, fragmented structure, rapid collage montage, closed subjective framing, soft focus, distorted angles, hand-held camera, flashbacks, flashforwards, and mixed genres; on the other hand, long takes, deep focus, wide-screen compositions, tracking/panning camera, grainy cinematography, actual locales, episodic structure, open framing, overhead mike and actual sounds, and a montage of songs and music from the time and setting of the film.[6]

The experimental qualities of this cinema ultimately prove unprofitable for the emergent postclassical Hollywood. By the release of Altman's *Buffalo Bill and the Indians* in 1976, and certainly by 1980 with his release of *Popeye,* the movement had run its course as a major phenomenon in the film industry. The box-office success of films likes *Jaws* (1975), *Rocky* (1976),

Star Wars (1977), and *Superman* (1978) established the blockbuster, high-concept films that characterize the Hollywood period style of the last quarter of the twentieth century. This cinema, like classical Hollywood cinema, remains committed to the stability and homogeneity of personality, social interchange, and narrative voice, as the causal coherence and closure of plot organize them. Straightforward stories, with big stars, big action, and big special effects characterize the fare of the new Hollywood. Its commitments furthermore to optimistic social values systematically hold in check political, psychological, and sociological forces that threaten to disrupt safe, mainstream cultural ideology.

Films like *McCabe & Mrs. Miller*, however, shape a different kind of American cinema. Altman's reconstruction of the traditional semantics and syntax of genre film, his critique of contemporary social values, his maverick stance within the Hollywood production system, his indebtedness to various European cinemas, his experimentation in technique and style certify his importance in the reawakening of American movies in the 1970s. Moreover, the film reflects both an artistic vision and aesthetic achievement that defines the art of cinematic modernism. Classical narrative cinema takes for granted the efficacy of human communication and a coherent social identity capable of intelligible, meaningful, ethical human action. Modernist cinema, in contrast, understands the world to be broken and chaotic, meaning to be ambiguous and precarious, and morality to be subjective and deceptive. It posits human identity as neither autonomous nor unified but a play of divergent and contradictory forces, both internal and external. It chronicles the failures of communication in the face of human greed, alienation, estrangement, and self-destruction. Rather than encouraging viewer identification with a coherent character psychology, not to mention a necessarily attractive one, it displays a variety of contradictory subject positions that finally belie the notion of explanatory discourse altogether. A central strategy of representation in modernist cinema is its effort to represent actual rather than idealized reality. Its actors portray ordinary "people," rather than literary "characters." Their behavior frequently seems motivated by apparently unmotivated events and causes that demand active audience participation to bridge narrative gaps for the construction of meaning. Reactions derive illogically from action. Narrative continuity disappears. Story lines multiply. Characters are alternatively major and minor figures in competing narratives.

Modernist narratives consequently develop fictions where story and plot time are fluid and fractured, where cause and effect are implicit or unknowable, where human identity is unstable and fragmented, and where narrative reflects on its own narration. The art cinema also conveys a sense of order that appears, not in the causal logic of transparent beginnings, middles, and ends, but in poetic metaphors, in symbolic registers, in formal designs. Modernist fiction thus seeks at once a lifelike reality and a formal vision that organizes the work as an artifact expressive of some truth about the human condition. Thus modernist cinema demands understanding character and identity, action and plot both realistically and formally, as expressive designs communicating values implicitly, indirectly, and ambiguously.

The films of Robert Altman everywhere reflect these modernist qualities. Their fractured and fragmentary narratives are not logically and causally inflected conflicts and resolutions but formal, lyrical designs that conceive social identity as multiple, unstable, and frequently shaped through the debasement of contemporary values by institutional authority. Altman's films may be best understood in terms of three particular aspects of art cinema narration: its interrogation of classical Hollywood storytelling and popular genres, its representation of debilitated and ineffectual social individuality, and its reflexive analysis of the entertainment industry as complicit in cultural alienation. *McCabe & Mrs. Miller* in particular substitutes structure for story and form for representation; it depicts debilitated individuals living in constrained circumstances of powerlessness and subservience. It displays a cynical view of the commercially motivated idealism of contemporary culture. It reflexively indicts the western itself as complicit in the malaise of contemporary American culture.

These very patterns of resistance to classical Hollywood moviemaking in Altman's films certainly endeared him to the counterculture audience of the 1970s. They have also constantly irritated the audience for postclassical Hollywood's high-concept form of entertainment, even as they have consistently defined the form and style of what Kristin Thompson calls the "Americanized art cinema."[7] Characteristic of art cinema narration, *McCabe & Mrs. Miller* systematically displays an open and poetic mode of storytelling; a trenchant perception of social identity as dependent, deficient, and imperfect; and a critical reflexivity about the nature of narrative communication itself. Altman expresses a "great affection" for the film: "I kept telling everybody all the time we were doing it that it was a poem." The film's blend of the lyrical and the narrative reflects the art cinema's blend of subjective and objective realism. It develops in particular, like all his films, from a narrative philosophy that Altman calls "subliminal reality." For over thirty years Altman followed this philosophy and worked out its various implications according to the possibilities afforded him by each new film. Life for him is not shaped by a causal narrative of two-dimensional events. Rather, its energies and its flow evolve through multiple, diverse, contradictory forces that lie below the surface, that resist logic, that escape attention. Film's great strength resides not in its narrative form but as a visual medium in its ability to capture the ebb and flow of human behavior in emotional and lyrical ways, like painting or music or poetry, and to leave its audience with intuitive rather than logical knowledge.[8]

The film recognizes this principle in the unspoken and unspeakable dimensions of human interactions. It employs lyrical and metaphoric style to suggest connections in the inexplicable partnership of John and Constance. It resides in the anxiety and doubt about the precariousness and meaning of their situation. The working title for the film was "The Presbyterian Church Wager," and it sees their behavior as a gamble with random consequences and defines their relationship in curious patterns of repetition. It glimpses the efforts of this marginal man and woman caught in irresistible systems that shape desire and action. It engages active audience awareness as necessary and complicit in the construction of consequence. It recognizes the authority of craft—like T. S. Eliot's "objective correlative"—to convey aesthetic insight indirectly. Emily Dickinson's poetic dictum similarly asserted: "Tell all the Truth but tell it slant— / Success in Circuit lies."[9] Subliminal reality paints numerous, divergent surfaces of the human enterprise to suggest subterranean roots of narrative potential.

An examination of Altman's adaptation of Edmund Naughton's *McCabe* offers significant insight into Altman's innovative approach to the story of the film. Kamilla Elliott's study of the *Novel/Film Debate* describes several concepts that underlie the adaptation of fiction to film, and two of these in particular illuminate Altman's work on the novel. Her "genetic" concept identifies adaptations in terms of the deep structure of narrative functions—of character, setting, action—shared by the literary and cinematic stories.[10] Despite Altman's accurate dismissal of the novel as a minor work, a "little story,"[11] *McCabe & Mrs. Miller* reveals a strong indebtedness to its "genetic" functions. The same characters—gambler "Pudgy" McCabe, prostitute Constance Miller, barkeep Patrick Sheehan, preacher Elliot, mining company officials, and hired guns—all work the growing streets of both the novelistic and cinematic frontier town Presbyterian Church. The same narrative conflict—small-town operator versus mining monopoly—organizes the development of these characters: McCabe is an itinerant gambler who finds in this far western community a social space sufficiently undeveloped to permit him a measure of independence and success. Mrs. Miller is a strong-willed and experienced madam who eventually hopes to free herself from prostitution and from the wilderness. Sheehan operates a mean saloon with an equally mean worldview. The minister cares only for his church building and resents the presence of community. And the mining company arrogantly means to control the whole town for its mineral deposits. Indeed, Altman argues that all these elements are generic not just to the novel but to the genre as well and that his reason for choosing this book derived from the freedom it thus allowed him to develop matters other than its traditional story told in traditional ways.

The novel demonstrates the kind of routine reading strategies audiences must employ to follow classical narrative. Significantly it begins with the impending showdown between McCabe and the killers sent by the mining company to acquire his property by violent means. McCabe thinks back on the series of events that brought him to this confrontation, and the next twelve chapters trace events over the last four years that logically have brought him to this confrontation. The novel recounts then through his retrospective mental recollections success at gambling; partnership with Mrs. Miller in saloon, casino, and brothel; romantic liaison between the two in opposition to the town's disapproving but grudging acceptance of their business; McCabe's realization of the mining company's plans for control of the town and the company's insulting offer to buy him out for half his worth; his pride and self-respect as both a gunman and a man of property. As the novel begins, all these factors motivate his waiting to face three gunman. The end of the story, the final showdown, is in the beginning, and the narrative employs a rhetoric of explanation: all these events follow each other sequentially and logically, leading inexorably to this last decisive moment. The last three chapters then detail the showdown: McCabe defeats the killers but is mortally wounded. Mrs. Miller in grief over her fallen lover and partner waits with McCabe's shotgun to kill the approaching Sheehan in revenge for his part in McCabe's death.

An effort to read the plot of the film causally could find a similarly coherent narrative logic. The itinerant gambler comes to Presbyterian Church looking for a new beginning; he wins sufficient capital from playing cards with the miners that he buys land, starts building a casino, and imports women for a brothel in the mining community. Word of his development reaches the professional madam who is also looking for new opportunity and who offers expertise and management skills as her contribution to a partnership in the vice business. The increasing potential of the zinc mine drives the mining company's desire to purchase all the property in town, but the gambler's unreasonably high asking price for his bathhouse/casino/brothel turns the company from negotiation to murder as a way to acquire his business. The gambler defends himself against the gunmen sent to exterminate him, kills them all, then dies in the snow from his wounds, while the madam mourns and escapes his death in an opium den. Within this broad outline of cause-effect logic, even small movements of significant character motivation apparently drive the plot: McCabe gets drunk in indignant reaction to Mrs. Miller's criticizing his business skills; his inebriation causes him to exaggerate his worth with the mining negotiators; exasperation with his insolence ends their effort to make a deal with him. And thus begins the confrontation with the company gunmen that will end his life.

This plot structure hardly accommodates all the action and human energy conveyed by the film's major episodes, however. Altman's film dramatically reveals his ongoing antipathy to straightforward, clearly delineated, and causally logical narratives. Throughout his career Altman has aggressively relegated motivation to the "subliminal reality" of conflicting, indeterminate, vague, inexpressible characterological desire. In his signature films, like *MASH, Nashville, A Wedding* (1978), *The Player* (1992), *Short Cuts* (1993), and *Gosford Park* (2001), he employs so many "major characters" as to demote the function of characters from fictive prominence. The story lines of twenty-four, forty-eight, fifty-six characters interweave in these films in ways that totally confuse narrative coherence. They ask the audience to understand the representation of some character at any one moment in the story not merely as part of an overarching cause-effect chain of events but as a comment or reflection on the preceding or following moments of the other characters in adjourning stories. Altman has argued that this is a "new way of telling stories" that leaves the audience wondering about what happens in any story while the narrative shifts from one character to another. His technique of story construction, however, makes it impossible to unweave the various character threads in order to make logical sense of any one story. An analysis, for instance, of the scenes cut from Altman's *Gosford Park* reveals that shots and scenes that would potentially have explained character motivation and behavior in individual stories have been systematically removed from the final cut of the film. The orderly development of plot implies an orderliness to life that is false. "We demand logic," he says, "but it doesn't necessarily have to be there."[12] The events and behaviors and motivations of life are inexplicable, random, disconnected, subliminal.

Thus when he reads the novel *McCabe,* he is uninterested in adapting Naughton's explanations of McCabe's coherent subjectivity. The novel extensively uses internal, third-person point of view to reveal character motivation. In particular, it organizes the predominant action of the story through McCabe's point of view: "he knew," "he understood," "he remembered," "he thought." A "faithful" approach to adaptation would require visual and aural means of conveying the explanatory power of his thoughts, his feelings, his memories, and his knowledge. Altman's excision of that perspective derives from his aesthetic interest in storytelling, where logical relationships are not delineated. Rather, his reading of the characters and situations of the novel results in a more open, more discontinuous, more ambiguous narrative. He has observed that he chose this simplistically generic western story on the one hand "because I'm not very inventive. I don't make up stories very well." On the other hand, that his film is "not a typical shoot-em-up western" is an aesthetic choice: "I wanted this to look a little different," with "an idea that you're peeking in on something" and that "it's not explaining too much." He articulates here the common artistic perspective that organizes most of the films in his thirty-five-year career: "I don't really care very much about story in a film. I think more of it as a painting." Setting out the western genre, with its expected plots, iconography, and ideological resolutions means that "I don't have to waste any time with that, and I can then mess around in the corners, in the details, and it allows the film to develop in a different way."[13]

Kamilla Elliott's concept of "de(re)composing" categorizes literary adaptations in terms of the cinematic reworking of the fiction according to the film's commitments to other texts than just the novel.[14] *McCabe & Mrs. Miller* reveals Altman's commitment both to an expressive aesthetic of story form and to a painterly aesthetic of film. These "corners" and "details" appear in a variety of reconstructions the film works on Naughton's novel, not only in narrative form but also in major story functions, moving them around in a space conceived as much as a canvas as a reel. It significantly revises the representations of all the major characters, while adding some and extending others, particularly the prostitutes themselves. The novel's lawyer, for instance, is the pedantically explicit, anticorporate cynic who recognizes the hopelessness of McCabe's resistance to the mining company: "They can't afford you around. Bad example. Pile all these mountains on you, if they have to." He insists, however, on the antiquarian importance of legally documenting all his futility: "They'll kill you, McCabe. Won't be chalk on the blackboard though. Won't wipe out. That's the sense there is in taking out warrants." His services are free because he "always hated big outfits, the lawyer said, big things.... I hate them."[15] He shows up at the end in order to be witness to the corporation's crimes. In the film, however, the lawyer's presence is rendered as a parody of the smarmy, populist politician, glibly spouting epigrammatic nonsense and empty promises as he looks toward a career in Washington. His condescension and pandering to McCabe function quickly to mark the larger political, like the corporate, forces that ignore and essentially isolate the movie's hero. In the film, Sheehan is not the resentful and jealous rival who constantly lurks in the background and schemes with the gunman to kill McCabe in the end. Like the townspeople, too, he shrinks in the film to a simpering, grinning foil to McCabe's success. The prostitutes, however, emerge from the background of the novel to become a major social and narrative presence on the film's canvas.

Equally significant is the dramatic manner in which narrative events are condensed, their connections implied, and their logical relationships blurred. What is the association between the film's first scene of McCabe's arrival at Presbyterian Church and his establishment of a card table in Sheehan's saloon and the second scene when McCabe leisurely rides into Bearpaw to buy prostitutes? What is the connection between McCabe's wrestling a knife from the prostitute who has attacked a customer and the arrival in camp of Mrs. Miller? What motivates fragmenting and then editing together the scene of Ida's entering Mrs. Miller's brothel and the arrival of the killers sent after McCabe? What is the implication of juxtaposing the killer Butler, who "can't make deals," and the lawyer Samuels whose services "are free of charge"? Does McCabe face the gunmen because somebody's "got to stand up for the little guy" or in self-defense? Why does Altman interrupt the scene of McCabe's and Mrs. Miller's last night together with the shooting of Cowboy? Answers to such discursive questions are multiple, and such editorial juxtapositions abound in the film.

The novel makes it clear that John McCabe is indeed "Pudgy" McCabe who killed Bill Roundtree for cheating at cards. In the film, Sheehan anxiously rushes after McCabe when it appears he is leaving just after establishing his card game. In a comical moment, McCabe responds to Sheehan's wondering "where you was going to go": "Well, I was going to go by that fence over there." In the next shot, Sheehan rushes back into the saloon declaring emphatically, "Yes sir, that man out there taking a pee is none other than Pudgy McCabe, the man who shot Bill Roundtree. He's got a big rep!" The information, its source, and its accuracy, is inexplicable and is never acknowledged by McCabe. What logic connects the two shots? The two scenes where Mrs. Miller aggressively confronts McCabe with assertions of his incompetence in running a whore house and in keeping his account books are followed by scenes of McCabe drunk; his inebriation is inconsequential in the first instance and significant in McCabe's miscalculation with Sears and Hollander in the second. But does McCabe drink because of the confrontations with Mrs. Miller? Such reasoning works only through the post hoc fallacy; one merely follows the other. Like all of the art cinema, *McCabe & Mrs. Miller* asks throughout to be read in its ambiguities.

The film's lack of interest in the clarity of coherent story relationships establishes, in part, its artistic effect as emotional and lyrical rather than narrative. One of the most striking sequences in the middle of the film dramatically illustrates the creative process that achieves this effect. On the evening the mining representatives arrive in town, the film intermixes a large number of events and situations that occur over a story time of less than twenty-four hours. That time is apparently Christmas, signaled by the opening shot of a couple dancing in the brothel before the elegant modern music box that plays the seasonal hymn, "Silent Night." In the next scene, a fight takes place in the street outside between Bart who is defending the honor of his mail-order bride Ida, and townsmen who assume she is "one of Mrs. Miller's girls." During the scuffle, which ends by mortally injuring Bart, the carriage chauffeuring Sears and Hollander arrives, pastor Elliot appears, and the black barber Sumner Washington and his wife step out of their barbershop. As Bart is carried inside then, all these characters retreat from the scene—the Washingtons nervously hurry back inside, the preacher hunched over with arms clenched at his side scurries away, and the businessmen drive off in silent wonder. The whole scene has occurred in the dark shadows of late dusk. Ida's, Sears's and Hollander's faces are reflected in close-up in the red-gold glow of interior lamps. An overhead camera shot captures the carriage as it drives through the streets, passes through a last golden gleam from the dying sunset and turns into a dark street full of miners' tents all lit by the small golden glow of numerous campfires. Over the whole scene continues the strains of "Silent Night" from the initial shot of the scene.

The play here of divergent, half-obscured action, chiaroscuro lighting, and Christmas music is rich in its sensuous complexity and ambiguity. But the sequence continues: it further contains the images from the brothel of the preparation of Birdie's birthday cake, McCabe's drunken interaction with Sears and Hollander, the birthday party, and McCabe sobering up in the tub at the bathhouse. Mrs. Miller retreats from the party whose cake and flaming candles fill the screen in close-up; she castigates McCabe for rejecting the offer from Harrison Shaughnessy. After McCabe's second meeting with the mining men and then his return as a client to the stoned Mrs. Miller, the negotiators decide to leave, McCabe discovers their departure the next morning, and finally everyone in town attends Bart's burial. Significantly this sequence begins with "Silent Night" and ends with the funeral service singing of "Asleep in Jesus."

The narrative referentiality of the sequence is at once difficult to follow, intricate in the multiplicity of motivations and associations it suggests, and typical of the film's patterns of imaginative construction. Preparations for the party precipitate the search for a lost bottle of gin and evoke an image of secret drinking. The prostitutes' celebration of the birth of Birdie resonates with the birth of Jesus. The preacher's abandonment of the fallen miner resonates with McCabe's disregard of the birthday party. Mrs. Miller's fee for services rendered parallels the negotiation for McCabe's property. McCabe's drunken and disheveled braggadocio contrasts to Sears's and Hollander's stylish and sober professionalism. The brilliant birthday candles contrast, and connect, the fading glow of day, the desolate campfires, and the glow of anxiety on the face of a mail-order bride. McCabe's goodnight words to Mrs. Miller, "Trust me," echo the end of McCabe's joke about the frog eaten by the eagle, "shit me." The Christmas hymn describes "sleep in heavenly peace," and the minister preaches about eternal damnation. As Helene Keyssar notes, "images and sounds and words that we overlooked in an initial recounting appear from the shadows of obscurity."[16] The sequence moves from connotations of holy birth to empty death.

The density of this sequence clearly involves far more than causal linearity. Rather, it reflects the fact that numerous discursive modes and channels of representation function concurrently. This explosive simultaneity derives both from Altman's dexterity with the craft of cinema and from the depth of his challenging imagination. The narrative of *McCabe & Mrs. Miller* involves many stories—some implied, some perceived indirectly, others drawn in discrete gestures, several dominating, all woven together into the vibrant tapestry that constitutes the film. One minor thread, for instance, traces the teenage prostitute Alma. Swathed in a woolen cap, hiding her face behind her hand, the young girl seems barely fifteen years old and is obviously on the verge of tears when she first appears as one of the "chippies" McCabe purchases in Bearpaw. The film captures her face again in terrified reaction to the men who pull one of the other three women off the horse upon their reaching Presbyterian Church. When McCabe finally gets the three women into his still unfinished quarters in the half-built saloon, Alma appears to be what the script calls a "catatonic-like waif." Before McCabe can leave to oversee the erection of their tents, Alma's quavering request for the potty stops him. Caught in close-up, Alma is a scared child, about to be deposited on the street as a "crib girl." The moment is crystalline with emotional depth. The next and last shot in her short story captures McCabe in the rocky trail before her tent wresting a large knife from the hysterical girl who has just repeatedly stabbed one of her customers. McCabe hardly knows how to deal with her, but the film quickly and succinctly sketches out the tragic sadness of prostitution for a homeless, orphan child with no place else to go, no other way to survive.

Unlike *Nashville* or *Gosford Park,* where narrative multiplicity circulates around the continuing appearance of numerous characters throughout the film, the canvas of *McCabe & Mrs. Miller* depicts many of these ministories, these brief shorthand tales, quickly and momentarily amid the larger stories of the title characters. Some, like Alma's, appear early. Others emerge as visual vignettes. Prostitutes arrive in Presbyterian Church at three moments in the film and constitute another narrative motif: when McCabe brings the three girls from Bearpaw, when the steam tractor brings Mrs. Miller to the camp, and when the five whores from Seattle traipse up the roadside to Mrs. Miller's house in the rain. Camera framing in which the women are set in opposition to the church marks each of these moments. It looms in bold silhouette against a golden setting sun on the first occasion, with Pastor Elliot affixing a cross to the top of the steeple. In low-angle medium shot, it looms up behind the snorting smokestack of the steam tractor transporting Mrs. Miller. It provides the site from which the preacher in extreme high-angle long shot stares down at the wet bedraggled women from Seattle. The importance of this last scene is reflected by the fact that in a production that routinely employs no more than five or six camera setups for a scene, this arrival required more than two dozen camera setups to capture its short seconds on the screen.[17] The juxtaposition of prostitute and church tells the story of clashing values and cultural opposition on the wilderness frontier; the changing spatial arrangements ring implicit changes on the unspoken but stereotypical relationships that pass quickly in and out of the narrative eye.

These abbreviated stories abound: the crippled Bart Coyle and his mail-order bride Ida. The enthusiastic Cowboy's visit to the brothel. The barber Washington and his wife. Mrs. Dunn who cooks and runs the counter for Sheehan. Sheehan himself. Altman's practice here and in all of his ensemble films develops a sense of lives that spill out of the frame, parts left out between momentary appearances within the film and parts outside the time of the narrative altogether. The generic story of gambler, whore, and killers, says Altman, "became an easy clothesline for me to hang my own essays on .... I was able to say, 'You think you know this story, but you don't know this story, because the most interesting part of it is all these little sidebars.'" The effect of these multiple strands, he argues, is that the audience becomes actively involved in the story, trying to fill the gaps, wondering about the missing, frequently "obligiatory" scenes of fictive lives.[18] The power of this creative construction of narrative film cuts two ways—it heightens the aura of reality as readers actively engage in a process of human interaction, and it motivates a greater involvement in the critical act of interpretation. Given their apparent divergence from other stories, how do they work in the overall trajectory of the film? The very abbreviated quality of their presence in the film works both realistically and expressionistically.

As these minor stories run parallel and peripherally to the dominant stories of the film, each individually raises the question of their significance collectively. The audience works to understand their relation to the overall narrative and must read their presence as a comment on the major stories, or as a supplement to them, or as a metaphoric reflection of plot or theme or style. Thus, for example, Ida's short, barely started relationship with both Bart and Cowboy may be seen to duplicate the relationship between McCabe and Mrs. Miller. The men are marginal; the women are prostitutes. Both relationships are brief and unstable, and both end in the death of the male that foreshadows the end of the film. Ironically, Ida happily waves goodbye to Cowboy as he rides unknowingly to his death. Mrs. Miller, in contrast, is not on hand to say goodbye to McCabe. She leaves their bed during their night in order to avoid McCabe's confrontation with the gunman because she fearfully anticipates what, as in the case of Bart and Cowboy, will be his death. Moreover, the accidental killing of Bart and the intentional murder of Cowboy prepare the audience for McCabe's death as well. Cowboy's death shockingly explodes into the story and heightens the emotional anxiety generated around McCabe's showdown at the end. Its violence provides the audience with an experience that grounds its shared apprehension with Mrs. Miller about the inevitable conclusion of that showdown.

Other moments in the film further reveal this strategy of indirection. Relationships, situations, and actions not apparently significant in the overall development of the story carry an emotional and rational weight that shapes audience engagement with the film. The episode involving Cowboy's happy sojourn in the brothel begins in the boyish innocence that characterizes Keith Carradine's performance of the role and ends sadly with his shooting death on the footbridge to Sheehan's saloon. A curious moment occurs in the middle of this short narrative sequence. Cowboy enters the parlor of the brothel in his long johns and asks, "who wants to be next? . . . Don't make no difference. I'm gonna have you all." Two of the prostitutes then giggle and whisper together as one makes a gesture of size with her fingers and laughs. What does this apparently gratuitous moment mean? Peter Lehman describes what he calls a crisis of shortness everywhere in Altman's films, routinely and perhaps most notably represented here in reference to a small penis size.[19] Penis size is a widespread marker of sexual prowess in the American male. It widely connotes strength, competence, and masculinity. Indeed in cultural psychoanalysis the phallus is the paramount signifier of desire, power, and authority. Apparently inconsequential references to the small penis uncannily appear throughout Altman's films from *That Cold Day in the Park* in 1969 to *Prairie Home Companion* in 2006. Its diminution throughout these films runs as a minor motif that parallels the representation of masculinity in crisis. Ineffectual, insecure, incompetent male characters fill Altman's canvases. Naughton's novel plays with this same signifier when it explicitly notes the importance for McCabe of the "tailored Colt in his tailored holster": "He would open the center drawer and strap it on . . . swelling himself with the authority of his pistol."[20] Altman's McCabe, however, finally kills Butler with a tiny derringer. Cowboy's small penis, his visual consternation at its joking mention, and McCabe's small pistol all implicitly coalesce into an image of inadequacy that metaphorically describes the hero who dies in the shootout at the end of this revised western. These are the figures a poem makes.

Another implied commentary on the central stories of the film emerges from the condensed story of Sumner Washington and his wife. When they drive into town in their barber's wagon, Mrs. Miller ignores them because of the wet plight of her newly arrived working girls. When Bart falls in the scuffle outside their shop, they appear briefly and then in the face of violence, quickly disappear. At Bart's funeral, they stand off by themselves, clearly uneasy in this community ritual around death. Finally, at the very end of the film, as the townspeople have extinguished the fire in the church, the couple flees from the scene. This dramatic moment during the ironic celebration of saving the church that no one frequents captures Sumner's wife with her face shrouded from sight running from the smoking building and cheering crowd with Sumner shielding her and glancing apprehensively over his shoulder at the scene. This is Altman's very painterly Orpheus and Eurydice, as the hero leads his love in flight from Hades. Racism certainly marks the marginality of this black couple who fears the potential of violence directed at them as scapegoats in the face of the destructive fire. McCabe and Mrs. Miller, at the same time, are marginal types who for a moment fill the business and social center in Presbyterian Church only to be swept away in the end by more central forces of civilization. These are the vocal images of painting.

The major stories of *McCabe & Mrs. Miller* are signaled by the title, which indicates again the multiplicity of narrative dimensions in the film. There are three major stories—McCabe's, McCabe's and Mrs. Miller's, and Mrs. Miller's—and they all drive in different directions. McCabe's effort to succeed as a gambler and establish his own business in town is greatly facilitated by his partnership with Mrs. Miller. His drinking in response to her challenges may be read as the cause of his failure to negotiate a sale of his property to the mining company. Multiple causes shape his misjudgment, however, including his own inadequacies as a dealer and the inexorable power of the company. McCabe's oft-repeated witticism—"If a frog had wings, he might not bump his tail so much"—aptly characterizes his bumping fits and starts as a gambler, businessman, lover, and gunfighter. Warren Beatty, fresh still from his dramatically successful portrayal of the likeable killer in *Bonnie and Clyde* (1967), actively pursued Naughton's novel as a property, sought this role, and constantly engaged Altman over the "right" development of McCabe's character. Beatty disliked the final results of the performance, but Altman called it one of the actor's very best roles.[21] That performance is as rich and compelling as Altman's multilayered narrative. He mixes the braggart, the wit, the boss, the drunk, the dandy, and the poet with fluid ease. He is gregarious and charming, blustering and self-confident, assertive and pompous, insecure and confused, mature and innocent, and ultimately brave and resolute by turns of gesture, body language, tone of voice, gaze. His performance is appealing and offensive and sympathetic in ways that ultimately make him an attractive character, if not a strong, forceful, and competent hero in the classical western way. His character is only partially responsible for the inevitable conclusion of his story; its drive to the end is deathward, his conflict with Harrison Shaughnessy beyond his power to conclude.

Mrs. Miller's story, however, has the opposite trajectory. Its end is in the beginning. Dependent upon the success of men like McCabe, she has made this journey from a Bearpaw to a Presbyterian Church before. And every time the end is the same. She brings experience and understanding and a sharp business sense to her partnership with McCabe, but in key moments her escape from prostitution must depend upon skills and knowledge and sensitivity less sure and effective than her own. McCabe's insensitivity to "that poor girl's birthday" conflicts with the caring Constance brings to the role of madam. McCabe's inability to add and subtract frustrates her economic sense. His failure, unlike the McCabe of the novel, to understand the power and business methods of the mining company dooms her interests as well as his. Julie Christie here leaves behind the romantic and tragic Lara of the epic *Doctor Zhivago* (1965) and the unhappy modern socialite of *Petulia* (1968). The power of her performance of Mrs. Miller's cockney determination, her assertive will, her quiet vulnerability, and her knowing dread of the inevitable garnered an Academy Award nomination for best actress, and its power shapes the nature of the partnership with John McCabe.

"Deals I don't mind. It's partners I don't like." But his partnership with Mrs. Miller is indispensable to his success. Her brothel brings in money, but it costs him "money and pain" and also challenges his sense of adequacy: "I guess I'm supposed to sit here and listen to a woman tell me how to negotiate with a mining company!" She tries to block his efforts to negotiate with the killers because she knows "they get paid for killing, nothing else!" McCabe's response is telling because it reflects the difficulty he brings to their partnership: "I guess if a man's fool enough to get in business with a woman, she ain't going to think much of him." Plaintively asserting, "I know what I'm doing," McCabe struggles to look competent in her eyes. Ultimately he wants her respect and her love. Moreover, she awakens a desire that reveals the inner man:

> Sometimes, sometimes when I take a look at ya, I just keep lookin' and a-lookin'. I want to feel your little body up against me so bad I think I'm go'n' bust. I keep tryin' to tell ya in a lot of different ways. Just one time if you could be sweet without no money around. I think I could—Well, I tell you something, I got poetry in me. I do! I got poetry in me. But I ain't goin' put it down on paper. I ain't no educated man. I got sense enough not to try. Cain't never say nothin' to you. If you just one time let me run the show, . . . You're just freezing my soul, that's what you're doing, . . . freezing my soul. . . . That's just my luck the only woman that's ever been one to me ain't nothing but a whore. But what the hell, I never was a percentage man. I suppose a whore's the only kind of woman I'd know.

This is an important speech in a number of ways. In production, Altman routinely would shoot a scene half a dozen times and then move on to the next one. Beatty always wanted more takes, and he and Altman competed throughout the shoot over matters of script and direction. In this scene, for which Altman used three cameras, Beatty kept wanting to reshoot. Altman finally got tired and went to bed, telling his assistant director to run as many takes as the actor needed. They ultimately logged 26 takes (from which Altman says he selected the third or fourth in editing).[22] Beatty's sense of perfection may well have grown from his realization of the importance of the speech. His longest speech, it reveals his desire and his feelings for Mrs. Miller. It reflects her sense of indifference toward him. And it discloses in a variety of ways his sense of insecurity and inadequacy around her—in expressing himself, in respecting his abilities, in their lovemaking, in running their business.

Unlike the novel where the two of them form both a business and a romantic relationship, the film draws a line between the two partners. McCabe wants her financial relationship, her respect, and her love. But Mrs. Miller only wants the partnership, because, as she tells Ida, getting involved romantically with men only brings trouble. Moreover, she needs competence in the relationship. When they go over the books after the first week of business, she accuses him:

> I say "we," Mr. McCabe, because you think small. You think small because you're afraid to think big. I'm telling you—you have to spend money to make money. You want to spend the rest of your life shopping cows in this dump—Fine! I don't! There's going to come a time, there's going to come a time when I'm taking me half interest and going to San Francisco and buying a legitimate boarding house, but right now I don't want no small timer screwing up me business!

The film then takes its major characters in different directions—McCabe inexorably toward his losing confrontation with Butler and his men, Mrs. Miller toward another lost opportunity to break away from prostitution. Their separate stories cross in the middle of the film as McCabe's incompetent dealing with Sears and Hollander sets in motion the ending that Mrs. Miller anticipates from the beginning. There is an imaginary past between a "John McCabe" and a "Constance Miller" and a metaphorical present between a traditional male and a new woman—both trying to succeed in a place of contact, a frontier where the very possibilities of success are still open, new, relatively unrestricted for these new "pioneers." Their partnership is another one of those third spaces where separate cultures, different personalities, and conflicting needs interact. Their desire as small-time entrepreneurs coincides, even as his pride and her determination clash; both are ultimately defeated by the power of big business. In the interim of stories that merge, cross, and conflict, they nevertheless construct a still warm space inside Mrs. Miller's house that momentarily offers that "shelter from the storm."

A significant part of the film's aesthetic complexity lies in this difference in narrative directions. Rather than any simple, straightforward narrative, the film overlays a number of related stories, kindred matters with divergent goals and conclusions. The complex layering of major and minor stories, of competing narratives is captured in the very temporal rhythms of the film's telling. In the first half of the film, the time of the town's construction expands as the time of the characters' actions is condensed. That is, images of the town's physical growth constantly accompany the actions of the story. The plot meanwhile develops with truncated and elliptical events, bits and pieces of several stories only implicitly connected. In the second half of the film this temporality reverses. The time of the town's development is condensed as the time of the characters' action expands. That is, the representation of growth reaches a plateau while the story traces in moment-by-moment detail the endgame of fire control and shootout. From McCabe's arrival in Presbyterian Church to the arrival of Sears and Hollander, the story of the town apparently occurs over many months, long enough for the town to grow from a small mining camp into a prosperous community with barber, general merchandise store, bakery, and pharmacy. This time itself is doubly marked, on the one hand by the slow, steady construction of the church through the singular efforts of the preacher and on the other by the large energetic labor of off-duty miners hired by McCabe to construct his saloon, bathhouse, and brothel. The time of the construction of the town becomes an impressionist whirl that transpires alongside, behind, and on the periphery of the various narrative lines that develop rapidly in singular, implicitly connected sequences, with minor motifs of character development interspersed. McCabe starts a card game. McCabe buys whores. Mrs. Miller proposes a partnership. Professional prostitutes come to town. The new businesses begin operation. As the history books are fond of saying, "Mining towns sprang up almost overnight." Nevertheless, several months of major construction activity occur expansively against a small number of story events.

Then the time of the story through the second half of the film apparently covers no more than a few days, from the night that Sears and Hollander leave town after their abortive conversations with McCabe until the arrival of the company's gunmen and the final gunfight. Time seems to stop in the middle sequence, crowded with Bart's dying, Birdie's birthday party, the offers from big business, and discussions of those offers between John and Constance. The final gunfight scene apparently takes no longer than the dramatic screen time of its telling, but the mutual stalking of the four opponents seems to go on forever. Actually shot over some eleven days in production during what developed as a major snowstorm, the scene literally condenses time as it expands the action. When it begins in the early morning, snow has just begun to fall; by the end of the scene, Butler and McCabe struggle through snow that has become several feet deep. Moreover, these temporal layers are magnified by the dual struggles occurring simultaneously at the end. The town's discovery of the fire started in the church when Butler kills the preacher, its frantic efforts to mobilize a firefight, the process and ultimate success of that fight—these activities all run in exact parallel to the process of the gunfight where one by one, McCabe kills all three of his opponents.

The time of the story, the multiple times of the narrative, and the time of the film—one now extended and the other foreshortened, one now condensed and the other expanded—produce a complex and rhythmic counterpoint and develop an ambiguous temporal dance among all the film's major components. Overriding the whole is the seasonal descent of the year. The production company, which shot the film in "dead sequence," lived in Vancouver for almost six months across the late summer and fall of 1970 and into the winter of 1971. Thus, in the fiction, McCabe arrives in Presbyterian Church with deciduous trees dressed in autumnal gold against the dark, wet green of fir and redwood trees and dies years later in the midst of a January blizzard. The film condenses the novel's lengthy and complex, four-year story time of individuals and community into the turning of a single autumnal season. To understand the artistry of the film is to recognize this remarkably poetic energy that freezes story movement into an aesthetic present, to hear the musical counterpoints that render the breathing in and out of life's hopes and its ends.

Perhaps one of the most striking aspects of the film's design of interwoven perspectives and temporal signatures is the point-of-view structure generated by the three Leonard Cohen songs that so prominently shape the film's emotional and rational effects. "The Stranger Song," "Sisters of Mercy," and "Winter Lady" are all contained on Cohen's popular debut album *The Songs of Leonard Cohen,* released in 1968. The film is full of the incidental music of flute, violin, and mechanical disk music, but its overall music track proved to be a problem during production. Altman's filmmaking is certainly the work of a painter as he has consistently asserted about his storytelling for over thirty years. It also is the work of a musician who constructs his stories and employs their sound tracks with the assurance of a composer. The structure and the music of *Nashville* sing its awareness of the spinning round of popular music, social desire, public death, and corporate entertainment. Keith Carradine's Academy Award–winning song "I'm Easy" is the film's singular inspiration. The hypnotic rhythms of *3 Women* derive from the eerie swimming pool murals painted in the southern California desert by Bodhi Wind and from the atonal woodwinds of Stomu Yamashta. *A Perfect Couple* tells its comic romance in the contrasting performances of the rock band Keepin' Em off the Streets and the Los Angeles Philharmonic Orchestra. The numerous stories that intersect in *Short Cuts* are organized around the competing sounds of jazz, classical, and new age music. *Kansas City* is full of contemporary jazz renditions of classical 1930s music, and its whole narrative is a jazz composition. Probably none of his films so dramatically reveals the musical and painterly imagination at work in Altman's fragmentary storytelling, his moving camera style, and his lyrical editing as *The Company* (2003), where rehearsal and recital, music and romance, dance and painting perform a stunning pas de deux.

The musical thinking that typifies his work is remarkably apparent in *McCabe & Mrs. Miller*. Considering at first the use of period music from the turn of the century and from the frontier, then considering music written for the film, Altman completed the production without having settled on any music at all. During postproduction, at a party in Paris where scotch and marijuana were in play along with Cohen's album, it occurred to the director that Cohen's music embodied the film. "That's my film!" he remembers exclaiming before he rushed immediately back to New York for the sole purpose of purchasing the music from Cohen. The production team wore out two copies of the album, which played continuously during the editing process on his earlier film, also shot in Vancouver, *That Cold Day in the Park*. Unrealized at the time, the music consequently, according to Altman, shaped the very rhythm of this western. In his oft-repeated story of how he came to Cohen's music for the film, it becomes clear that in an unconscious way the music motivated the film. Moreover, within Cohen's extensive body of work, these three songs have come to be symbiotically associated with the film.

The three songs influence more than rhythm, however; they also work as musical equivalents of the three major narrative perspectives of the film. The order of their occurrence in the film also matches the order of their significance in these different narrative trajectories: The film begins with "The Stranger Song" and conveys Mrs. Miller's point of view from the perspective of her final contemplation in the opium den at the end of the film.

"Sisters of Mercy" occurs in the first third of the film and represents the joint vision of the partnership signaled by the title. "Winter Lady" develops the point of view of McCabe and courses throughout the final sequence of the film. The lyrics and the location of each song further engage the audience in the superimposition of signifiers that constitute the artistic opulence of the film, all mediated by the poet's overarching perspective. When the film opens, the lyrics of "The Stranger Song" accompany the image of the lone rider on the screen and identify him individually as a "dealer," and collectively as another of "all the men you knew." They also introduce him as the object of the contemplative "you." They establish a third person observing. Stephen Scobie describes this persona as "one of the major paradoxes of Cohen's work: namely that the theme of the loss of personality is projected in terms of what appears to be a very strong personality and ego, that of the artist himself."[23]

Robert Kolker observes that, from the perspective of Mrs. Miller's gaze at the very end of the film,

> if we recall those opening shots, the enclosed space they embrace, McCabe mumbling to himself as he dismounts from his horse, the vacant and directionless stares of the men hanging about in the cold, it is clear that Mrs. Miller's state of isolation and self-absorption is only an intensification of the state of things at the beginning. If we realize, in retrospect, how the cutting of the film and its crowded, fragmented spaces and sound create a sense of pervasive isolation in the midst of community, the end comes as little surprise.[24]

This is an important and subtle understanding of how the film works as narrative art. It develops in a more complex way than Naughton's novel, where McCabe's anticipation of the gunfight motivates the novel's survey of the years that have brought him to this point of showdown. The very end of the film indeed motivates the beginning and the entire story told then throughout the film. The viewing subject enters the film in sympathetic understanding with a woman mourning the loss of yet another man who "did not leave you very much / not even laughter." The film begins apparently under the retrospective gaze of the woman whose opium haze contains the stories of John McCabe and Constance Miller just recounted or about to be recalled. The "Stranger Song" here both foreshadows the personality of McCabe and locates his loss as just another in a string of failed relationships. It identifies "you" as a place of shelter. It describes "that kind of man" as a loser, desperate to succeed, "watching for the card / that is so high and wild / he'll never have to deal another," making empty promises, and unable to enter a sound relationship because of "reaching for the sky just to surrender." He remains the stranger, just passing through, who finally blames "your love and warmth and shelter" for weakening his will. The film here just introduces John McCabe, but Mrs. Miller has already "seen that man before"—dissembling about the "burden of his dreams," trading his faded skill for the shelter of her partnership, luring her to "meet between the trains we're waiting for." The narrative now begins, but the story is already over, and she has just had "to watch another tired man / lay down his hand." The man would be on a divine mission, "some Joseph looking for a manger," but here is no savior or blessed virgin but a prostitute. Mrs. Miller has listened to McCabe talk "his dreams to sleep" and has watched both his and her hope for escape vanish like that "highway / that is curling up like smoke above his shoulder." The song establishes an intimate colloquy of recognition and understanding between the voice of the poem and Mrs. Miller; it simultaneously includes the audience as sharing this knowledge that the film will now reveal and its conclusion ratify.

The viewing subject in the first two sequences of the film watches McCabe set about the operation that the narrative already contains as a failure. It watches these actions with the sadness of empathy for the trapped Mrs. Miller. It establishes the narrator as the "I" who would touch "you" in her loss of him, who finally asserts the distance between the "I" as observer and the "traveling" lady now appearing in the third sequence of the film as this song fades from the sound track: "It's you, my love, you who are the stranger." Sympathetic, understanding, repeating it now in this telling but ultimately unable to convey the tragedy:

> I never had a secret chart
> to get me to the heart of this
> or any other matter
> Well he talks like this
> You don't know what he's after.

Certainly the lyrics suggest other readings as well. The "you" may associate with the shrouded figure riding into the frame. It may be the alter ego of the poetic voice in colloquy with itself. The dominant emotional logic of the music, however, added by Altman at the completion of the production process, conveys from the end of the narrative the sad trajectory of the story that here begins. Cohen's speaker invites the listener into a disconsolate reflecting on attachment, futility, and loss. Mrs. Miller is "left behind" by just another man seeking shelter and divinity, asking for more than she can give. As the narrative opens with this retrospective lament, the story is already closed on the stoned oblivion induced by the fact that "he did not leave you very much."

This song shapes response to the first two sequences of the film and from Mrs. Miller's point of view characterizes the man whose death in the last sequence will continue her captivity in "the life." The wordless notes of "The Stranger Song" return momentarily, uncannily, one last time in the scene where she begs McCabe not to meet Butler but to leave town and save himself. Its music is now replaced by the strains of the song that arises when he goes to bed with her and that will play intermittently across the last four sequences of the film. If the first song reflects Mrs. Miller's perspective, the last song, "Winter Lady," reflects McCabe's. The title captures Mrs. Miller's emotional distance from her partner who knows in repeated refrain "I'm not your lover." It conveys his romantic wish for a mutual relationship, rather than one for which he has to pay, and it conveys these emotions through the recollection of a past and obsolescent defense of a "child of snow" by a "soldier" who "fought every man for her." The warmth of his feeling is cast against her coldness; it understands her desire to be "on your way"; it senses her sadness, "you so quiet now," as she contemplates her ongoing journey. The poignancy of the song sounds most dramatic as Mrs. Miller leaves their bed the night before McCabe's showdown with the company gunmen. Its irony cuts two ways in the final scene of the film. The lyrics plead with her to stay when it is he who leaves in death; they lament the lost "child of snow" as the camera zooms in on the snow-covered, mortally wounded lover. When the camera zooms in finally to that remarkable extreme closeup of Mrs. Miller's opiated gaze, the lyrics, like the film itself, contrast her to that nostalgic and sentimental image of the lover who "used to wear her hair like you" and "weave it on a loom / of smoke and gold and breathing."

The lament of these two songs catches the narrative energies of these two very separate and equally sad stories, and between them occurs the third Cohen song "Sisters of Mercy." It occurs only in the third sequence of the film where it indicates the emotional center of warmth and shelter and community that grows temporarily out of the business partnership "McCabe & Mrs. Miller." Now the point of view derives from the soul seeker who has found refuge in their brothel and from a feeling of fellowship with "you who've been traveling so long." The prostitutes in this space are cast by the song as religious acolytes, like nuns in a monastery, waiting for sinners in their darkest hour when they "just can't go on." The solace is sexual where "they've sweetened your night." Their sanctuary brings "comfort," refreshment, and also even inspiration, as "later they brought me this song." In a story space where fall is descending and the year is dying, they offer restoration:

> If your life is a leaf
> That the seasons tear off and condemn
> They will bind you with love
> That is graceful and green as a stem.

The sense of renewal in the song is magical. Most important, perhaps, the "sisters" bring redemption "when you're not feeling holy." They hear confessions, they restore sight, and they heal with "the dew of their hem."

This place of refuge beckons the lonely, the sinful, the weary—travelers, clients, the prostitutes themselves. The song accompanies the business that McCabe will start badly and that the partnership with Mrs. Miller will employ to establish the "clean, well-lighted space" of the film's middle. For a moment in this place the "sisters of mercy," the prostitutes, the brothel offer another third space, here between the opportunity calling from the wilderness and its failure. Like the mythic ideal of the frontier itself, it beckons:

> Yes, you who must leave everything
> That you can not control;
> It begins with your family,
> But soon it comes round to your soul.

A major achievement of the structure in the film is not only the way that the bleak understandings reached at the conclusion color the characters, the action, the mood of the film from the beginning. That conclusion further motivates the middle of the narrative as well. *McCabe & Mrs. Miller* everywhere asks to be read simultaneously as a realistic film and as an impressionistic one. The flashing of the film stock casts a golden glow over all the events, transmuting its action into the canvas of painting. The music of Leonard Cohen also shapes narrative events at the same time that it imprints those events with a melancholy mood and a meditative rhythm.

Mrs. Miller's story also asks to be read in both realistic and impressionistic ways. Her experience in the West, her dependency on masculine capital, her captivity in the hands of male "small-timers," and her knowledge of the inevitability of death in this place of opportunity drive the construction of her house. The middle of the narrative contains a number of scenes that reflects Mrs. Miller's spaces of refuge in opposition to "screwing with the wind whistling up your khyber" and to the deathwardness of McCabe's narrative. In contrast to his drunken attempt to assert authority over the management of the whorehouse as he stands outside in the cold, the film conveys her sitting on her bed, rubbing her foot, and reading a book with utter delight, her small space warmly lit by the golden glow of a lamp and filled with the gentle music box sounds of "Brahms' Lullaby." In the midst of the long sequence that begins with Sears's and Hollander's arriving, the tensions of Bart's fatal injury and the mining company's offers contrast strikingly with the images of warmth, peace, and harmony that emanate from the brothel and the communal celebration of Birdie's birthday.

If Altman had no music track for his film till the end of production, he identifies specific diegetic music for this middle section in the script that precedes the production. When Mrs. Miller makes her proposal to McCabe in Sheehan's saloon, the local violinist plays "Beautiful Dreamer." The script also specifies this music when Mrs. Miller's girls arrive. The prostitute Lily opens the valve to bring hot water into the bathhouse for the Seattle prostitutes recovering from their wet travels to Presbyterian Church; their revel in this steamy warmth is marked by the transition from their playing together to their communal harmonizing of "Beautiful dreamer, awake unto me" as Lily sways in smiling contentment with their singing: "Sounds of the rude world, heard in the day, / Lull'd by the moonlight have all pass'd away!" This is at once one of the major dramatic moments in the story of McCabe's and Mrs. Miller's business and one of the most poetically evocative images of the film. The sisters of mercy themselves find here the shelter from the cold wind that continually blows outside in the wilderness world.

This center cannot hold for long, however. The harsh reality of Bart's death, of Cowboy's killing, of McCabe's plight with the gunman, indeed even of McCabe's crying in Constance's room—these mean that the cold outside, that winter, that death prevail. The expressive refuge of this middle space in the film is motivated by the fear of the reality of the final space. The clean well-lighted place of the brothel gives way to the white glare of snow and death and to the darkened shadows of the Chinese opium den. Just, however, as this end lies in the film's beginning, the narrative suggests in its very telling a transcendence of that end. McCabe is dead, but Mrs. Miller is still a "traveling lady." Helene Keyssar argues: "What we see at the end of *McCabe & Mrs. Miller* is a woman who endures."[25]

The experience of subliminal reality in *McCabe & Mrs. Miller* derives from the overlay of multiple stories, from the multiplicity of the perspectives conveyed by the lyrics of Cohen's songs, from the simultaneity of both realistic and expressive motivations of the same space and actions, from the temporal complexities of narrative that reflect both literal and metaphoric time. It also derives from a characteristic quality of Altman's accomplishments in art cinema narration. Narrative logic cedes its place of central importance in classical cinema and works in parity with the temporal and spatial systems of cinematic discourse. *McCabe & Mrs. Miller* clearly reflects the extensive research that traditionally characterizes the western effort to convey a realistic West. The advertisements for the film touted its historical representations: "This is what the West was like: primitive, miserable and full of violence and despair." At the same time, however, audiences and reviewers everywhere complained that the story was hard to follow, that the sound was impossible to understand, and that its cinematography was too erratic and moody. The film's muddy soundtrack remains famous and has been variously described as the result of poor recording conditions in the Vancouver setting where the film was shot, as the sign of Altman's carelessness as a director, and as the result of Altman's significant experiments in sound. Like art cinema generally, *McCabe & Mrs. Miller* strives for a greater verisimilitude, in distinction from the shooting-stage look and sound of realism in most classical Hollywood filmmaking. Location shooting, natural lighting, and live sound attempt to capture "actual" life. Similarly, art cinema stories reject the clear-cut logic of Aristotelian structure for plots that meander, multiply, drift away, refuse to close—again in some sort of imitation of how life's events actually move.

At the same time, the art cinema foregrounds the work of the director, who emerges as the auteur with a vision, a signature style, a thematic worldview. From the time that *MASH* appeared in 1970 to the release of his last film, *Prairie Home Companion,* in 2006, Altman's work has demanded attention as among the most significantly experimental in contemporary cinema. In addition to the famous multiple casts and divergent narrative lines, these films in particular call attention to the use of sound, mise-en-scène, and cinematography. On the one hand, he mobilizes these aspects of film style in aggressively realistic ways and—in the context of the Hollywood Renaissance of the late sixties and early seventies—in ways that call attention to themselves as different from standard Hollywood practice. Twenty-four tracks of sound recording, multiple and overlapping tracks of sound editing, cinematography marked by dramatic pan and zoom shots, metaphoric editing, ensemble acting—these conjure the Altman film. On the other hand, as a self-consciously painterly auteur, Altman writes and shoots and edits according to an expressive sense of style and values that motivate him as an expressive artist.

In this meeting ground of the realistic and the expressive, David Bordwell has argued, the art cinema asks to be read in ambiguity.[26] The spatial and temporal systems of cinematic discourse support the logical system in the classical cinema to ground the time and place of the diegesis. But film style may work to authenticate and compliment the realism of story, to support it metaphorically as its supplement, or to play against it as an altogether alternative narrative. An ambiguity derives from the overlapping quality of several stories being told simultaneously, such that the metaphorical quality of the style must be read ambiguously because of its potential support of any one of those stories or all of them, or perhaps alternatively none. When the spatial and temporal systems of cinematography, editing, mise-en-scène, and sound rise to parity with the narrative system, they encourage both a reading that complements story and that runs alongside it in visual and aural supplement. The resulting ambiguities of *McCabe & Mrs. Miller* rest in its rich and accomplished amalgamation of multiple and divergent stories, intricate and conflicting modes of discourse, elaborate and contrasting stylistic registers, and competing commitments to representation. Sound, for instance, is at once hard to understand in numerous places in the film because of the overlapping conversations that permit the audience to hear only occasional words. Arguably the words understood by the audience are all the editors want heard: for instance, the phrase "What kind of gun was that?" in the conversations when McCabe first enters Sheehan's establishment. Or the word "gunfighter" later in the conversations about Pudgy McCabe's past. In some scenes, sound has obviously had to be dubbed in postproduction (dialogue and music during the funeral scene, for instance), but key speeches in the film stand out quite clearly—Mrs. Miller's proposal of partnership, the negotiations between McCabe and the mining company, lawyer

Samuels's plan for protecting McCabe, Mrs. Miller's last despairing conversation with McCabe, McCabe's "poetry in me" speech. Sound is at once a marker of social reality, a point of narrative development, and shorthand for individual characters (McCabe's mumbling, the fiddler's playing scales on his instrument, building foreman Jeremy's ramblings, Sheehan's pompous assertings). Over the years, Altman became famous for letting his actors improvise in large dramatic spaces where they are not aware of the camera, but in the final cut of the film, he claimed, all the language on the screen was also in the script.[27] Vocal sound asks variously to be heard realistically, expressionistically, and narratively from one moment to the next.

Cohen's music more than the dialogue, of course, indicates how the sound contributes significantly to expressionist readings. With the appearance of *The Graduate* in 1967 and *Easy Rider* in 1969, the movies discovered the value of using contemporary popular songs to develop soundtracks complementary to the narrative. This practice, which actively and popularly continues in postclassical Hollywood, works with particular success in *McCabe & Mrs. Miller*. If Cohen works perhaps anachronistically by associating popular contemporary music with a period film, his music also illustrates the complexity that occurs when linking musical lyrics with narrative images. The juxtaposition creates ambiguous visual and aural relationships in which the two media interactively comment upon each other. While the three songs here certainly focus central narrative perspectives, their cryptic imagery raises questions of local interpretation throughout the film. More than just the analysis of lyrics, what does it mean that the words "he was just some Joseph looking for a manger" play over the shot of McCabe about to cross the rope bridge to Sheehan's? Or that the words "you hate to see another tired man / lay down his hand / like he was giving up the holy game of poker" accompany McCabe as he rides among the great piles of logged trees going to Bearpaw's lumber mills? One of the most striking images in the film combines the long-shot silhouette of the preacher's putting the cross atop the church steeple against a brilliant golden sunset as Cohen's music celebrates the healing efficacy of the "sisters of mercy." A misanthropic preacher placing a cross on an empty church, a gambling entrepreneur importing three sad prostitutes, a song of restoration at the golden end of day—these constitute an intricate and ambiguous nexus of expression. Such occurrences juxtapose images, actions, and music in ways that diverge from classical cinema's redundant linkage of sight and sound. Throughout the film they produce nodes of complex meaning that transcend narrative coherence and realistic representation and demand that the film be read with a sensitivity to the ambiguous play of associations.

After leaving the sleeping McCabe on the cold blue night before his death, Mrs. Miller stops to gaze at the water amid the lightly falling flakes of snow, the angled braces and bars of the bridge and her bedroom stairs, and the soft notes of "Traveling lady stay a while / Until the night is over." The complexity of this shot brings the narrative to an emotional stop, as so often in this film, throwing the present moment into a lyrical tableau of multiple times, varied points of view, diverging characterizations, and numerous poignant associations that diverge in many directions at once. The difficulty in unpacking this single and profound moment is magnified by the many moments like it across the film. The mise-en-scène is replete with these tableaux that convey the marvelous mixture of stylistic effects working together simultaneously.

The camera pans along with the movement of two horses during the opening credits until they follow an invisible trail toward a redwood church rising out of the wet misty gray wilderness of mountains and evergreen trees; the lone rider enshrouded in a red bear fur coat plods slowly toward the beacon of the church's spire. The point-of-view shot of Mrs. Miller gazing from the window of McCabe's unfinished saloon captures in shades of gray and green a mining street littered with mining and building debris where three tents provide the homes and the worksites for McCabe's three crib-girl prostitutes. In a late dusk shot as the ubiquitous wind moans and the low notes of "Traveling Lady" fill the soundtrack, Mrs. Miller walks up the hill from the brothel to the saloon in a landscape of black trees and snow-topped houses that stretch downward to the slate-colored Pacific, seen here for the only time in the film, faintly lit by the last white glare of a lone cloud reflecting the long-set sun. The camera opens on a close-up of a gravestone, zooms out, and cranes up to reveal the green mountainside sloping down toward the redwood buildings that fill the valley bottom and the townspeople who surround a grave and a gleaming white coffin as that wind moans, as the glaring white light of the sky rolls down the frame, and as the minister warns of the "swift and powerful blade of justice that lays open the serpent of evil and leaves its putrid flesh to rot under the sun of heaven."

McCabe stands with his back to the camera, a stovepipe splitting the screen, his face visible in a small mirror in the middle of the frame, a black and white window on the right displaying the wet, frozen world outside and a blue and gold window on the left revealing the stairs to Mrs. Miller's bedroom. McCabe dresses, loads his pistol, and declares "I got poetry in me"—all under the soft strains of "The Stranger Song." Frames within frames, images within images, sounds upon sounds. When Sheehan looks down the street upon hearing that the church is burning, the reverse shot provides one of the clearest views of the entire town in the film: an ironically quiet and peaceful panoramic shot in depth with the church at the far back center of the frame, a tiny gold light just visible through a window; the town is everywhere shrouded in heavy snow, trees and buildings alike weighed down in a blanket of white as thick flakes fill the frame against the leaden gray sky and somber dark of the mountains.

Each of these single and singular tableaux is a painting that deserves a title. Each stops the viewer's attention to story as it enters the stream of images seen in the film now as art museum. Each is stunning in the play of place and form, light and color. *McCabe & Mrs. Miller* impresses beyond its narrative force as a lovely work of visual art.

Editing also creates intricate visual juxtapositions like these, in both small moments of transition and in larger units of discursive construction. When the first card game gets under way in the brown-gold light of the film's initial sequence, the camera zooms in to McCabe's face as he puffs on a cigar and grins with easy camaraderie and shows off a prominent gold tooth. The next shot is a close-up of feet walking across the rope bridge in black and white, introducing the figure who in a moment will be identified as the preacher. The preacher is introduced metonymically. Such editing differs strikingly from classical analytical editing that introduces scenes broadly and then analytically edits in its dramatic action. Similarly, when his manager tells McCabe that the company negotiators had returned to Bearpaw because they knew they weren't dealing with a "tinhorn," the camera shows McCabe's face in a close-up reaction shot of surprise, dismay, anxiety, wonder—emotions partially generated by Beatty's wordless expression, and partially by the cut to a close-up of a tombstone and the beginning of the funeral scene for Bart Coyle. Editorial transitions like this are routine. Their sudden contrasts of subject, lighting, locale, movement, and perspective motivate questions about relationships and ambiguities of meaning that must be understood not analytically but metaphorically. Such is the editorial movement from the close-up of the teenage prostitute to the zoom on McCabe's face to the medium-close telephoto shot of the preacher that blurs and flattens his face against the flames of a campfire in the extreme foreground before opening up to show in medium shot the crib tents of McCabe's women. All three shots accompany the return to the soundtrack of Cohen's singing "They were waiting for me" from "Sisters of Mercy," and they perfectly illustrate the kind of transitions in the film that condense time and space into the separate lines of a lyrical poem.

Two larger editorial movements in the film further demonstrate how this element of style carries much of the multiple perspectives so central to the film's aesthetic achievement. In the bathhouse scene where the newly arrived whores soak away the cold journey from Seattle, the editing cuts among the shot of men gambling in McCabe's saloon, the women bathing, and the gaze of the fat prostitute Lily. The men sit in a circle round a card table and talk in gossiping tones of wonderment about the physical anatomy of Chinese women as they play, the women gambol and sing together in a round tub of steaming water, and Lily looks on with both a glum detachment and finally a dreamy, swaying contentment. The edited shots separate the spaces by gender, by community, by attention; they link cards and baths and circles and a desiring gaze. Their associations are ambiguous, multiple, implied, rich in the images of refuge that fill the middle of the film.

The multiple scenes that conclude the film, of course, reflect the harsher reality of the life of prostitutes, gamblers, and fragile partnerships on the frontier. The long scene of McCabe's confrontation with the killers intercut with the scene of the fight to save the church finally intercut with the long zoom shot of Mrs. Miller in the opium den closes the multiplicities of captivity and hope, opportunity and chance, and value and power on the cold of death and the heat of opium.

The play of lighting, framing, and camera movement, set design, character behavior, and sound in such scenes constitute individual paintings that stand out for a moment and then are swept along on the editing currents that propel the film narratively, musically, and poetically. At different times the film echoes other painters—classical, impressionist, regional—in its development of these shots, and its temporal journey develops the most penetrating and engaging gallery of images of all the Altman films. Critics find differing visual styles in the film. Paul Arthur, for instance, describes its "rigid interior/exterior color scheme—Rembrandt inside, Caspar David Friedrich outside." Adrian Danks asserts that its images "resemble a painting by the sixteenth-century artist Pieter Bruegel, broken up into interlocking tableaux and brought up to date."[28] Altman's film *Vincent & Theo*

(1990) examines the relationship of Van Gogh with his brother and watches the painter in the midst of some of his more important work in Arles. The film visually is a kind of homage to Van Gogh, and so is *McCabe & Mrs. Miller,* where Altman's use of brown tones and light recalls the Dutch artist's work. The scene in particular when Sheehan lights the lamp over the poker table particularly evokes Van Gogh's "Potato Eaters." The final scene of the film as McCabe is stalked by the company gunmen is marked not only by a heavy snowfall in the scene itself but by snow that has been enhanced in the printing stage of production, creating an effect of flakes that seem at time painted on the surface of the film; the scene recalls the pointillism of postimpressionist Georges Seurat. Throughout the film, red/gold and blue/green images of the surrounding mountains, trees, and valley variously evoke the regional northwest mountainscapes of painters like William Keith, Thomas Moran, Worthington Whittredge, Thomas Hill, and Albert Bierstadt. Altman's film must take a place of prominence as a cinematic contribution to the "Rocky Mountain School" of American art.

As a painting in motion, however, the film's set design must also be read as poetry whose stanzas are organized around a stunning palette of black and white and gray, of blue and green and brown, of red and gold. As set designer or art director, Leon Ericksen developed this and similar looks for Altman's *Images* (1972), *California Split* (1974), and *Quintet* (1979). At times its dark tones overwhelm the surfaces of its action: The pale-face preacher hunched over in his black frock coat and wide brimmed black hat repeatedly punctuates other dark spaces across the film. McCabe riding to Bearpaw to buy his whores pushes his horse through black and white water into a gray town. The killers arrive on a icy night in a scene similarly colored in somber gray and black, light glaring white off the ice in front of Sheehan's saloon, and we watch them in medium long shot cross the rope bridge in the midst of a frozen, black-and-white winter world.

Two patterns of imagery in particular dominate the lyrical organization of the film, however (as they will again later in *Quintet*): The heavy dark patterns of gray skies and green trees under the almost constant rain of late autumn resonate with the muddy brown and gray tones of the human space designated initially by Sheehan's saloon. Running through this darkness are a series of golden-red lights that rise to crescendo inside Mrs. Miller's baby-blue whorehouse. In a striking telephoto shot much admired by Stanley Kubrick,[29] the filtered camera watches McCabe in long shot doubly filtered through the glass of the saloon as he pauses at the bridge to light his cigar. The tiny flame of his match against the otherwise dark wet surroundings dramatically opens this metaphoric pattern. When the camera initially enters Sheehan's, the film offers another of its captivating tableaux: Sheehan kneels before a statue of the Madonna, in the shadowy, iron-barred liquor closet that doubles as holy grotto where he lights a candle and prays for blessing; for a quick moment the light of a religious candle glows in the dark. When McCabe and the miners gather round the newly designated poker table, Sheehan lights the lamp overhead and a soft golden glow suffuses the faces of the men, and the red-clothed table becomes a scarlet altar.

These little gold lights are everywhere, cutting, shaping, molding the darkness of Sheehan's and the early darkness of the film. The glowing red wood of newly milled trees gives the growing town of Presbyterian Church itself a golden gleam that seems to hold back a wilderness gloom. The light of the bathhouse fire heats the water, steams the air, and casts a golden-red glow over the bodies of the sisters of mercy as they recover from their wet, cold, muddy journey from Seattle. Mrs. Miller finds refuge against that dark night in the golden-red warmth of her room. The human faces in all these spaces lit momentarily, briefly, minutely by these little fires themselves become golden lanterns in the dark. The light of new wood and numerous lamps turn McCabe's new House of Fortune and Mrs. Miller's whorehouse into the glowing warm spaces at the center of this film. Both the literal and expressive heart of *McCabe & Mrs. Miller,* these sites differ in their cinematography. One style captures McCabe's saloon in a sharply edged, glossy, satin sheen. Mrs. Miller's brothel, however, is suffused in a soft, diffusion-filtered glow. Its welcoming, communal warmth visually, dramatically, thematically is caught in the extreme close-up of the candles on Birdie's birthday cake; flaming, golden, unfocused, their fire fills the screen, the celebrants, the room, the very heart of darkness itself.

Ernest Hemingway's conception of "a clean, well-lighted place" (which he presented in a short story of the same name) imagines a space that is a refuge, a home, a site of solace against the turmoil and darkness that precedes and follows it.[30] It provides momentary respite from the storms perceived as the twentieth century's bequest to the modernist imagination. The howling wind of wilderness opens and closes the film. The fire and warmth at the center of the film slowly fade, extinguished by the cold of nature and the cold of man's violence. Metaphorically, this transformation is caught by two shots of the town in the last sequence of the film. When

McCabe climbs the church belfry to watch for his stalkers, the camera reveals the town spread out below in a panning shot that remarkably conveys the gleaming red buildings across the little valley as the light of civilization prevailing against the gloom of wilderness. The production design that has been constructing this set across the months of the shooting of the film is here fully revealed in its final completion. But literally seconds later, the ground-level shot of the burning church at the far end of the street of this frontier town conveys the desolating power of winter to defeat man's constructions and his puny light. The final three shots of the film describe an ironically exuberant townspeople who have extinguished the fire that threatened their meaningless symbol of civilization, a frozen "child of snow" whose life has been extinguished by the ruthless power of corporate civilization, and a once "traveling lady" whose illusory lamps of solace have been replaced by the realistic glow of the opium gaze.

When *McCabe & Mrs. Miller* appeared in 1971, its alternative narrative structure and stylistic expression were dramatically obvious to an audience still trained either to appreciate the strictures of classical Hollywood or resistant to their formal and ideological constraints. What seemed remarkable then in overlapping sound, metaphoric editing, expressive cinematography, multiple narrative, and painterly perspectives had by the end of the century become commonplace aspects of postclassical Hollywood. Unlike *Nashville, Buffalo Bill and the Indians, The Player,* and *Prêt-à-Porter* (1994), which achieve their reflexivity through a critique of the process of entertainment itself, *McCabe & Mrs. Miller*'s apparent reflexivity derives from ways that style and storytelling then called attention to themselves as innovative. Reflexivity and aesthetic self-consciousness are central features that the art cinema shares with modernism, and this film looks at itself in a reflexive manner that transcends its creative artistry. On one hand, the film clearly continues the modernist disaffection with the values of modernity. The sense of alienation and despair that express the counterculture's rejection of middle-class values also figures in the sense of cultural alienation that underlies modernist art since the early part of the twentieth century.

On the other hand, that sense of estrangement motivates a central aspect of the narrative structure of the film. The narrative begins with the bleak point of view upon which it ends: McCabe dead, Mrs. Miller trapped still in prostitution and drug addiction, their just-successful partnership crushed by corporate ruthlessness and greed. The fidelity of this conclusion to a lifelike fatalism motivates the luminosity and optimism of the brothel and the film's middle section. But that pessimistic ending also reflects an understanding of the West as the motive for westerns themselves. The mythic western included hard work, sacrifice, and commitment that pay off in happy endings and achieved goals—families made, fortunes gained, wilderness defeated, democracy spread. But if history had ignored it before, contemporary western historians recall that the frontier West was full of death, disease, grinding labor, limited resources, geographic and climatic extremes, and failure. The face of prostitution gives ample evidence of these conditions. *McCabe & Mrs. Miller* argues that the confrontation of hope and failure motivates the middle space of desire, which in this film is the clean, well-lighted space of the brothel, and in cultural history the space of the western myth itself. Tough times, difficult circumstances, and marginal existence are not the stuff of popular fiction. The makers of westerns in particular reshape the travails of life in the desert West, the mining and cattle Wests, and the small-town frontiers into stories suffused with the golden haze of reminiscence. The Myth of the West reflects a land of heart's desire, mindful of the struggle to survive but confident that heroic deeds will build the new nation. The film then, like Mrs. Miller's creation of a place of warmth in the space of death, like Cohen's musical invention in the knowledge of surrender and jokers left behind, like the western genre's romantic conception of happy trails and happy endings in face of hardship and loss, constitutes another set of artistic images shored against cultural ruin.

Revisionist historians and storytellers rewrite this tale to bring back the multiplicity of ethnic faces, the genocide of native peoples, the conflicting economic and social values, and the mix of success and failure of a more historic West. The dramatic, stylistic, historical, and cultural interactions of *McCabe & Mrs. Miller* variously establish that frontier as a space where such differences collide. As Altman's adaptation of Naughton's novel reconstructs the story by confusing narrative causality, the film becomes more complicated to follow, more impossible for the audience hypnotically to consume its story. As it reconstructs character, time, and space, it also displays a heterogeneous array of other social texts. Into these spaces of ambiguity and complexity, then, flood the contextual implications always working in storytelling but generally subordinate to the dominance of action. All narrative discourse is situated by an intricate intertextuality, in which prior texts of history, politics, philosophy, and aesthetics determine how meaning is possible in any present textual moment. The rich narrative profuseness of *McCabe & Mrs. Miller* more actively sends its audience to this intertextual space in order to construct meanings out of what Walt Whitman called "diffused faint clews and indirections."[31] The film resides within, reconstructs, and explains the classical western genre. It reflects Altman's significant definition of a new American cinema. It echoes the new western history's revision of the mythical views of the West as the site of heroic individualism and burgeoning democratic nationalism. It participates in the 1960s call for cultural alternatives to regnant American social values. It sees the possibility of women in partnership with men, even as it chronicles the power that stands in their mutual way. Aesthetically its fiction is poetry; it lyrically combines haunting music, probing zoom shots, rhythmic editing, and a somber palette of blues and greens, golds and reds. Its narrative structures invoke the affiliation of John McCabe and Constance Miller and "weave it on a loom / Of smoke and gold and breathing."

Epilogue: Violence, Decline, and Death

Early in Robert Altman's revision of the detective genre, *The Long Goodbye* (1973), Philip Marlowe is being interrogated by a gangster who demonstrates his tough determination by suddenly smashing a Coke bottle across the face of his girlfriend. In the last scene of *Nashville* (1975), while country music star Barbara Jean is singing at a political rally, a member of the crowd suddenly starts shooting at her. In the middle of his Hollywood satire *The Player* (1992), the studio script producer without warning violently attacks a writer whom he suspects is sending him death threats. At the end of *Short Cuts* (1993) a mild-mannered family man suddenly begins to smash the head of a young girl he has attempted to pick up. These vicious attacks occur at different parts of their stories. They appear unexpectedly. They shock onlookers in the film, and their suddenness and violence stun the audience as well. Furthermore, they significantly change the tone and meaning of the story.

During the 1960s an American president had been assassinated. Two prominent civil rights leaders had been assassinated. The former U.S. attorney general and brother of the president had been assassinated while running for president. The nightly news announced the daily body count and detailed the latest violence from the Vietnam battlefields. Demonstrations on campuses across the country erupted in violent encounters between students and police over numerous issues of political and institutional policies. Race riots broke the peace of large American cities. Violence had become a very visible part of the American experience. Altman's first big

Hollywood hit—indeed, his biggest film at the box office—was *MASH* in 1970. Its black humor and antiwar sentiment is punctuated by the bloody violence of the battlefield operating tent. Its huge popularity among young people derived in part from its ability to laugh in the middle of carnage. Almost all of Altman's films in the 1970s end in death. Indeed, as he remarked repeatedly in interviews, "Death is the only end I know."[1] These films reached a young audience for whom innocence and traditional values collided with the harshness of the world they saw around them and the government that drafted them into adulthood. The creative energies of *McCabe & Mrs. Miller* engage and reflect these social conditions that have been a major legacy of the last quarter of the twentieth century.

In the middle of the film, Cowboy has ridden a long way from some cattle range to these Pacific Coast mountains to find sex and momentary companionship. As played by Keith Carradine, he exudes youthfulness, enthusiasm, and innocence, and the girls in Mrs. Miller's brothel make him a home there. When he leaves to return to that generic range, the girls fondly hug and kiss him and wish him farewell. He stops at Sheehan's to buy new socks to replace the ones worn out running around without shoes at Mrs. Miller's and there suddenly is shot to death by Kid. Cowboy's gawky simplicity contrasts with violence and menace in the same effective way that Carradine's characterizations do in Altman's *Thieves Like Us* (1974) and *Nashville*. Cowboy's boyishness and popularity with the prostitutes in many ways characterize the space of retreat and community represented in the middle of the film. In particular, his effect on Ida has been to convert her fear and apprehension over prostitution into the giddy infatuation apparent in her repeated farewell, "Bye, Cowboy!" His small penis may have been the object of an affectionate joke at Mrs. Miller's, but inadequacies and fears there are momentarily washed away. Nevertheless, that dark night and the winter wind wait just outside.

The short narrative around Cowboy's arrival and fate in Presbyterian Church reflects the aesthetic shorthand that characterizes the film. When he heads off to the brothel after his first tense encounter with McCabe, the film cuts from the hazy golden valley to the black and white glare of three horsemen riding through the woods. Between their traveling and their arrival is interposed the scene where Mrs. Miller welcomes Ida to her house. Then Cowboy's stay there, the killers' arrival, and McCabe's growing apprehension over his plight are interwoven strands throughout this sequence that lead to the ultimate showdown at the end of the film. All these scenes dramatically juxtapose the film's opposing color palettes, sharply contrasting the warm, golden light of the brothel with the stark black and white darkness of the killers.

Cowboy's encounter then with Kid on the footbridge to Sheehan's shatters the golden fantasy of solace and redemption from the "sisters of mercy." Like their generic names, these two adversaries cut opposite stereotypes—one in the oversized ten-gallon hat and chaps of the movie cowpuncher, the other in the "Dutchboy" cap, tie, and jacket of the urban immigrant ghetto. Cowboy's gun is half hidden under his leather coat; Kid wears his low, like the quick-draw gunman he would emulate. To this point, the narrative has only implied the menace of the mysterious threesome. Now their identity becomes patent. They are killers, and none more sadistically so than the kid. Immediately before Cowboy reaches Sheehan's, Kid has been showing off with his pistol to Breed. When he misses the whiskey jug resting on the frozen pond, he defensively insists, "I wasn't trying to hit it. The trick's not to hit it but to make it float." When Cowboy calls out, "Hold it, sonny . . . . I don't want to get shot," he further engages Kid's defensiveness. He calls Cowboy names and taunts him with the sole purpose of allowing Kid to draw down on the harmless cattle rider. When he shoots Cowboy in cold blood, everyone watches in stunned and utter silence—his companion gunmen, Sheehan and other townspeople, and especially the audience. The sudden and inexplicable killing violates the mythic code of the gunfight. It breaks the middle peace of the film. It shatters the innocence of the movie's central story. It immediately foreshadows the impending confrontation of McCabe and the company killers, as well as the film's tragic conclusion. It brings cold-blooded violence to the surface of this hitherto quiet frontier story. Altman underlines its shock with an echo on the two gun shots and a slow-motion zoom in to Cowboy's body floating on its back in the pond, and then he repeats the climax of the shot for emphasis.

Sheehan's footbridge is a striking and repeated part of the film's set design that finally, like so much else in the film, must be understood impressionistically. The various crossings of this bridge from rocky road to shelter take on symbolic weight. McCabe crosses it in light upon his entrance to Presbyterian Church, and he crosses it again in winter darkness to deal for his life. It represents the many transitions at work in the story, as McCabe gets a female partner, as Mrs. Miller finds the opportunity for economic deliverance from the captivity of prostitution, as the grungy mining camp becomes a bustling town, as big business seeks to expand its profits. It also represents the transitions developing in Altman's film itself—into the new western, into a revised view of the historic West, into a new dispensation for women in the culture, into a new aesthetic of filmmaking. But the cowboy cannot make the crossing. Helene Keyssar observes: "Traditionally a sign of hope, transcendence, of the ability of human beings to make connections, to overcome the obstacles of nature, the bridge now becomes an ominous sign of vulnerability and disassociation."[2] The scene breaks the intimacy of John and Constance's last night together. Its cold gray light replaces the warm glow of the brothel. It presages the five deaths that will follow on this wintry day. Cowboy's death on the bridge and then McCabe's death in the snow at the end reverberate across the film. Innocence collapses in the face of sudden and inexplicable violence. The stunned gaze of the audience replicates Mrs. Miller's stoned oblivion as an inexorable closure to any celebration of "love and warmth and shelter."

The scene of Cowboy's death resonates with the rich visual, narrative, and thematic complexities of the entire film and with the unique vision of Altman's best work. *MASH* crossed the bloody gore of the Vietnam War with the wise-cracking irreverence of smart-ass surgeons in frontline operating tents. *Nashville* balanced an exuberant view of popular country music with an awareness of the bleakness in American lives that motivates the music. *The Player* exposed the cynicism and greed that underlie Hollywood's commitment to happy endings. *Short Cuts* transformed Raymond Carver's grim fiction of the Northwest into kaleidoscopic meditations on Los Angeles as life and death in contemporary America. *Gosford Park* (2001) engaged the fiction of murder mysteries to examine the humor and the trauma of social class distinctions. The Academy of Motion Picture Arts and Sciences nominated all of these films for the Best Picture of the Year. These five works also enshrine what must be recognized as the Altman vision. His films constitute a synthesis of enthusiasm for life's play and potential with despair over failures in the human enterprise, all captured with an energetic cinematic style that relishes in the innovative joy of filmmaking. When Altman died in November 2006 at the age of 81, the mass media eulogized him with specific reference to these films—and one other: *McCabe & Mrs. Miller* was remembered as one of Altman's best and his most beautiful film. The film stands as one of the major artistic achievements in Altman's momentous Hollywood career from 1969 to 2006. Its representation of prostitution as a kind of restitution, its recognition that wilderness potential supports a merciless capitalist enterprise, its discovery that, as William Butler Yeats put it, "Love has pitched his mansion in / The place of excrement"[3]—these reflect Altman's understanding that the golden glow of life's energy everywhere confronts the inevitability of death's dark descent. *McCabe & Mrs. Miller* is an artistic accomplishment that at once sings its narrative acknowledgment of the end. It narrates emotional possibility against rational inevitability. It paints a cinematic picture of the West that shimmers in all the idealistic desire to escape the past that lies inexorably ahead. It stands as Altman's great poem to autumn's golden decline into winter.

NOTES

INTRODUCTION: NEGOTIATIONS AND DEALS

1. Mark Twain, *Roughing It* (Hartford, Conn.: American Publishing Company, 1871), 340.
2. Paul Arthur, "How the West Was Spun: *McCabe & Mrs. Miller* and Genre Revisionism," *Cineaste* 28 (Summer 2003): 19.
3. Richard Slotkin, *Gunfighter Nation: The Myth of the Frontier in Twentieth-Century America* (New York: Atheneum, 1992), 278. Also Janet Walker, "Introduction: Westerns through History," in *Westerns: Films through History,* ed. Janet Walker (New York: Routledge, 2001), 1–4.
4. Robert Altman, director's scene commentary/behind-the-scenes documentary, in *McCabe & Mrs. Miller,* DVD (1971; Burbank, Calif.: Warner Home Video, 2002).
5. John Keats, "To Autumn," *John Keats: Selected Poetry,* http://englishhistory.net/keats/poetry/toautumn.html.
6. Altman, director's scene commentary.
7. James Joyce, "The Dead," in his *Dubliners,* http://whitewolf.newcastle.edu.au/words/authors/J/JoyceJames/prose/dubliners/dubliners15.html.

CHAPTER ONE. THE REAL AND MYTHIC WEST

1. Henry David Thoreau, *Walden* (Boston: Houghton Mifflin, 1960), 81.
2. Steven D. Lavine, "Introduction: Museums and Multiculturalism," in *Exhibiting Cultures: The Poetics and Politics of Museum Display,* ed. Ivan Karp and Steven D. Lavine (Washington, D.C.: Smithsonian Institution Press, 1991), 5.
3. Ludmilla Jordanova, "Objects of Knowledge: A Historical Perspective," in *The New Museology,* ed. Peter Vergo (London: Reaktion Books, 1989), 26.
4. Richard Slotkin, *Gunfighter Nation: The Myth of the Frontier in Twentieth-Century America* (New York: Atheneum, 1992), 29–32.
5. Richard White, "Frederick Jackson Turner and Buffalo Bill," in *The Frontier in American Culture: An Exhibition at the Newberry Library, August 26, 1994–January 7, 1995,* ed. James R. Grossman (Berkeley: University of California Press, 1994), 45.
6. Ibid., 9, 11.
7. Elliott West, "A Longer, Grimmer, but More Interesting Story," in *Trails: Toward a New Western History,* ed. Patricia Nelson Limerick, Clyde A. Milner II, and Charles E. Rankin (Lawrence: University Press of Kansas, 1991), 105.
8. Patricia Nelson Limerick, *Something in the Soil: Legacies and Reckonings in the New West* (New York: W. W. Norton, 2000), 292.
9. Robert Burgoyne, *Film Nation: Hollywood Looks at U.S. History* (Minneapolis: University of Minnesota Press, 1997), 35.

10. Janet Walker, "Introduction: Westerns through History," in *Westerns: Films through History*, ed. Janet Walker (New York: Routledge, 2001), 13.
11. Limerick, *Something in the Soil*, 79.
12. Patricia Nelson Limerick, *The Legacy of Conquest: The Unbroken Past of the American West* (New York: W. W. Norton, 1987), 29–30.
13. Ibid., 62.
14. Walker, "Introduction," 15.
15. Jordanova, "Objects of Knowledge," 25.
16. Janet Walker, "Captive Images in the Traumatic Western: *The Searchers, Pursued, Once upon a Time in the West,* and *Lone Star,*" in *Westerns: Films through History*, ed. Janet Walker (New York: Routledge, 2001), 222.
17. Ibid., 225.
18. Ibid., 226.
19. Elliott West, revision of Rodman W. Paul, *Mining Frontiers of the Far West, 1848–1880* (Albuquerque: University of New Mexico Press, 2001), 210.
20. Ibid.
21. Robert Altman and David McKay, "McCabe & Mrs. Miller," film script (Robert Altman Collection, Wisconsin Center for Film and Theater Research, Wisconsin Historical Society, Madison, Wis.), 1.
22. Ibid., 2.
23. West, *Mining Frontiers*, 166.
24. Patricia Nelson Limerick, "The Adventures of the Frontier in the Twentieth Century," in Grossman, *Frontier in American Culture*, 74.
25. Limerick, *Something in the Soil*, 215–216.
26. Richard White, *"It's Your Misfortune and None of My Own": A New History of the American West* (Norman: University of Oklahoma Press, 1991), 244.
27. West, *Mining Frontiers*, 235.
28. W. Sherman Savage, *Blacks in the West* (Westport, Conn.: Greenwood Press, 1976), 120.
29. West, *Mining Frontiers*, 199.
30. Ibid., 227.
31. Roy Rosenzweig, "The Rise of the Saloon," in *Eight Hours for What We Will: Workers and Leisure in an Industrial City, 1870–1920* (New York: Cambridge University Press, 1983), 142–143.
32. Carlos Arnaldo Schwantes, *The Pacific Northwest: An Interpretive History* (Lincoln: University of Nebraska Press, 1996), 155.
33. West, *Mining Frontiers*, 280.
34. Limerick, *Legacy of Conquest*, 106.
35. Altman and McKay, "McCabe & Mrs. Miller," script, 1.
36. West, *Mining Frontiers*, 69.
37. Limerick, *Something in the Soil*, 216.
38. Paula Petrik, *No Step Backward: Women and Family on the Rocky Mountain Mining Frontier, Helena, Montana, 1865–1900* (Helena: Montana Historical Society Press, 1987), 4.
39. White, *"It's Your Misfortune,"* 267, 325.
40. Schwantes, *Pacific Northwest*, 272.
41. White, *"It's Your Misfortune,"* 266.
42. Ibid., 381.

43. Cited in Limerick, *Something in the Soil*, 293.
44. Lyric recorded by Robert V. Hine and John Mack Faragher, *The American West: A New Interpretive History* (New Haven, Conn.: Yale University Press, 2000), 265.
45. West, *Mining Frontiers*, 166.
46. Ibid., 198, 211.
47. Hine and Faragher, *American West*, 364.
48. White, *"It's Your Misfortune,"* 309.
49. Ibid.
50. West, *Mining Frontiers*, 220.
51. Sandra L. Myres, *Westering Women and the Frontier Experience, 1800–1915*. (Albuquerque: University of New Mexico Press, 1982), 7.
52. White, *"It's Your Misfortune,"* 307.
53. Anne M. Butler, *Daughters of Joy, Sisters of Misery: Prostitutes in the American West, 1865–90* (Urbana: University of Illinois Press, 1985), 65.
54. Petrik, *No Step Backward*, 4.
55. Limerick, *Something in the Soil*, 35.
56. White, *"It's Your Misfortune,"* 260.
57. West, *Mining Frontiers*, 214.
58. Ibid., 215.
59. Myres, *Westering Women*, 11.
60. Limerick, "Adventures of the Frontier," 75.
61. Myres, *Westering Women*, 4.
62. Susan H. Armitage, "Through Women's Eyes: A New View of the West," in *The Women's West*, ed. Susan H. Armitage and Elizabeth Jameson (Norman: University of Oklahoma Press, 1987), 11.
63. Limerick, *Something in the Soil*, 49.
64. Jane Tompkins, *West of Everything: The Inner Life of Westerns* (New York: Oxford University Press, 1992), 39.
65. Slotkin, *Gunfighter Nation*, 86.
66. Petrik, *No Step Backward*, xvii.
67. Tompkins, *West of Everything*, 38.
68. Quoted in ibid., 43.
69. Butler, *Daughters of Joy*, xi.
70. Ibid., xix.
71. Petrik, *No Step Backward*, 56.
72. West, *Mining Frontiers*, 267.
73. Chris Enns, *Hearts West: True Stories of Mail-Order Brides on the Frontier* (Guilford, Conn.: Globe Pequot Press, 2005), xi, 106.
74. White, *"It's Your Misfortune,"* 278.
75. West, *Mining Frontiers*, 266.
76. Limerick, *Something in the Soil*, 49.
77. Myres, *Westering Women*, 256.
78. Petrik, *No Step Backward*, 38.
79. Butler, *Daughters of Joy*, 59.
80. Petrik, *No Step Backward*, 33.
81. Ibid., 49.
82. Limerick, *Something in the Soil*, 49.
83. West, *Mining Frontiers*, 267.

84. Petrik, *No Step Backward,* 56.
85. Ibid., xvii.
86. White, *"It's Your Misfortune,"* 304–305.
87. Petrik, *No Step Backward,* 35.
88. Mary Murphy, "The Private Lives of Public Women: Prostitution in Butte, Montana, 1878–1917," in Armitage and Jameson, *Women's West,* 195.
89. Butler, *Daughters of Joy,* 27, 46.
90. Petrik, *No Step Backward,* 56.
91. Limerick, *Something in the Soil,* 50–51, 52.
92. Altman and McKay, "McCabe & Mrs. Miller," script, 37.

CHAPTER TWO. REVISIONIST WESTERN

1. David Lusted, *The Western* (Harlow, England: Pearson Education, 2003), 32.
2. Lee Clark Mitchell, *Westerns: Making the Man in Fiction and Film* (Chicago: University of Chicago Press, 1996), 163.
3. Jane Tompkins, *West of Everything: The Inner Life of Westerns* (New York: Oxford University Press, 1992), 41.
4. J. Hoberman, "How the West Was Lost," in *The Western Reader,* ed. Jim Kitses and Gregg Rickman (New York: Limelight Editions, 1998), 91.
5. Michael Dempsey, "Altman: The Empty Staircase and the Chinese Princess," *Film Comment,* September 1974, 15.
6. Quoted in Rita Parks, *The Western Hero in Film and Television: Mass Media Mythology* (Ann Arbor, Mich.: UMI Research Press, 1982), 130.
7. Phil Hardy, *The Encyclopedia of Western Movies* (Minneapolis, Minn.: Woodbury Press, 1984), 322–351.
8. Rick Altman, *Film/Genre* (London: British Film Institute, 1999), 62.
9. Tag Gallagher, "Shoot-Out at the Genre Corral: Problems in the 'Evolution' of the Western," in *Film Genre Reader II,* ed. Barry Keith Grant (Austin: University of Texas Press, 1995), 202, 206. See also Matthew R. Turner, "Cowboys and Comedy: The Simultaneous Deconstruction and Reinforcement of Generic Conventions in Western Parodies," in *Hollywood's West: The American Frontier in Film, Television, and History,* ed. Peter C. Rollins and John E. O'Connor (Lexington: University Press of Kentucky, 2005), 220.
10. Jim Kitses, "Introduction: Post-modernism and the Western," in Kitses and Rickman, *Western Reader,* 17.
11. Ibid., 16.
12. William Cronon, George Miles, and Jay Gitlin, "Becoming West: Toward a New Meaning for Western History," in *Under an Open Sky: Rethinking America's Western Past,* ed. William Cronon, George Miles, and Jay Gitlin (New York: W. W. Norton, 1992), 25.
13. Steve Neale, *Genre and Hollywood* (London: Routledge, 2000), 134.
14. Elliott West, "American Frontier," in *The Oxford History of the American West,* ed. Clyde A. Milner II, Carol A. O'Connor, and Martha A. Sandweiss (New York: Oxford University Press, 1994), 105.
15. Lusted, *The Western,* 210.

16. Paul Arthur, "How the West Was Spun: *McCabe & Mrs. Miller* and Genre Revisionism," *Cineaste*, Summer 2003, 18.
17. John Cawelti, "*Chinatown* and Generic Transformation in Recent American Films," in *Film Theory and Criticism*, ed. Gerald Mast and Marshall Cohen, 3rd ed. (New York: Oxford University Press, 1985), 518.
18. Jack Nachbar, "Riding Shotgun: The Scattered Formula in Contemporary Western Movies," in *Focus on the Western*, ed. Jack Nachbar (Englewood Cliffs, N.J.: Prentice Hall, 1974), 103.
19. Kitses, "Introduction," 19.
20. "Bets and Bawds," pictorial, *Playboy*, September 1971, 103.
21. Robert Altman, "Robert Altman, Julie Christie, and Warren Beatty Make the Western Real," interview by Jacoba Atlas and Ann Guerin, *Show*, August 1971, 18.
22. Paul Zimmerman, "Virgin Wood," review of *McCabe & Mrs. Miller*, directed by Robert Altman, *Newsweek*, 5 July 1971, 71.
23. Stuart Rosenthal, "McCabe and Mrs. Miller," review of *McCabe & Mrs. Miller*, directed by Robert Altman, *Focus on Film*, Spring 1972, 8.
24. David Brudnoy, "Home on the Range," review of *McCabe & Mrs. Miller*, directed by Robert Altman, *National Review*, 22 October 1971, 1119.
25. George M. Boyd, "All Is Vanity," review of *McCabe & Mrs. Miller*, directed by Robert Altman, *Christian Century*, 27 October 1971, 127.
26. Jan Dawson, "*McCabe and Mrs. Miller*," review of *McCabe & Mrs. Miller*, directed by Robert Altman, *Sight and Sound* 40 (Autumn 1971): 221.
27. Quoted in Ernest Parmenter, "McCabe & Mrs. Miller," *Filmfacts* 14, no. 9 (1971): 192.
28. *McCabe & Mrs. Miller*, DVD (1971; Burbank, Calif.: Warner Home Video, 2002).
29. Robert Altman, *Altman on Altman*, ed. David Thompson (London: Faber & Faber, 2006), 59; Charles A. Baker, "The Theme of Structure in the Films of Robert Altman," *Journal of Popular Film* 2 (Summer 1973): 259.
30. Bruce Cook, "Hooray! 'McCabe' Is the Real McCoy!" review of *McCabe & Mrs. Miller*, directed by Robert Altman, *Washington Post*, 7 July 1971, 90.
31. Quoted in Parmenter, "McCabe & Mrs. Miller," 192.
32. William Pechter, "Stop That Cult," Review of *McCabe & Mrs. Miller*, directed by Robert Altman, *Commentary* 52 (November 1971): 40.
33. Cawelti, "*Chinatown* and Generic Transformation," 519.
34. Robert Altman, interview by Atlas and Guerin, 18, 21.
35. Altman, *Film/Genre*, 208.
36. F. Scott Fitzgerald, *The Great Gatsby*, chap. 9, http://etext.library.adelaide.edu.au/f/fitzgerald/f_scott/gatsby/chapter9.html.
37. Altman, *Film/Genre*, 89.
38. Ibid.
39. Thomas Schatz, *Hollywood Genres: Formulas, Filmmaking, and the Studio System* (New York: Random House, 1981), 31.
40. Louis L'Amour, *Hondo* (New York: Bantam, 1953), 1.
41. Kitses, "Introduction," 22.
42. Edward Buscombe, "Inventing Monument Valley: Nineteenth-Century Landscape Photography and the Western Film," in Kitses and Rickman, *Western Reader*, 118.
43. Ibid., 127.
44. Tompkins, *West of Everything*, 71, 74.

45. Lusted, *The Western*, 253.
46. Edmund Naughton, *McCabe* (New York: Berkley, 1959), 7.
47. Ibid., 7, 31.
48. John G. Cawelti, *Adventure, Mystery, and Romance: Formula Stories as Art and Popular Culture* (Chicago: University of Chicago Press, 1976), 39–40.
49. Frank McConnell, *Storytelling and Mythmaking: Images from Film and Literature* (New York: Oxford University Press, 1979), 17.
50. Richard Slotkin, *Regeneration through Violence: The Mythology of the American Frontier, 1600–1860* (Middletown, Conn.: Wesleyan University Press, 1973), 269.
51. Michael Marsden, "Savior in the Saddle: The Sagebrush Testament," in Nachbar, *Focus on the Western*, 95.
52. Mitchell, *Westerns*, 81–82.
53. Patricia Nelson Limerick, *The Legacy of Conquest: The Unbroken Past of the American West* (New York: W. W. Norton, 1987), 29.
54. Tompkins, *West of Everything*, 41.
55. Mitchell, *Westerns*, 17.
56. Susan Lee Johnson, "'A Memory Sweet to Soldiers': The Significance of Gender in the History of the 'American West,'" in *Women and Gender in the American West*, ed. Mary Ann Irwin and James F. Brooks (Albuquerque: University of New Mexico Press, 2004), 91.
57. Mitchell, *Westerns*, 3.
58. Johnson, "'A Memory Sweet,'" 92.
59. Blake Lucas, "Saloon Girls and Ranchers' Daughters: The Woman in the Western," in Kitses and Rickman, *Western Reader*, 301.
60. Pam Cook, "Women and the Western," in Kitses and Rickman, *Western Reader*, 293.
61. Robert Warshow, "Movie Chronicle: The Westerner," in *The Immediate Experience* (Garden City, N.J.: Doubleday, 1962), 137.
62. Cawelti, *Adventure, Mystery, and Romance*, 193.
63. Jim Kitses, *Horizons West: Anthony Mann, Budd Boetticher, Sam Peckinpah: Studies of Authorship within the Western* (Bloomington: Indiana University Press, 1969), 10–11.
64. Frank Gruber, "The 7 Ways to Plot a Western," *TV Guide*, 30 August 1958, 5–7.
65. Will Wright, *Sixguns and Society: A Structural Study of the Western* (Berkeley: University of California Press, 1975), 12.
66. Cawelti, *Adventure, Mystery, and Romance*, 194.
67. Wright, *Sixguns and Society*, 32.
68. Naughton, *McCabe*, 35–36.
69. Roger Ebert, "McCabe & Mrs. Miller (1971)," review of *McCabe & Mrs. Miller*, directed by Robert Altman, *RogerEbert.com: Movies and More*, 14 November 1999, http://rogerebert.suntimes.com/apps/pbcs.dll/article?AID=/19991114/REVIEWS08/911140301/1023.
70. Lauren Berlant, *The Anatomy of National Fantasy: Hawthorne, Utopia, and Everyday Life* (Chicago: University of Chicago Press, 1991), 5, 20.
71. Slotkin, *Regeneration through Violence*, 94.
72. Mitchell, *Westerns*, 135.
73. Sara L. Spurgeon, *Exploding the Western: Myths of Empire on the Postmodern Frontier* (College Station: Texas A&M University Press, 2005), 75.
74. William R. Handley, *Marriage, Violence, and the Nation in the American Literary West* (Cambridge: Cambridge University Press, 2002), 15.

75. Christopher Castiglia, *Bound and Determined: Captivity, Culture-Crossing, and White Womanhood from Mary Rowlandson to Patty Hearst* (Chicago: University of Chicago Press, 1996), xi.
76. Jane Tompkins, *Sensational Designs: The Cultural Work of American Fiction, 1790–1860* (New York: Oxford University Press, 1986), 145.
77. Mitchell, *Westerns*, 141.
78. Mary Murphy, "The Private Lives of Public Women: Prostitution in Butte, Montana, 1878–1917," in *The Women's West*, ed. Susan H. Armitage and Elizabeth Jameson (Norman: University of Oklahoma Press, 1987), 195.
79. Paula Petrik, *No Step Backward: Women and Family on the Rocky Mountain Mining Frontier, Helena, Montana, 1865–1900* (Helena: Montana Historical Society Press, 1987), 139.
80. Castiglia, *Bound and Determined*, 10.
81. Mitchell, *Westerns*, 143–144, 124.
82. Slotkin, *Regeneration through Violence*, 564.
83. Cawelti, *Adventure, Mystery, and Romance*, 38.
84. Robert Frost, "The Figure a Poem Makes," in *The Complete Poems of Robert Frost* (Boston: Holt, Rinehart & Winston, 1948), v.
85. Spurgeon, *Exploding the Western*, 3.
86. Cawelti, *Adventure, Mystery, and Romance*, 194.
87. Arthur, "How the West Was Spun," 18.
88. Adrian Danks, "Just Some Jesus Looking for a Manger: *McCabe & Mrs. Miller*," August 2002, *Senses of Cinema*, http://www.sensesofcinema.com/contents/cteq/00/9/mccabe.html.
89. Frost, *Complete Poems*, 53.
90. Slotkin, *Regeneration through Violence*, 564–565.

CHAPTER THREE. COUNTERCULTURAL CONTEXTS

1. Quoted in Terry Anderson, *The Sixties* (New York: Longman, 1999), 181.
2. Frank Davey, "Leonard Cohen and Bob Dylan: Poetry and the Popular Song," in *Leonard Cohen: The Artists and His Critics*, ed. Michael Gnarowski (Toronto: McGraw-Hill-Ryerson, 1976), 114.
3. Anderson, *The Sixties*, 181.
4. Ibid.
5. Bruce J. Schulman, *The Seventies: The Great Shift in American Culture, Society, and Politics* (New York: Free Press, 2001), 24.
6. Ibid., 145.
7. For example, Thomas Schatz, *Hollywood Genres: Formulas, Filmmaking, and the Studio System* (New York: Random House, 1981), 61.
8. John H. Lenihan, *Showdown: Confronting Modern America in the Western Film* (Urbana: University of Illinois Press, 1980), 4.
9. Ibid., 20.
10. Peter N. Carroll, *It Seemed Like Nothing Happened: The Tragedy and Promise of America in the 1970s* (New York: Holt, Rinehart & Winston, 1982), 24.
11. Schulman, *The Seventies*, 17.
12. Davey, "Leonard Cohen and Bob Dylan," 115, 118.

13. Quoted in Carroll, *It Seemed Like Nothing Happened*, 5.
14. Ibid., 87.
15. Ibid., 20, 21.
16. Patricia Nelson Limerick, *Something in the Soil: Legacies and Reckonings in the New West* (New York: W. W. Norton, 2000), 284.
17. "Codes of the West," at *Phantom Ranch*, http://www.phantomranch.net/bwestern/creeds.htm.
18. Students for a Democratic Society, "Port Huron Statement of the Students for a Democratic Society, 1962," http://coursesa.matrix.msu.edu/~hst306/documents/huron.html.
19. Annette Kolodny, *The Land before Her: Fantasy and Experience of the American Frontiers, 1630–1860* (Chapel Hill: University of North Carolina Press, 1984), 255.
20. Carroll, *It Seemed Like Nothing Happened*, 243.
21. Robert Altman, director's scene commentary/behind-the-scenes documentary, in *McCabe & Mrs. Miller*, DVD (1971; Burbank, Calif.: Warner Home Video, 2002).
22. Carroll, *It Seemed Like Nothing Happened*, 247.
23. Anderson, *The Sixties*, 99.
24. Lenihan, *Showdown*, 164.
25. Anderson, *The Sixties*, 88.
26. Edmund Naughton, *McCabe* (New York: Berkley, 1959), 336.
27. Sandra Kay Schackel, "Women in Western Films: The Civilizer, the Saloon Singer, and Their Modern Sister," in *Shooting Stars: Heroes and Heroines of Western Film*, ed. Archie P. McDonald (Bloomington: Indiana University Press, 1987), 197.
28. Carroll, *It Seemed Like Nothing Happened*, 34.
29. Anderson, *The Sixties*, 195.
30. Ibid., 217.
31. Quoted in Schulman, *The Seventies*, 164.
32. Ibid., 178.
33. Susan Lee Johnson, "'A Memory Sweet to Soldiers': The Significance of Gender in the History of the 'American West,'" in *Women and Gender in the American West*, ed. Mary Ann Irwin and James F. Brooks (Albuquerque: University of New Mexico Press, 2004), 101.
34. Helene Keyssar, *Robert Altman's America*, 3rd ed. (New York: Oxford University Press, 2000), 178.
35. Kolodny, *The Land before Her*, 11.
36. Naughton, *McCabe*, 18, 20.
37. Keyssar, *Robert Altman's America*, 182.
38. Ibid., 190.
39. Krista Comer, *Landscapes of the New West: Gender and Geography in Contemporary Women's Writing* (Chapel Hill: University of North Carolina Press, 1999), 56.
40. Robert Kolker, *A Cinema of Loneliness: Penn, Stone, Kubrick, Scorsese, Spielberg, Altman*, 3rd ed. (New York: Oxford University Press, 2000), 327.
41. Anderson, *The Sixties*, 35.
42. Paula Petrik, *No Step Backward: Women and Family on the Rocky Mountain Mining Frontier, Helena, Montana, 1865–1900* (Helena: Montana Historical Society Press, 1987), 25–58.
43. Comer, *Landscapes of the New West*, 6, 54, 57.
44. Patricia Nelson Limerick, "The Adventures of the Frontier in the Twentieth Cen-

tury," in *The Frontier in American Culture: An Exhibition at the Newberry Library, August 26, 1994–January 7, 1995,* ed. James R. Grossman (Berkeley: University of California Press, 1994), 76.
45. Kolodny, *The Land before Her,* 4.
46. Mary Louise Pratt, "Arts of the Contact Zone," *Profession,* Modern Language Association, 1991, 33–40; Gloria E. Anzaldúa, *Borderlands/La Frontera: The New Mestiza* (San Francisco: Spinsters/Aunt Lute Press, 1987).
47. Quoted in Claire Kramsch, "Thirdness: The Intercultural Space," in *Language, Culture and Identity,* ed. Torben Vestergaard (Aalborg, Denmark: Aalborg University Press, 1999), 14, 47.
48. Bhabha quoted in ibid., 47.
49. Quoted in ibid., 26.
50. Keyssar, *Robert Altman's America,* 198.
51. Carroll, *It Seemed Like Nothing Happened,* 267.
52. Schulman, *The Seventies,* 145.

CHAPTER FOUR. ALTMAN'S ART

1. Robert Altman, *Altman on Altman,* ed. David Thompson (London: Faber & Faber, 2006), 60. Vilmos Zsigmond, "A Conversation with Vilmos Zsigmond, ASC," by Bob Fisher, in *International Cinematographer's Guild,* June 2002, http://www.cameraguild.com/index.html?interviews/chat_zsigmond/index.htm~top.main_hp.
2. Ibid.
3. Robert Altman, ". . . They Take on a Life of Their Own . . . ," interview by Richard T. Jameson and Kathleen Murphy, *Movietone News* 55 (September 1977): 4.
4. Vilmos Zsigmond, "Moving Cameras, Moving Stories: An Interview with Vilmos Zsigmond," by Antony Teofilo, *Interviews from the Set of "Jersey Girl,"* n.d., http://www.jerseygirl-movie.com/interviews/12.html.
5. Thomas W. Bohn and Richard L. Stromgren, *Light and Shadows: A History of the Motion Picture* (Port Washington, N.Y.: Alfred Publishing, 1975), 460.
6. Glenn Man, *Radical Visions: American Film Renaissance, 1967–1976* (Westport, Conn.: Greenwood Press, 1994), 105.
7. Kristin Thompson, *Storytelling and the New Hollywood: Understanding Classical Narrative Techniques* (Cambridge, Mass.: Harvard University Press, 1999), 10.
8. Altman expresses the paradigms of this aesthetic in interviews throughout his career. See, e.g., Robert Altman, "Robert Altman: An Interview with the Noted Film Director," by James Martin, *In Touch* (July 1974), 72; and Robert Altman, "Reflections on *Short Cuts,*" interview in *Luck, Trust, and Ketchup: Robert Altman in Carver Country,* documentary, in *Short Cuts,* DVD (1993; Chatsworth, Calif.: Home Vision, Image Entertainment, 2004).
9. Emily Dickinson, 1129, "Tell all the Truth but tell it slant," http://poetry.eserver.org/dickinsonpoems.html.
10. Kamilla Elliott, *Rethinking the Novel/Film Debate* (New York: Cambridge University Press, 2003), 150.
11. Robert Altman, director's scene commentary/behind-the-scenes documentary, in *McCabe & Mrs. Miller,* DVD (1971; Burbank, Calif.: Warner Home Video, 2002).
12. Connie Bryne and William Lopez, "*Nashville* (an Interview 'Documentary')," *Film*

Quarterly 29 (Winter 1975–1976): 25. Altman expands on these views particularly in "Reflections on *Short Cuts*."
13. Altman, director's scene commentary, *McCabe & Mrs. Miller*.
14. Elliott, *Rethinking the Novel/Film Debate*, 157.
15. Edmund Naughton, *McCabe* (New York: Berkley, 1959), 56, 59, 60.
16. Helene Keyssar, *Robert Altman's America*, 3rd ed. (New York: Oxford University Press, 2000), 184.
17. *McCabe & Mrs. Miller* Archive, Daily Shooting Record, Robert Altman Collection, Wisconsin Center for Film and Theater Research, Wisconsin Historical Society, Madison.
18. Robert Altman, *Robert Altman Interviews*, ed. David Sterritt (Jackson: University Press of Mississippi, 2000), 196, and "Reflections on *Short Cuts*."
19. Peter Lehman, *Running Scared: Masculinity and the Representation of the Male Body* (Philadelphia: Temple University Press, 1993), 122.
20. Naughton, *McCabe*, 26.
21. Altman, *Altman on Altman*, 65.
22. Ibid., 64–65; Altman, director's scene commentary, *McCabe & Mrs. Miller*; *McCabe & Mrs. Miller* Archive, Daily Shooting Record, Robert Altman Collection, Wisconsin Center for Film and Theater Research, Wisconsin Historical Society, Madison.
23. Stephen Scobie, *Leonard Cohen* (Vancouver, B.C.: Douglas & McIntyre, 1978), 11.
24. Robert Kolker, *A Cinema of Loneliness: Penn, Stone, Kubrick, Scorsese, Spielberg, Altman*, 3rd ed. (New York: Oxford University Press, 2000), 327–328.
25. Keyssar, *Robert Altman's America*, 197.
26. David Bordwell, *Narration in the Fiction Film* (Madison: University of Wisconsin Press, 1985), 88.
27. Robert Altman, director's scene commentary, in *Gosford Park*, DVD (2001; Universal City, Calif.: Universal Studios Home Video, 2002).
28. Paul Arthur, "How the West Was Spun: *McCabe & Mrs. Miller* and Genre Revisionism," *Cineaste* 23 (Summer 2003): 19; Adrian Danks, "Just Some Jesus Looking for a Manger: *McCabe & Mrs. Miller*," *Senses of Cinema*, August 2002, http://www.sensesofcinema.com/contents/cteq/00/9/mccabe.html.
29. Altman, director's scene commentary, *McCabe & Mrs. Miller*.
30. Ernest Hemingway, "A Clean, Well-Lighted Place," in his short-story collection, *Winner Take Nothing* (New York: Scribner's, 1933); the text of the short story can be found at http://www.mrbauld.com/hemclean.html.
31. Walt Whitman, "When I Read the Book," in *Leaves of Grass*, http://whitman.classicauthors.net/leavesofgrass/leavesofgrass11.html.

EPILOGUE: VIOLENCE, DECLINE, AND DEATH

1. Robert Altman, *Robert Altman Interviews*, ed. David Sterritt (Jackson: University Press of Mississippi, 2000), 109.
2. Helene Keyssar, *Robert Altman's America*, 3rd ed. (New York: Oxford University Press, 2000), 188.
3. William Butler Yeats, "VI. Crazy Jane Talks with the Bishop," http://gutenberg.com/eBooks/BlackMask_Online/ytwist.htm#1_1_1.

BIBLIOGRAPHY

Altman, Rick. *Film/Genre.* London: British Film Institute, 1999.
Altman, Robert. *Altman on Altman.* Edited by David Thompson. London: Faber & Faber, 2005.
———. Director's Scene Commentary, Behind-the-Scenes Documentary. *McCabe & Mrs. Miller,* 1971. DVD. Burbank, Calif.: Warner Home Video, 2002.
———. Director's Scene Commentary, Behind-the-Scene Documentary, Background Documentary. *Gosford Park,* 2001. DVD. Universal City, Calif.: Universal Studios Home Video, 2002.
———. "M*A*S*H, McCloud and McCabe: An Interview with Robert Altman." By John Cutts. *Films and Filming* 18 (November 1971): 40–44.
———. *McCabe & Mrs. Miller* Archive. Robert Altman Collection. Wisconsin Center for Film and Theater Research. Wisconsin Historical Society, Madison, Wis.
———. "Reflections on *Short Cuts.*" Interview in *Luck, Trust, and Ketchup: Robert Altman in Carver Country.* Documentary in *Short Cuts,* 1993. DVD. Chatsworth, Calif.: Home Vision, Image Entertainment, 2004.
———. "Robert Altman: A Conversation." By Russell Auwerter. *Action!* 6 (January–February 1971): 2–4.
———. "Robert Altman: An Interview with the Noted Film Director." By James Martin. *In Touch,* July 1974, 67–76.
———. "Robert Altman, Julie Christie, and Warren Beatty Make the Western Real." Interview with Robert Altman. By Jacoba Atlas and Anne Guerin. *Show,* August 1971, 18–21.
———. "... They Take on a Life of Their Own ..." Interview by Richard T. Jameson and Kathleen Murphy. *Movietone News* 55 (September 1977): 2–13.
Altman, Robert, and David McKay. "McCabe & Mrs. Miller." Film Script. *McCabe & Mrs. Miller* Archive. Robert Altman Collection. Wisconsin Center for Film and Theater Research. Madison, Wisconsin.
Anderson, Terry. *The Sixties.* New York: Longman, 1999.
Armitage, Susan H. "Through Women's Eyes: A New View of the West." In *The Women's West,* edited by Susan H. Armitage and Elizabeth Jameson, 9–18. Norman: University of Oklahoma Press, 1987.
Arthur, Paul. "How the West Was Spun: *McCabe & Mrs. Miller* and Genre Revisionism." *Cineaste* 23 (Summer 2003): 18–20.
Baker, Charles A. "The Theme of Structure in the Films of Robert Altman." *Journal of Popular Film* 2 (Summer 1973): 243–261.
Berlant, Lauren. *The Anatomy of National Fantasy: Hawthorne, Utopia, and Everyday Life.* Chicago: University of Chicago Press, 1991.
Blair, Karen J., ed. *Women in Pacific Northwest History.* Rev. ed. Seattle: University of Washington Press, 2001.
Bohn, Thomas W., and Richard L. Stromgren. *Light and Shadows: A History of the Motion Picture.* Port Washington, N.Y.: Alfred Publishing, 1975.

Bordwell, David. *Narration in the Fiction Film.* Madison: University of Wisconsin Press, 1985.

Boyd, George M. "All Is Vanity." Review of *McCabe & Mrs. Miller,* directed by Robert Altman. *Christian Century,* 27 October 1971, 127.

Brauer, Ralph. "Who Are Those Guys? The Movie Western during the TV Era." In *Focus on the Western,* edited by Jack Nachbar. Englewood Cliffs, N.J.: Prentice Hall, 1974. 118–128.

Brudnoy, David. "Home on the Range." Review of *McCabe & Mrs. Miller,* directed by Robert Altman. *National Review,* 22 October 1971, 1119.

Bryne, Connie, and William Lopez. "*Nashville* (an Interview 'Documentary')." *Film Quarterly* 29 (Winter 1975–1976): 13–25.

Burgess, Jackson. "*McCabe and Mrs. Miller.*" *Film Quarterly* 25 (Winter 1971–1972): 49–53.

Burgoyne, Robert. *Film Nation: Hollywood Looks at U.S. History.* Minneapolis: University of Minnesota Press, 1997.

Buscombe, Edward. "Inventing Monument Valley: Nineteenth-Century Landscape Photography and the Western Film." In *The Western Reader,* edited by Jim Kitses and Gregg Rickman, 115–132. New York: Limelight Editions, 1998.

Butler, Anne M. *Daughters of Joy, Sisters of Misery: Prostitutes in the American West, 1865–90.* Urbana: University of Illinois Press, 1985.

Buttkus, Glenn. "Pudgy's Pipedream." Tacoma Film Club Annex, 16 July 2006. http://tfca.blogspot.com/2006/07/mccabe-mrs-miller-1971-by-buttkus.html.

Canby, Vincent. "*McCabe and Mrs. Miller.*" Review of *McCabe & Mrs. Miller,* directed by Robert Altman. *New York Times,* 26 June 1971, 87.

Carroll, Peter N. *It Seemed Like Nothing Happened: The Tragedy and Promise of America in the 1970s.* New York: Holt, Rinehart & Winston, 1982.

Castiglia, Christopher. *Bound and Determined: Captivity, Culture-Crossing, and White Womanhood from Mary Rowlandson to Patty Hearst.* Chicago: University of Chicago Press, 1996.

Cavallo, Dominick. *A Fiction of the Past: The Sixties in American History.* New York: St. Martin's Press, 1999.

Cawelti, John G. *Adventure, Mystery, and Romance: Formula Stories as Art and Popular Culture.* Chicago: University of Chicago Press, 1976.

———. "*Chinatown* and Generic Transformation in Recent American Films." In *Film Theory and Criticism,* edited by Gerald Mast and Marshall Cohen, 503–520. 3rd ed. New York: Oxford University Press, 1985.

———. "Reflections on the New Western Films." In *Focus on the Western,* edited by Jack Nachbar, 113–117. Englewood Cliffs, NJ: Prentice Hall, 1974.

———. *The Six-Gun Mystique.* Bowling Green, Ohio: Bowling Green University Popular Press, 1971.

Cocks, Jay. "*McCabe and Mrs. Miller.*" Review of *McCabe & Mrs. Miller,* directed by Robert Altman. *Time,* 27 July 1971, 51.

"Codes of the West." Phantom Ranch. http://www.phantomranch.net/bwestern/creeds.htm.

Cohen, Leonard. "Cohen's New Skin." Interview by Harvey Kubernik and Justin Pierce. *Melody Maker,* 1 March 1975. http://www.leonardcohenfiles.com/melmak2.html.

———. "Interviews and Newspaper Articles." *The Leonard Cohen Files.* http://www.leonardcohenfiles.com/.

Comer, Krista. *Landscapes of the New West: Gender and Geography in Contemporary Women's Writing.* Chapel Hill: University of North Carolina Press, 1999.

Cook, Bruce. "Hooray! 'McCabe' Is the Real McCoy!" Review of *McCabe & Mrs. Miller,* directed by Robert Altman. *Washington Post,* 7 July 1971, 90.

Cook, Pam. "Women and the Western." In *The Western Reader,* edited by Jim Kitses and Gregg Rickman, 293–300. New York: Limelight Editions, 1998.

Corkin, Stanley. *Cowboys as Cold Warriors: The Western and U. S. History.* Philadelphia: Temple University Press, 2004.

Coyne, Michael. *The Crowded Prairie: American National Identity in the Hollywood Western.* London: I. B. Tauris, 1998.

Cronon, William. "Kennecott Journey: The Paths out of Town." In *Under an Open Sky: Rethinking America's Western Past,* edited by William Cronon, George Miles, and Jay Gitlin, 28–51. New York: W. W. Norton, 1992.

Cronon, William, George Miles, and Jay Gitlin. "Becoming West: Toward a New Meaning for Western History." In *Under an Open Sky: Rethinking America's Western Past,* edited by William Cronon, George Miles, and Jay Gitlin, 3–27. New York: W. W. Norton, 1992.

Danks, Adrian. "Just Some Jesus Looking for a Manger: *McCabe & Mrs. Miller.*" *Senses of Cinema,* August 2002. http://www.sensesofcinema.com/contents/cteq/00/9/mccabe.html.

Davey, Frank. "Leonard Cohen and Bob Dylan: Poetry and the Popular Song." In *Leonard Cohen: The Artist and His Critics,* edited by Michael Gnarowski, 111–124. Toronto: McGraw-Hill-Ryerson, 1976.

Dawson, Jan. "*McCabe and Mrs. Miller.*" Review of *McCabe & Mrs. Miller,* directed by Robert Altman. *Sight and Sound* 40 (Autumn 1971): 221.

Dempsey, Michael. "Altman: The Empty Staircase and the Chinese Princess." *Film Comment,* September 1974, 10–17.

Denby, David. "The Sense of Period." Review of *McCabe & Mrs. Miller,* directed by Robert Altman. *Atlantic,* September 1971, 109–111.

Durham, Philip, and Everett L. Jones, eds. *The Western Story: Fact, Fiction, and Myth.* New York: Harcourt Brace Jovanovich, 1975.

Djwa, Sandra. "Leonard Cohen: Black Romantic." *Canadian Literature* 34 (Autumn 1967): 32–42.

Ebert, Roger. "McCabe & Mrs Miller." Review of *McCabe & Mrs. Miller,* directed by Robert Altman. *RogerEbert.com: Movies and More,* 14 November 1999. http://rogerebert.suntimes.com/apps/pbcs.dll/article?AID=/19991114/REVIEWS08/911140301/1023.

Elder, Sean. "Take This Longing from My Tongue." Salon Brilliant Careers, 15 June 1999. http://www.salon.com/people/bc/1999/06/15/cohen/index.html.

Elliott, Kamilla. *Rethinking the Novel/Film Debate.* New York: Cambridge University Press, 2003.

Engle, Gary. "*McCabe and Mrs. Miller:* Robert Altman's Anti-western." *Journal of Popular Film* 1 (Fall 1972): 268–287.

Enns, Chris. *Hearts West: True Stories of Mail-Order Brides on the Frontier.* Guilford, Conn.: Globe Pequot Press, 2005.

Etulain, Richard W. *Does the Frontier Experience Make America Exceptional?* New York: Bedfords/St.Martin's, 1999.

―――. "The Historical Development of the Western." *Journal of Popular Culture* 7 (Winter 1973): 717–727.

―――. *Re-imagining the Modern American West: A Century of Fiction, History, and Art.* Tucson: University of Arizona Press, 1996.

Gaines, Jane Marie, and Charlotte Cornelia Herzog. "The Fantasy of Authenticity in Western Costume." In *Back in the Saddle Again: New Essays on the Western,* edited by Edward Buscombe and Roberta E. Pearson, 182–196. London: British Film Institute, 1998.

Gallagher, Tag. "Shoot-Out at the Genre Corral: Problems in the 'Evolution' of the Western." In *Film Genre Reader* II, edited by Barry Keith Grant, 202–216. Austin: University of Texas Press, 1995.

Gerard, Lillian. "Belles, Sirens, Sisters." *Film Library Quarterly* 5 (Winter 1972): 14–16.

Goetzmann, William H., and William N. Goetzmann. *The West of the Imagination.* New York: W.W. Norton, 1986.

Goodwin, Michael. "*McCabe and Mrs. Miller.*" Review of *McCabe & Mrs. Miller,* directed by Robert Altman. *Take One* 2 (October 1971): 19–20.

Gnarowski, Michael, ed. *Leonard Cohen: The Artist and His Critics.* Toronto: McGraw-Hill, Ryerson, 1976.

Gruber, Frank. "The Basic Western Plots." *Writers Yearbook,* 49–53, 160. Cincinnati, Ohio: F & W Publications, 1955.

―――. "The 7 Ways to Plot a Western." *TV Guide,* 30 August 1958, 5–7.

Handley, William R. *Marriage, Violence, and the Nation in the American Literary West.* Cambridge: Cambridge University Press, 2002.

Hardy, Phil. *The Encyclopedia of Western Movies.* Minneapolis, Minn.: Woodberry Press, 1984.

Harmetz, Aljean. "The 15th Man Who Was Asked to Direct 'M*A*S*H' (and Did) Makes a Peculiar Western." *New York Times Magazine,* 20 June 1971, 10–11, 46–47, 49, 52–54.

Herron, William. "*McCabe and Mrs. Miller.*" Review of *McCabe & Mrs. Miller,* directed by Robert Altman. *Films in Review* 20 (August/September 1971): 440–41.

Hine, Robert V., and John Mack Faragher. *The American West: A New Interpretive History.* New Haven, Conn.: Yale University Press, 2000.

Hoberman, J. "How the West Was Lost." In *The Western Reader,* edited by Jim Kitses and Gregg Rickman, 85–92. New York: Limelight Editions, 1998.

Horwitz, James. *They Went Thataway.* New York: Ballantine Books, 1976.

Irwin, Mary Ann, and James F. Brooks, eds. *Women and Gender in the American West.* Albuquerque: University of New Mexico Press, 2004.

Johnson, Susan Lee. "'A Memory Sweet to Soldiers': The Significance of Gender in the History of the 'American West.'" In *Women and Gender in the American West,* edited by Mary Ann Irwin and James F. Brooks, 89–109. Albuquerque: University of New Mexico Press, 2004.

Jordanova, Ludmilla. "Objects of Knowledge: A Historical Perspective." In *The New Museology,* edited by Peter Vergo, 22–40. London: Reaktion Books, 1989.

Kael, Pauline. "Pipe Dream." Review of *McCabe & Mrs. Miller,* directed by Robert Altman. *New Yorker,* 3 July 1971, 40–42.

Kauffman, Stanley. "McCabe and Mrs. Miller." Review of *McCabe & Mrs. Miller,* directed by Robert Altman. *New Republic,* 4 September 1971, 26, 33.

Keller, Alexandra. "Historic Discourse and American Identity in Westerns since the Reagan Era." In *Hollywood's West: The American Frontier in Film, Television, and History,* edited by Peter C. Rollins and John E. O'Connor, 239–260. Lexington: University of Kentucky Press, 2005.

Keyssar, Helene. *Robert Altman's America*, 3rd. ed. New York: Oxford University Press, 2000.

Kitses, Jim. *Horizons West: Anthony Mann, Budd Boetticher, Sam Peckinpah: Studies of Authorship within the Western*. Bloomington: Indiana University Press, 1969.

———. "Introduction: Post-modernism and the Western." In *The Western Reader*, edited by Jim Kitses and Gregg Rickman, 15–34. New York: Limelight Editions, 1998.

Knight, Arthur. "SR Goes to the Movies." Review of *McCabe & Mrs. Miller*, directed by Robert Altman. *Saturday Review*, 24 July 1971, 51.

———. "The Technics and Techniques of Film." Review of *McCabe & Mrs. Miller*, directed by Robert Altman. *Saturday Review*, 7 August 1971, 31.

Kolker, Robert. *A Cinema of Loneliness: Penn, Stone, Kubrick, Scorsese, Spielberg, Altman*. 3rd ed. New York: Oxford University Press, 2000.

Kolodny, Annette. *The Land before Her: Fantasy and Experience of the American Frontiers, 1630–1860*. Chapel Hill: University of North Carolina Press, 1984.

———. "Letting Go of Our Grand Obsessions: Notes Toward a New Literary History of the American Frontiers." *American Literature* 64 (1992): 1–18.

Kowalewski, Michael, ed. *Reading the West: New Essays on the Literature of the American West*. New York: Cambridge University Press, 1996.

Kramsch, Claire. "Thirdness: The Intercultural Space." In *Language, Culture and Identity*, edited by Torben Vestergaard, 41–58. Aalborg, Denmark: Aalborg University Press, 1999.

Lackmann, Ronald. *Women of the Western Frontier in Fact, Fiction, and Film*. Jefferson, N.C.: McFarland & Co., 1997.

L'Amour, Louis. *Comstock Lode*. New York: Bantam, 1982.

———. *Hondo*. New York: Bantam, 1953.

Langford, Barry. "Revisiting the 'Revisionist' Western." *Film and History* 33 (2003): 26–35.

Lavine, Steven D., and Ivan Karp. "Introduction: Museums and Multiculturalism." In *Exhibiting Cultures: The Poetics and Politics of Museum Display*, edited by Ivan Karp and Steven D. Lavine, 1–10. Washington, D.C.: Smithsonian Institution Press, 1991.

Lehman, Peter. *Running Scared: Masculinity and the Representation of the Male Body*. Philadelphia: Temple University Press, 1993.

Lenihan, John H. *Showdown: Confronting Modern America in the Western Film*. Urbana: University of Illinois Press, 1980.

Levy, Peter B., ed. *America in the Sixties—Right, Left, and Center: A Documentary History*. Westport, Conn.: Greenwood Press, 1998.

Lewis, R. W. B. *The American Adam: Innocence, Tragedy, and Tradition in the Nineteenth Century*. Chicago: University of Chicago Press, 1955.

Limerick, Patricia Nelson. "The Adventures of the Frontier in the Twentieth Century." In *The Frontier in American Culture: An Exhibition at the Newberry Library, August 26, 1994–January 7, 1995*, edited by James R. Grossman, 67–102. Berkeley: University of California Press, 1994.

———. "Borderland vs. Frontier: Redefining the West: A Conversation with Patricia Nelson Limerick." *Humanities*, September/October 1996, 4–9, 47–51.

———. *The Legacy of Conquest: The Unbroken Past of the American West*. New York: W. W. Norton, 1987.

———. *Something in the Soil: Legacies and Reckonings in the New West.* New York: W. W. Norton, 2000.

Limerick, Patricia Nelson, Clyde A. Milner II, and Charles E. Rankin, eds. *Trails: Toward a New Western History.* Lawrence: University Press of Kansas, 1991.

Lipset, Seymour Martin. *American Exceptionalism: A Double-Edged Sword.* New York: W.W. Norton, 1997.

Lucas, Blake. "Saloon Girls and Ranchers' Daughters: The Woman in the Western." In *The Western Reader,* edited by Jim Kitses and Gregg Rickman, 301–320. New York: Limelight Editions, 1998.

Lusted, David. *The Western.* Harlow, England: Pearson Education, 2003.

Man, Glenn. *Radical Visions: American Film Renaissance, 1967–1976.* Westport, Conn.: Greenwood Press, 1994.

Marsden, Michael. "Savior in the Saddle: The Sagebrush Testament." In *Focus on the Western,* edited by Jack Nachbar, 93–100. Englewood Cliffs, N.J.: Prentice Hall, 1974.

Marx, Leo. *The Machine in the Garden: Technology and the Pastoral Ideal in America.* London: Oxford University Press, 1964.

Mayerson, Donald. "A Second Look at the Real *McCabe and Mrs. Miller. Cue,* 2 October 1971, 64.

McConnell, Frank. *Storytelling and Mythmaking: Images from Film and Literature.* New York: Oxford University Press, 1979.

Meyers, Robert B. "Theory Number One: Dissecting an Interpretation." *Journal of Popular Film* 2 (Summer 1973): 300–315.

Milner, Clyde A., II, Anne M. Butler, and David Rich Lewis, eds. *Major Problems in the History of the American West: Documents and Essays.* 2nd ed. Boston: Houghton Mifflin, 1997.

Mitchell, Lee Clark. *Westerns: Making the Man in Fiction and Film.* Chicago: University of Chicago Press, 1996.

Morgenstern, Joseph. "Up from the Anthill." Review of *McCabe & Mrs. Miller,* directed by Robert Altman. *Newsweek,* 2 August 1971, 9.

Murphy, Kathleen. "Anecdote of a Jar: On *McCabe and Mrs. Miller.*" Review of *McCabe & Mrs. Miller,* directed by Robert Altman. *Movietone News* 6 (September 1971): 5, 18–21.

Murphy, Mary. "The Private Lives of Public Women: Prostitution in Butte, Montana, 1878–1917." In *The Women's West,* edited by Susan H. Armitage and Elizabeth Jameson, 193–206. Norman: University of Oklahoma Press, 1987.

Myres, Sandra L. *Westering Women and the Frontier Experience, 1800–1915.* Albuquerque: University of New Mexico Press, 1982.

Nachbar, Jack. "Riding Shotgun: The Scattered Formula in Contemporary Western Movies." In *Focus on the Western,* edited by Jack Nachbar, 101–112. Englewood Cliffs, N.J.: Prentice Hall, 1974.

Nachbar, Jack, and Ray Merlock. "Bibliography: Trail Dust. Books about Western Movies: Selected Classics and Works since 1980." In *Hollywood's West: The American Frontier in Film, Television, and History,* edited by Peter C. Rollins and John E. O'Connor, 322–344. Lexington: University of Kentucky Press, 2005.

Naughton, Edmund. *McCabe.* New York: Berkley, 1959.

Neale, Steve. *Genre and Hollywood.* London: Routledge, 2000.

———. "Vanishing Americans: Racial and Ethnic Issues in the Interpretation and Context of Post-war 'Pro-Indian' Westerns." In *Back in the Saddle Again: New Essays on the*

Western, edited by Edward Buscombe and Roberta E. Pearson, 8–28. London: British Film Institute, 1998.

O'Connor, John E., and Peter C. Rollins. "The West, Westerns, and American Character." In *Hollywood's West: The American Frontier in Film, Television, and History*, edited by Peter C. Rollins and John E. O'Connor, 1–36. Lexington: University of Kentucky Press, 2005.

Ondaatje, Michael. *Leonard Cohen*. Toronto: McClelland & Stewart, 1970.

Parks, Rita. *The Western Hero in Film and Television: Mass Media Mythology*. Ann Arbor, Mich.: UMI Research Press, 1982.

Parmenter, Ernest. "McCabe & Mrs. Miller." Review of *McCabe & Mrs. Miller*, directed by Robert Altman. *Filmfacts* 14, no. 9 (1971): 192.

Paul, Rodman W. *Mining Frontiers of the Far West, 1848–1880*, revised by Elliott West. Albuquerque: University of New Mexico Press, 2001.

Pechter, William S. "Block That Cult." *Commentary* 52 (November 1971): 34–42.

Petrik, Paula. *No Step Backward: Women and Family on the Rocky Mountain Mining Frontier, Helena, Montana, 1865–1900*. Helena: Montana Historical Society Press, 1987.

Ravage, John W. *Black Pioneers: Images of the Black Experience on the North American Frontier*. Salt Lake City: University of Utah Press, 1997.

Rosenthal, Stuart. "McCabe and Mrs. Miller." Review of *McCabe & Mrs. Miller*, directed by Robert Altman. *Focus on Film*, Spring 1972, 8–9.

Rosenzweig, Roy. "The Rise of the Saloon." In *Eight Hours for What We Will: Workers and Leisure in an Industrial City, 1870–1920*, 35–64. New York: Cambridge University Press, 1983.

Sarris, Andrew. "Films in Focus." Review of *McCabe & Mrs. Miller*, directed by Robert Altman. *Village Voice*, 8 July 1971, 49.

Saunders, John. *The Western Genre: From Lordsburg to Big Whiskey*. London: Wallflower Press, 2001.

Savage, W. Sherman. *Blacks in the West*. Westport, Conn.: Greenwood Press, 1976.

Schackel, Sandra Kay. "Women in Western Films: The Civilizer, the Saloon Singer, and Their Modern Sister." In *Shooting Stars: Heroes and Heroines of Western Film*, edited by Archie P. McDonald, 196–217. Bloomington: Indiana University Press, 1987.

Schatz, Thomas. *Hollywood Genres: Formulas, Filmmaking, and the Studio System*. New York: Random House, 1981.

Schickel, Richard. "*Life* Goes to the Movies." Review of *McCabe & Mrs. Miller*, directed by Robert Altman. *Life*, 17 September 1971, 15.

Schjeldahl, Peter. "McCabe and Mrs. Miller: A Sneaky-Great Movie." Review of *McCabe & Mrs. Miller*, directed by Robert Altman. *New York Times*, 24 July 1971.

Schulman, Bruce J. *The Seventies: The Great Shift in American Culture, Society, and Politics*. New York: Free Press, 2001.

Schwantes, Carlos Arnaldo. *The Pacific Northwest: An Interpretive History*. Lincoln: University of Nebraska Press, 1996.

Scobie, Stephen. "The Counterfeiter Begs Forgiveness: Leonard Cohen and Leonard Cohen." *Canadian Poetry* 33 (Fall/Winter 1993). http://www.uwo.ca/english/canadian poetry/cpjrn/vol33/scobie.htm.

———. *Leonard Cohen*. Vancouver, Canada: Douglas & McIntyre, 1978.

Seagraves, Anne. *Soiled Doves: Prostitution in the Early West*. Hayden, Idaho: Wesanne Publications, 1994.

Sears, Roebuck & Co. *Consumers Guide,* catalog no. 110 (Fall 1900). Northfield, Ill.: Gun Digest Publishing, 1970.

Self, Robert. "Author, Text, and Self in *Buffalo Bill and the Indians.*" In *Ambiguity in Literature and Film,* edited by Hans Braendlin, 104–116. Gainesville: University Press of Florida, 1998.

———. "The Modernist Art of Robert Altman." *Senses of Cinema.* n.d. http://www.sensesofcinema.com/contents/directors/05/altman.html.

———. "Ritual Patterns in Western Film and Fiction," In *Narrative Strategies: Original Essays in Film and Prose Fiction,* edited by Syndy Conger and Janice Welsch, 105–114. Macomb: Western Illinois Press, 1981.

———. *Robert Altman's Subliminal Reality.* Minneapolis: University of Minnesota Press, 2002.

Shalit, Gene. "Beatty and Christie and *McCabe and Mrs. Miller*—Stop." Review of *McCabe & Mrs. Miller,* directed by Robert Altman. *Look,* 10 August 1971, 44.

Siemerling, Winfried. *Discoveries of the Other: Alterity in the Work of Leonard Cohen, Hubert Aquin, Michael Ondaatje, and Nicole Brossard.* Toronto: University of Toronto Press, 1994.

Simmon, Scott. *The Invention of the Western Film: A Cultural History of the Genre's First Half-Century.* Cambridge: Cambridge University Press, 2003.

Simon, John. "An Appalling Plague Has Been Loosed on Our Films." Review of *McCabe & Mrs. Miller,* directed by Robert Altman. *New York Times,* 18 September 1971, 132–133.

Simonson, Harold P. *The Closed Frontier: Studies in American Literary Tragedy.* New York: Holt, Rinehart & Winston, 1970.

Slotkin, Richard. *Gunfighter Nation: The Myth of the Frontier in Twentieth-Century America.* New York: Atheneum, 1992.

———. *Regeneration through Violence: The Mythology of the American Frontier, 1600–1860.* Middletown, Conn.: Wesleyan University Press, 1973.

Smith, Henry Nash. *Virgin Land: The American West as Symbol and Myth.* New York: Vintage, 1950.

Spurgeon, Sara L. *Exploding the Western: Myths of Empire on the Postmodern Frontier.* College Station: Texas A&M University Press, 2005.

Steckmesser, Kent Ladd. *The Western Hero in History and Legend.* Norman: University of Oklahoma Press, 1965.

Sterritt, David, ed. *Robert Altman Interviews.* Jackson: University Press of Mississippi, 2000.

Students for a Democratic Society. "Port Huron Statement of the Students for a Democratic Society, 1962." http://coursesa.matrix.msu.edu/~hst306/documents/huron.html.

Thompson, Kristin. *Storytelling and the New Hollywood: Understanding Classical Narrative Techniques.* Cambridge, Mass.: Harvard University Press, 1999.

Thoreau, Henry David. *Walden.* Boston: Houghton Mifflin, 1960.

Tompkins, Jane. *Sensational Designs: The Cultural Work of American Fiction, 1790–1860.* New York: Oxford University Press, 1986.

———. *West of Everything: The Inner Life of Westerns.* New York: Oxford University Press, 1992.

Turner, Frederick Jackson. "The Significance of the Frontier in American History." In *Proceedings of the Forty-First Annual Meeting of the State Historical Society of Wiscon-*

sin, 79–112 . Madison: State Historical Society of Wisconsin, 1894.

Turner, Matthew R. "Cowboys and Comedy: The Simultaneous Deconstruction and Reinforcement of Generic Conventions in Western Parody." In *Hollywood's West: The American Frontier in Film, Television, and History*, edited by Peter C. Rollins and John E. O'Connor, 218–238. Lexington: University Press of Kentucky, 2005.

Turner, Ralph Lamar, and Robert J. Higgs. *The Cowboy Way: The Western Leader in Film, 1945–1995*. Westport, Conn.: Greenwood Press, 1999.

Twain, Mark. *Roughing It.* Hartford, Conn.: American Publishing Co., 1871.

Vergo, Peter. "The Reticent Object." In *The New Museology*, edited by Peter Vergo, 41–59. London: Reaktion Books, 1989.

Walker, Janet. "Captive Images in the Traumatic Western: *The Searchers, Pursued, Once upon a Time in the West*, and *Lone Star*." In *Westerns: Films through History*, edited by Janet Walker, 219–252. New York: Routledge, 2001.

———. "Introduction: Westerns through History." In *Westerns: Films through History*, edited by Janet Walker, 1–26. New York: Routledge, 2001.

Walsh, Moira. "*Hoa Binh*." Review of *McCabe & Mrs. Miller*, directed by Robert Altman. *America*, 11 September 1971, 153.

Warshow, Robert. "Movie Chronicle: The Westerner." In *The Immediate Experience*, 135–154. Garden City, N.J.: Doubleday, 1962.

West, Elliott. "American Frontier." In *The Oxford History of the American West*, edited by Clyde A. Milner II, Carol A. O'Connor, and Martha A. Sandweiss, 115–150. New York: Oxford University Press, 1994.

———. "Beyond Baby Doe: Child Rearing on the Mining Frontier." In *The Women's West*, edited by Susan H. Armitage and Elizabeth Jameson, 179–192. Norman: University of Oklahoma Press, 1987.

———. "A Longer, Grimmer, but More Interesting Story." In *Trails: Toward a New Western History*, edited by Patricia Nelson Limerick, Clyde A. Milner II, and Charles E. Rankin, 103–111. Lawrence: University Press of Kansas, 1991.

Westerbeck, Colin L. "Revamping the Vamp." Review of *McCabe & Mrs. Miller*, directed by Robert Altman. *Commonweal* 94 (August 1971): 407–408.

White, Richard. "Frederick Jackson Turner and Buffalo Bill." In *The Frontier in American Culture: An Exhibition at the Newberry Library, August 26, 1994–January 7, 1995*, edited by James R. Grossman, 67–70. Berkeley: University of California Press, 1994.

———. *"It's Your Misfortune and None of My Own": A New History of the American West*. Norman: University of Oklahoma Press, 1991.

Williams, Carol J. *Framing the West: Race, Gender, and the Photographic Frontier in the Pacific Northwest*. Oxford: Oxford University Press, 2003.

Worland, Rick, and Edward Countryman. "The New Western American Historiography and the New American Westerns." In *Back in the Saddle Again: New Essays on the Western*, edited by Edward Buscombe and Roberta E. Pearson, 182–196. London: British Film Institute, 1998.

Wright, Will. *Sixguns and Society: A Structural Study of the Western*. Berkeley: University of California Press, 1975.

Wyatt, Justin. "Economic Constraints/Economic Opportunities: Robert Altman as Auteur." *Velvet Light Trap* 38 (1996): 51–67.

Zimmerman, Paul. "Virgin Wood." Review of *McCabe & Mrs. Miller*, directed by Robert Altman. *Newsweek*, 5 July 1971, 71–72.

Zone, Ray, ed. *New Wave King: The Cinematography of Laszlo Kovacs.* Hollywood, Calif.: ASC Press, 2002.

Zsigmond, Vilmos. "A Conversation with Vilmos Zsigmond, ASC." By Bob Fisher. *International Cinematographer's Guild,* 1 June 2002. http://www.cameraguild.com/index.html?interviews/chat_zsigmond/index.htm~top.main_hp.

———. "Moving Cameras, Moving Stories: An Interview with Vilmos Zsigmond," by Antony Teofilo. *Interviews from the Set of "Jersey Girl."* n.d. http://www.jerseygirl-movie.com/interviews/12.html.

———. "SOC Interview with Vilmos Zsigmond, ASC." *Operating Cameraman,* Spring 1995. http://www.soc.org/opcam/06_sp95/mg06_vilmos.html.

———. "Vilmos Zsigmond, ASC Shares Some Thoughts about the Art and Craft of Motion-Picture Lighting." By Jon Silberg. *American Cinematographer,* October 2004. http://www.theasc.com/magazine/oct04/vilmos/page1.html.

INDEX

Academy Awards, 122, 153, 158, 178
adaptation, film. *See under McCabe (novel)*
African Americans, 23, 84
alcoholism, 42
Allen, Woody, 52
Almighty Alma, 38, 149
Altman, Rick, 58, 59
Altman, Robert, 52, 105–106, 133–134, 138
    as auteur, 165
    award nominations, 178
    on cinematography, 137
    death, 178
    as director, 57, 133
    filmmaking style, 8, 9, 10, 56, 58, 137, 138, 140–142, 144–145, 158, 164–165, 169, 172, 178
    films of (*see individual titles*)
    on genre, 6
    on narrative film, 11
    photos, 100
    as popular director, 57, 133
    reputation for misogyny, 133
    on subliminal reality, 142, 144
    television work, 56
    use of soundtrack, 157–158, 165
    on westerns, 55–56
American Art Cinema, 3, 12, 138. *See also* art cinema
Anderson, Terry, 116, 119
antiwar movement, 109–110
antiwesterns, 5, 54
Anzaldúa, Gloria, 130
art cinema, 9, 11, 138, 141, 142, 147, 164, 165, 172
Arthur, Paul, 2, 88, 169
auteurs, 138–139, 164
Autry, Gene, 16, 111

baby boomers, 110–111

Ballad of Little Jo, The, 53
Bart Coyle, 46–47, 84, 85, 115, 150, 168
Beatles, 108
Beatty, Warren, 91 (photo), 100 (photo), 100113–114, 133, 153, 154
"Beautiful Dreamer," 20–21, 41, 163
Bergman, Ingmar, 138
Berlant, Lauren, 76
Bhabha, Homi, 130, 131
Bierstadt, Albert, 61–62, 170
Birdie, 148
Blazing Saddles, 54, 89, 103
Bohn, Thomas, 139
Bonanza, 29, 51, 56
Bonnie and Clyde, 110, 113, 133, 153
Boone, Daniel, 78
Bordwell, David, 165
"Brahms Lullaby," 163
Breed, 177
Brewster McCloud, 8, 103, 106, 133
brothels, 115, 124–126, 129. *See also* prostitutes, creation of community
Brunetière, Ferdinand, 52
Buffalo Bill (William F. Cody), 9–10, 17–18, 52, 65, 77, 104
Buffalo Bill and the Indians, or Sitting Bull's History Lesson, 6, 9–10, 19, 51, 57, 133, 139, 172
Bullette, Julia C., 20
Bumppo, Natty, 65, 66
Buñuel, Luis, 138
Burgoyne, Robert, 19
Buscombe, Edward, 62
business, 2, 4, 26, 49, 75, 114–118
    corporate greed, 9, 74, 104, 128, 172
Butch Cassidy and the Sundance Kid, 54, 89
Butler, 49, 64, 70, 75, 97 (photo), 116, 146, 152, 155, 157, 161
Butler, Anne, 31, 35, 36, 41, 42

201

California Split, 8, 106, 133, 170
camera work, 137, 150
capitalism, 13, 90, 111
captivity narratives, 5–8, 76, 78–81, 83–84
Carradine, Keith, 151, 158, 176
Cassavetes, John, 9, 52, 138
Castiglia, Christopher, 80, 81
Cat Ballou, 52, 132
Cawelti, John, 54, 57, 64, 71, 72, 87, 88
Champlin, Charles, 56
Cheyenne Autumn, 89
Chicago Jo. *See* Hensley, Josephine
Chinese, 23–24
Chinese Exclusion Act of 1886, 23
Christie, Julie, photo, 91 (photos), 122, 126, 153
churches
    in mining camps, 8, 29, 30, 62
    as symbols, 31
church in Presbyterian Church, Wash., 1, 20, 22, 27, 29, 31, 39, 44, 115–116, 127–128, 143, 149–150, 156, 157, 166, 167, 171
    fire at, 41, 42, 75, 84, 115–116, 152, 168, 169, 172
cinematography, 165, 170–171
civil rights movement, 110
Classical Narrative Cinema, 11, 140
"Clean Well-Lighted Place, A," 171
Close Encounters of the Third Kind, 136
Code of the West, 111
Cody, William F. *See* Buffalo Bill
Cohen, Leonard, 12, 17, 158, 162, 166, 173
    lyrics, 119, 136, 138, 159, 164
    popularity of, 108–109
    "Sisters of Mercy," 82, 115, 125, 157, 159, 161–162, 169
    "Suzanne," 109
    "The Stranger Song," 1, 4, 21, 85, 86, 157, 158, 159–161, 168
    "Winter Lady," 86, 157, 159, 161
colonialism, 130
Colt .45, 16
Come Back to the 5 & Dime, Jimmy Dean, Jimmy Dean, 134
Comer, Krista, 124, 126
Company, The, 158
Comstock Lode, 65–66

Cookie's Fortune, 134
Cooper, Gary, 5, 113, 120
Cooper, James Fenimore, 52, 65, 66
Coppola, Francis Ford, 9, 52
counterculture, 101–109, 114, 116, 118, 132–134. *See also* antiwar movement; civil rights movement; women's movement
Cowboy, 41, 68, 74, 134, 147, 150–152, 163, 176–178
cowboy creeds, 111
Crane, Stephen, 52
Custer, George Armstrong, 104–105

Dances with Wolves, 21, 53
Danks, Adrian, 88, 169
Davey, Frank, 101, 108
Deadly Affair, The, 135
Dead Man, 53
Deer Hunter, The, 136
Deliverance, 136
Dempsey, Michael, 50
Destiny Rides Again, 50, 63
Devane, William, 111
directors, 52, 54, 138–139, 164. *See also* auteurs
diversity, ethnic and racial, 23
Domesticity, Cult of, 21, 31, 34, 35
Dr. T & the Women, 133
drugs, 42, 107–108, 114
Dunn, Mrs., 24, 31, 82, 150
Duvall, Shelly, 36, 124
Dylan, Bob, 87, 101–102, 106–107, 108–109, 124, 132

East, 71
Eastwood, Clint, 68
Easy Rider, 166
Ebert, Roger, 57, 75
economy, western, 27
editing, 168–169
Elliot, Reverend, 30, 143, 147, 150
Elliott, Kamilla, 142, 145
environmentalism, 58–59
Ericksen, Leon, 11, 137, 170
expressionism, 150, 166
extraction industry, 12, 14, 22, 24–26, 73. *See also* mining

202 **INDEX**

families, 30–31, 32
Far Country, The, 29, 50
fashion, 27–28, 47
Fellini, Federico, 138
feminism, 9, 36, 106, 118, 133. *See also* women's movement
feminist criticism, 68, 80, 120–121
film criticism, 10
Fitzgerald, F. Scott, 59
flashing, 135–137, 162
Flynn, Errol, 104
Fonda, Jane, 52, 132
footbridge. *See under* Sheehan's Saloon
Ford, John, 16, 89, 104
frontier, 5, 7, 49. *See also* Turner, Frederick Jackson
   as borderland, 71, 76, 129
   definition of, 19, 127
   economy of, 50
   history of, 18, 173
   myth of, 43, 130, 162
   and national identity, 53–54
   in revisionist westerns, 43
   women on, 35, 40, 42, 68
Frontier Thesis. *See* Turner, Frederick Jackson
Frost, Robert, 88, 89
funerals, 46, 47

gamblers, 32, 66, 67, 81, 89, 169
gambling, 2, 4, 32–33, 73, 113, 114, 127
   on mining frontier, 22, 30, 31, 41, 43
   and prostitution, 122
Garner, James, 5
gender roles, 4, 71, 83–84, 101, 123, 131
genre, 6, 50, 57–63
   revisions of, 51–52, 88–89, 132
   transformation of, 54
genre criticism, 52
genre fiction, 87
Geronimo, 53
Gilded Age, 31, 35
Gingerbread Man, The, 89, 133
Godard, Jean-Luc, 138
gold rush, 28
Good, the Bad, the Ugly, The, 54
Gosford Park, 89, 133, 134, 144, 145, 149, 178
Graduate, The, 109, 113, 116, 133, 166

Grateful Dead, 108
Great Northfield Minnesota Raid, The, 54
Grey, Zane, 84
Gruber, Frank, 72
Gunfighter, The, 53
gunfighters, 33
gunfights, 47–48, 49, 71, 74, 98 (photo), 116, 177
guns, 4, 5, 20
Gunsmoke, 5, 47, 51, 63

Hanging Tree, The, 7
Hannie Caulder, 89, 132
Hardy, Phil, 51
Harrison Shaughnessy Mining Company
   conflict with McCabe, 74, 125, 130, 148, 153
   hitmen of, 43, 115–116 (*see also* killers)
   plot to take Presbyterian Church, 1–2, 40, 117
   power of, 28
   significance of corporate name, 26
   as villain, 63, 73
Hart, William S. ("Two-Gun"), 16, 65, 87
Harte, Bret, 66, 67
Heaven's Gate, 16
Hemingway, Ernest, 16, 48, 87–88, 171
Hendrix, Jimi, 108
Hensley, Josephine (Chicago Jo), 2
heroes, 64–65, 72, 73, 76, 89–90, 113, 120, 132
Heston, Charleton, 113
heterosexuality, 80
High Noon, 49, 50, 53, 63, 89
High Plains Drifter, 54, 103
historiography, 15, 17, 19, 21, 44
Hoffman, Dustin, 113, 116
Hollywood Production Code, 37
Hollywood Renaissance, 52, 138, 139, 165
homosociality, 68
Hopalong Cassidy, 111

Ida Coyle, 124
Images, 106, 134, 170
immigrants, 23–24
impressionism, 162, 163
improvisation, 166
Indians (Native Americans), 44–45, 77–78, 79, 130

Indians, 57
individualism, 28, 54, 89
International Art Cinema, 9, 11, 138. *See also* art cinema
Irish, 23

James, Jesse, 104
Jaws, 139
Jeremiah Johnson, 54
Johnny Guitar, 53, 89
Johnson, Susan, 68, 120
Joplin, Janis, 108
Joyce, James, 11
juxtaposition, 146–147, 150, 168

Kansas City, 134, 158
Keaton, Buster, 52
Kellerman, Sally, 133
Keyssar, Helene, 120, 122, 123, 131, 148, 164, 178
Kid, 20, 176, 177
killers
    arrival of, 170
    McCabe's negotiations with, 3, 117, 154
    McCabe's shootout with, 47, 49, 74, 169
    in novel *McCabe*, 48, 143
    as stereotypical villains, 63
Kitses, Jim, 53, 55, 71
Klute, 132–133
Kolker, Robert, 125, 159
Kolodny, Annette, 111, 121, 128
Kopit, Arthur, 57
Kubrick, Stanley, 9, 138, 170
Kurosawa, Akira, 138

L'Amour, Louis, 61, 65
landscape, 62
Last of the Mohicans, The, 53
Lehman, Peter, 151
Lenihan, John, 104, 116
Leone, Sergio, 4, 55
Limerick, Patricia, 18, 19, 22, 26, 33, 38, 42, 67, 110–111
Little Big Man, 4, 54, 89, 103, 105, 110, 113
logging, 24–25
Lone Ranger, 111
lone rider, 1, 21, 29, 61, 159, 167

Long Goodbye, The, 106, 133, 175
Lucas, George, 52
Luhrmann, Baz, 60
Lumet, Sidney, 135
Lusted, David, 47, 63

Maclean, Norman, 29
mail-order brides, 8, 36, 46, 82, 85, 124, 147, 148
Man, Glenn, 139
Manifest Destiny, 6, 8, 15, 21, 42, 54, 57, 77, 90
Mann, Anthony, 29
Man Who Shot Liberty Valance, The, 17, 46, 89
masculinity, 4, 29, 34, 67–68, 70, 81, 84, 113, 151–152
MASH, 8, 88, 103, 106, 115, 133, 144, 164, 176, 178
Maverick, 5, 61
McCabe (novel), 63–64, 74, 111–112, 118, 121–123
    adaptation of, 123, 142–143, 145–146, 173
    showdown as structural device in, 48, 159
McCabe, John, 1, 2, 61, 63–64, 72, 74, 90, 114, 152, 154–155
    photos, 91–93, 95, 97, 99
    as western hero, 66–67
McCabe & Mrs. Miller
    advertising for, 55
    as cinema painting, 169–170
    cinematography, 12, 135–137, 164
    DVD release, 56, 88
    editing, 12
    feminist perspectives on 126, 129, 131
    location, 45
    as museum, 20, 23, 45, 46, 168
    music, 157, 158–159, 162, 163, 166
    plot, 143–144
    production, 3, 8, 12, 29, 44, 105, 109, 150, 154, 156–158, 160, 165, 170, 172
    reviews, 55–57, 164
    set design, 11, 26–27, 137, 169, 170, 172, 177
    shoot, 107, 157
    sound, 165–166
    soundtrack, 12, 20, 108–109, 164, 169

204 **INDEX**

synopsis, 48–49
time of action, 156–157
McCrea, Joel, 120
McKinley, William, 28, 29, 43, 44
McMurtry, Larry, 65
Mean Streets, 110
Midnight Cowboy, 113
Millais, Hugh, 114
mining, 22–26, 32, 46, 128. *See also* extraction industry
mining camps, 22–23, 27, 62
misogyny, 81, 133
Miss Kitty, 5, 63, 106
Mitchell, Lee, 47, 66, 67, 79, 83
modernism, 172
modernist cinema, 140–141
Monte Walsh, 89
Moulin Rouge! 60–61
Miller, Mrs. Constance, 1, 2, 33, 68, 90, 91 (photo), 94–97 (photos), 99 (photo), 121–125, 131, 153, 155
museums, 15–16, 19–20, 37
musicals, 6, 59–60
My Darling Clementine, 62, 89
Myres, Sandra, 34
myth, 88, 89–90, 126, 173

Nachbar, Jack, 55
Nashville, 88, 107, 115, 144, 149, 157, 172, 175, 176, 178
national identity, 5, 12, 53, 76, 102, 131–132
national narratives, 6, 76–77, 78
Native Americans, 44–45, 77–78, 79, 130
Naughton, Edmund, 48, 118, 142, 173
Neale, Steve, 53
New Hollywood Cinema, 52, 103, 106, 139, 174
New Left, 111
New Western History, 17–19, 45, 106
Nichols, Mike, 9, 52
Nixon, Richard, 47, 53, 103, 106, 109, 112, 132, 133
North to Alaska, 7
nudity, 107

Once Upon a Time in the West, 4, 21
Oregon Trail, 28
Ox-Bow Incident, The, 53

Paleface, 52
Pechter, William, 57
Peck, Gregory, 113
Peckinpah, Sam, 4, 9, 52, 55
Penn, Arthur, 4, 9, 52, 55, 105
Perfect Couple, A, 134, 158
Petrik, Paula, 27, 31, 36, 39, 41, 42, 126
Pinto Kate, 38, 82
Pioneers, The, 52
Player, The, 144, 172, 175, 178
politicians, 112–113
Pollack, Sidney, 52
Popeye, 134, 139
Port Huron Statement, 111, 118
Prairie Home Companion, 151, 164
Pratt, Mary Louise, 130
Presbyterian Church, Wash., 14, 22–28, 30, 31, 66, 72, 81, 126–129
growth of, 1, 26–27, 86, 156
photos, 92, 94–96
prostitution in, 5, 8, 38–41, 82, 149
target of Harrison Shaughnessy Mining Company, 2, 73, 116–118
Prêt-à-Porter, 172
progressive movement, 28, 35
prospecting, 32
prostitutes
creation of community, 41, 124–126, 162
drug use among, 107
life of, 41–42
in mining camps, 30
as natural resource, 129
photos, 93
in western history, 19, 106
in westerns, 67, 89
prostitution, 132–133, 178
as captivity narrative, 5, 8, 80–81, 82, 123
demographics of, 40, 149
in Helena, Mont., 31–32, 39, 41
and substance abuse, 108
in western history, 2, 33–34, 41–42, 46, 173
in westerns, 67
as women's work, 36–40

Quick and the Dead, The, 53
Quintet, 170

INDEX 205

Ready to Wear. See Prêt-à-Porter
realism, 137, 142, 150, 162–165
reflexivity, 6, 9, 138, 141, 172
religion, 5, 39, 46, 62, 75, 80, 114–118, 119, 128
Riders of the Purple Sage, 84
Ride the High Country, 7
Rio Bravo, 63
River Runs through It, A, 29
Rocky, 139
Rocky Mountains, 61–62
Rogers, Roy, 16, 111
"room of one's own," 123
Roosevelt, Theodore, 17, 28–29, 35, 43, 77
Rowlandson, Mary, 121
Run of the Arrow, 53

saloons, 24, 62–63
Scarecrow, 139
Schackel, Sandra, 118
Schatz, Thomas, 52, 60
Schatzberg, Jerry, 139
Schulman, Bruce, 103, 108, 132
Scobie, Stephen, 159
Searchers, The 21, 46, 50, 79, 82, 83, 89
Secret Honor, 133
semantics (of genre), 59
set design. *See under* McCabe & Mrs. Miller
sex trade. *See* prostitution
Shampoo, 113
Shane, 7, 46, 62, 63, 72
Sheehan, Patrick, 147, 166, 168, 170, 171, 177
    on Chinese, 23
    deal with Harrison Shaughnessy Mining Company, 117
    in film adaptation, 143, 146
    negotiation with McCabe, 127
    in novel *McCabe,* 75, 122, 143
    Sheehan's Saloon, 3, 33, 127, 128, 146, 170–171
    description of, 22, 63
    footbridge, 63, 151, 166–168, 170, 177–178
    and immigrant community, 8, 24
    photo, 92
    and set design, 27
shootouts. *See* gunfights

Short Cuts, 144, 158, 175, 178
showdowns. *See* gunfights
"Silent Night," 20, 41, 115, 147, 148
Simon and Garfunkel, 109
"Sisters of Mercy" (Cohen), 82, 115, 125, 157, 159, 161–162, 169
sixties, 102, 103, 131–132
Slotkin, Richard, 17, 78, 85, 89
space, 117–118, 126–134, 129
    third, 126, 130–131
spaghetti westerns, 4
Spielberg, Steven, 52, 139
spirituality, alternative, 114
Spurgeon, Sara, 88
Stagecoach, 50, 51, 52, 89, 104
Stars in My Crown, 62
Star Wars, 140
storytelling, 141, 144–151, 155–156, 173
"Stranger Song, The" (Cohen), 1, 4, 21, 85, 86, 157, 158, 159–161, 168
Stromgren, Richard, 139
subliminal reality, 142, 144, 164
Superman, 140
"Suzanne," 109
syntax (of genre), 59–60

Tanner '88, 133
Tanner on Tanner, 134
That Cold Day in the Park, 106, 151, 158
They Died with Their Boots On, 104–105
Thieves like Us, 106, 133, 134, 176
Thompson, Kristin, 141
Thoreau, Henry David, 14
3 Women, 134, 158
Tompkins, Jane, 34, 48, 50, 62, 67, 80
"traumatic" westerns, 21
True Womanhood, Cult of, 35, 46, 66
Truffaut, François, 138
Tumbleweeds, 16, 17, 87
Turner, Frederick Jackson, 7, 17–18, 22, 35, 43, 58, 65, 77
Twain, Mark, 2, 32, 52, 111
Two-for-One Lil, 38, 82

Unforgiven, 21, 53, 68

Vancouver, B.C., 105
Van Gogh, Vincent, 170

Vietnam War, 109–114, 116
villains, 63, 73
Vincent & Theo, 169–170
violence, 110, 175–176
Virginia City, Nev., 2, 32, 65
Virginian, The, 52, 65, 84, 120

Walker, Janet, 19, 21
Warshow, Robert, 71
Washington, Sumner, 23, 84, 147, 150, 152
Wayne, John, 5, 56, 65, 79, 113
Wedding, A, 144
West, 8, 56, 164
    African Americans in, 23
    Asians in, 23
    conceptualizations of, 7, 17–19, 71
    democracy of, 111
    development of, 106
    economy of, 22
    feminist perceptions of, 121
    gamblers in, 30–31, 32
    gunfighters in, 33
    immigrants in, 23
    masculinity in, 120–121
    mining in, 22, 32
    myth of, 173, 174
    and national identity, 6–7, 77
    opium trade in, 24
    prostitution in (*see* prostitutes; prostitution)
    relation to East, 27–28
    as setting, 15
    settlement of, 14, 22, 26, 54, 71, 128
    story of, 5, 6
    women in, 34, 119–121
West, Elliott, 18, 22, 23, 30, 32, 36, 40, 54
western history
    prostitutes in, 19, 34, 35, 38, 42
    revisions of, 35, 43, 55, 138
    women in, 24, 34, 35, 38
    See also New Western History
westerns, 1, 4, 5, 6, 15, 34, 44, 46, 55, 71, 79, 87, 110–111
    adult, 104
    archetypal, 65
    B, 103
    central tenets, 53–54
    classical, 19, 21, 43, 56, 72
    decline of, 53, 89
    feminist critiques of, 68
    heterosexuality in, 80
    as historiography, 12, 19
    Hollywood productions of, 51
    ideology of, 17, 19
    Indians in, 79
    landscapes of, 62
    and masculine identity, 67–68
    missionaries in, 114
    as museums, 12, 16
    myth of, 33, 173
    parodies of, 52–53
    revisionist, 16, 43, 51–57, 63, 88, 101, 103, 105, 174
    and social issues, 105, 118
    television, 51
    transformation of, 126
    "traumatic," 21
    and West, 16, 173
    women in, 67, 132
    See also antiwesterns
White, Richard, 17, 31, 37, 41
Whitman, Walt, 25
Wild Bunch, The, 4, 54, 89, 103, 110, 133
wilderness, 1, 2, 6–7, 14, 15, 30, 44, 45, 49, 61–62, 67, 77, 78, 84, 85, 105, 110–112, 124, 127, 129–131, 138
    conflict with civilization, 4, 17–18, 42, 54, 55, 65–66, 71–72, 74–76, 79, 88–90, 101, 103, 104, 121, 128, 131
Wild West Show, Cody's, 10, 17
Winchester '73, 16
Winning of the West, 17
"Winter Lady" (Cohen), 86, 157, 159, 161
Wister, Owen, 52, 65, 84, 120
women
    creation of community, 40–41, 124–125, 129
    representations of, 34–35, 120, 131
    roles of, 30–31, 34–37, 43, 50, 63, 106, 119, 132
    in West, 121
    in westerns, 67
    and western writing, 121, 126
women's movement, 106, 118–126, 132, 133
Wright, Will, 72

Yeats, William Butler, 77, 179
Young, Fred, 135
youth culture, 9, 107–108, 110, 114

Zandy's Bride, 132
Zsigmond, Vilmos, 12, 100 (photo), 135–136, 137, 139